The U.S. Marine Corps
Mountain Warfare Training Center
1951-2001

by
Major General Orlo K. Steele, U.S. Marine Corps (Retired)
Lieutenant Colonel Michael I. Moffett,
U.S. Marine Corps Reserve (Retired)

History Division
United States Marine Corps
Washington D.C.
2011

Other Volumes in the Marine Corps Base and
Training Center History Series

Quantico: Crossroads of the Marine Corps, 1978
U.S. Marines at Twentynine Palms, California, 1989

PCN 106 0000 7600

Foreword

The following account represents a significant look at a half century of U.S. Marine Corps effort in the Sierra Nevada mountain range of California. This has been and is still the location of the Corps cold weather and mountain training facility. Over time the needs and demands for Marines and units prepared to operate under these conditions waxed and waned with the real world requirements of deployed forces. This was reflected in the realities of conflicts in the Korean Peninsula, the Cold War's northern and southern flanks, and in the current Global War in Terrorism fight in Afghanistan and elsewhere. While the future is often uncertain, this firm look at the past is useful to show how previous challenges have prompted creative and innovative responses. This is as much a story of evolution as an institution.

The primary author, Major General Orlo K. "O.K." Steele took on this project based on personal experience as a mountain leader instructor, and unit commander. His purpose was to document the 1951 through 2001 story to demonstrate the continued relevance of mountain and cold weather training at Bridgeport and Pickel Meadow. A native of Oakland, California, General Steele's Marine Corps' active career spanned the years 1955 through 1990. As an infantry officer he served with distinction at every level from platoon, battalion, regiment, amphibious unit, amphibious brigade, division through expeditionary force. Other tours of duty included Marine Corps Recruit Depot, San Diego; the Mountain Warfare Training Center; Marine Detachment, USS *America* (CVA 66); NROTC officer instructor Dartmouth College; Marine Barracks Guantanamo Bay, Cuba; Marine Barracks, Washington, D.C.; and Headquarters, U.S. Marine Corps. He is a graduate of Stanford University, Marine Corps Amphibious Warfare School, Marine Corps Command and Staff College, and the National War College. Since retirement he has been active on advisory boards, mentoring, and with this project which he conceived, resourced, and executed.

The coauthor Lieutenant Colonel Michael I. "Mike" Moffett took part in this effort as a member of the History Division's Field History Branch. He assisted in the review and revision of the entire manuscript and authored the sidebars and final chapter. A New Hampshire native, he served as a regular and reserve infantry officer at the platoon, company, and battalion level. His service also included his attendance at the mountain leader winter course at the Mountain Warfare Training Center. Lieutenant Colonel Moffett's other significant duties have been with the Marine Enlisted Commissioning Program Preparatory Course, as well as serving a field historian tour in Afghanistan. He is a graduate of the University of New Hampshire and Plymouth State University. Mr. Ken Williams's editing and design branch prepared the manuscript for publication with editing by Ms Wanda Renfrow and layout by Mr. W. Stephen Hill.

Dr. Charles P. Neimeyer
Director of Marine Corps History

Preface

In mid-April 2000, I put a telephone call into the late Colonel John W. Ripley who was a longstanding friend and a former messmate from our days together in the 2d Marine Division. John had just recently been appointed to be the Director, Historical Division at Headquarters Marine Corps. After congratulating him on his new duties, I mentioned to him that during the previous month I had been to the Marine Corps Mountain Warfare Training Center (MWTC) to observe a Marine air-ground task force exercise conducted by 65 students from Colonel John A. Keenan's Expeditionary Warfare School. That trip reminded me that in September 2001, MWTC would celebrate its 50th Anniversary. "Shouldn't the History Division commemorate the event by publishing an historical monograph?" I asked. "Perhaps we can do that," John agreed. The following week I followed that call up with an e-mail suggesting to John that as soon as he had selected an author for the MWTC project to please let me know, as I would be happy to provide some photographs and background material that I held from the mid 1960s.

After six months of silence I telephoned John again. "How is the MWTC project progressing?" I asked. "It hasn't begun yet," he responded, "too many other priorities." "Listen," John said to me, "you are probably as familiar with the training center as anyone; why don't you write it?" "Let me think about it and I will get back to you," I told him as I rang off.

John's instincts were close to the mark. I had always considered Pickel Meadow to be a special place. During my 35 years of active duty, the training center had either directly, or indirectly touched my life at practically every rank. I had first walked into that meadow as a private first class in February 1956 for 10-days of cold weather indoctrination. Then, I returned as a first lieutenant in December 1960 as a student in the Escape, Evasion, and Survival School. In January 1963, I reported there for duty as a captain and for the next two years served as the senior instructor-guide of the Mountain Leadership School. I took command of the 2d Battalion, 1st Marines as a major in May 1973, two weeks later we deployed to Bridgeport for a month of summer mountain training while the base was still in a caretaker status. I had served as the 1st Marine Division's training officer as a lieutenant colonel when in 1975 we started the first winter mountain operations training course for a rifle company of the 7th Marines. As a colonel in Policies Plans and Operations at Headquarters U.S. Marine Corps in 1981, I was present at the decision briefing given to General Robert H. Barrow as he pondered on what the fate of MWTC should be. Finally, as a major general I was privileged to command the 2d Marine Division from 1987 to 1989 when MWTC played a pivotal role in preparing our Marines and sailors for the most likely contingency operation that was then facing the division: the prospect of fighting a winter campaign in north Norway.

After I had considered the matter, I telephoned John and told him that I would be happy to take a stab at authoring the monograph. However to do so, I would need some financial assistance to help underwrite my out-of-pocket expenses for research at both the Washington Navy Yard historical library and the Marine Corps University archives at Quantico. John said that he would speak to Lieutenant General George R. Christmas to see whether the Marine Corps Heritage Foundation might be willing to provide a small grant for that purpose.

It so happened that Ron Christmas and I had a longstanding relationship that dated back to 1963, at what was then the Cold Weather Training Center. At the time, Ron was a student second lieutenant from the 2d Reconnaissance Battalion. I on the other hand had just arrived for a two-year tour of duty at Bridgeport, when we were put into the same six-man team of students in the February Winter Mountain Leadership Course. Thus for the next four weeks, the two of us and our four other teammates shared an improvised parachute shelter at 9,000 feet elevation, while trying to master the techniques of day and night cross-country skiing with a 50-pound pack strapped to our backs. Fortunately, General Christmas did indeed approve the request for a grant. Therefore, I am very grateful to Ron, Susan Hodges and the Heritage Foundation Executive Committee for providing the financial assistance that I needed for my initial research trips. I am also grateful to them for their extreme patience during the nine years that it has taken me to complete this project.

After drafting an outline and developing a working bibliography, I devoted the first 10 days of February

2001 and an additional five days in July researching primary source documents at the Historical Division's Navy Yard library and at the Gray Research Center archives at Quantico. I am indebted to Chief Historian Charles D. Melson, Dr. David B. Crist; Mr. Robert Aquilina, the assistant head of the Reference Branch at the History Division; History Division Executive Assistant Cynthia Meyer; and to Ms. Kerry A. Strong, the director of the Gray Research Center Archives, and her staff.

Unfailingly, each person managed to ferret out all of my special requests, thereby enabling me to acquire copies of most of the official source documents that are cited and referenced throughout this work. I also benefited greatly from the many articles that appeared in *Leatherneck* magazine on CWTC and MWTC over the past half century, which my good friend Colonel Walter G. Ford, kindly compiled and sent to me.

It was during that first research period that I also realized it would speed things up if I had an assistant to help me go through the vast amount of material on cold-weather operations that was held in the Breckenridge library at Quantico. I therefore turned to another friend and former Marine Barracks, Washington D.C., mess-mate, Colonel John R. Allen. At that time, John was the commanding officer at The Basic School. I asked Colonel Allen whether he might have a second lieutenant who was in a temporary "holding pattern" who could be made available on a part-time basis to carry out specific research tasks at Quantico over the next several months? The next morning, Second Lieutenant Sean J. Schickle reported to me for temporary duty at Breckenridge library. Sean was a graduate of Illinois State University and had just been commissioned three months prior, after spending eight years in the Marine Corps Reserve as a combat engineer. Further, I learned, he was not scheduled to start The Basic School until May. Sean immediately demonstrated a keen interest in the project and I wasted no time in putting him to work. During the following month, Colonel John Keenan also kindly added Lieutenant Schickle to his manifest of students who were being flown out to Bridgeport for the annual Expeditionary Warfare School Mountain Marine air-ground task force operation. While together at Bridgeport, Sean and I were able to screen documents held locally, and among other things, spend four hours audio taping the personal recollections of the legendary retired Master Gunnery Sergeant John Marjanov. I have good reason to be very grateful to Sean for all of his contributions to this monograph and especially for his invaluable research into many of the official reports used in Chapters 4 and 5. I trust the commanding knowledge and appreciation that Sean acquired for cold weather and mountain operations during those early months of 2001 still stand him in good stead today.

On 6 September 2001, the Marine Corps Mountain Warfare Center celebrated its 50th Anniversary with a ceremony and open house at the training center. Several hundred people were in attendance, including a number of former Marines who had served tours of duty there. By this time, I had the first three chapters in draft form, and was gleaning through the material I intended to use in the fourth. Therefore, I was glad to accept Colonel James M. Thomas's invitation to be one of the guest speakers and to make a few brief remarks describing what conditions must have been like for those Leathernecks who served at Pickel Meadow during its first year. Following the ceremony, I had the good fortune to meet Mr. and Mrs. Harold Haberman of Denver Colorado. Staff Sergeant Haberman had been among those first pioneers to serve in the Cold Weather Battalion during 1951-1952. After exchanging cards, Harold promised to send me some photographs he had taken during his first winter at Bridgeport. When I saw the photos I was elated. Readers will see why in Chapters 3 and 4. They portray the severe blizzard conditions that repeatedly swept across the Sierra's that year, far better than any narrative could possibly describe them.

During the course of writing this history, my co-author and I have done our utmost to reach out and learn the personal stories of those who had either served at MWTC, or who had undergone training there. To my former S-3 officer at MWTC, Lieutenant Colonel Edwin A. Deptula, Retired go special thanks for enabling me to conduct personal interviews with Colonels Walter Moore and Richard Johnson whose insights on how the Cold Weather Battalion first came into being proved invaluable. We are equally indebted to First Sergeant Carl. H. Raue Jr.; Major Anthony F. Milavic; Gunnery Sergeant Henry Vozka; and Major James N. A. Goldsworthy OBE, Royal Marines; Colonel Jeffery W. Bearor; and Major General Harry W. Jenkins, Jr., for the wealth of material, personal accounts and photographs, which they have so generously provided for inclusion to this history.

This project received assistance from many retired Marines and other persons living in the nearby communities to MWTC. Included among this list are: Bob Peters, owner of the Bridgeport Inn who helped research records held at the Mono County Courthouse and articles from the *Bridgeport Chronicle-Union;* Gunnery Sergeant Coy D. Ziglar, also of Bridgeport; Gunnery Sergeant Eugene L. Ewing and former Corporal William A.

"Bing" Blood, both of Carson City, Nevada; Captain Wiley M. Clapp Jr. of Minden, Nevada, Rita Richardson, widow of the late Lieutenant Colonel Rodney C. Richardson, also of Minden; Gunnery Sergeant Richard N. Denhoff of Gardnerville, Nevada; Mr. Eric M. Williams, Archaeologist for the Bridgeport Ranger District Office, Humboldt-Toiyabe National Forest; and Mr. Kent Stoddard, President of the Mono County Historical Society, at Bridgeport, California.

Valuable insights were also gained through either telephone or audio taping interviews with former commanding officers at MWTC. Personal recollections were taken from the late Brigadier General Donald M. Schmuck; Colonel Glen E. Martin; Mrs. Darlene Guy, widow to the late Colonel John Guy; Colonel William H. Osgood; Colonel John F. Stennick,, and Colonel Raymond L. Polak. Additionally, since the onset of writing this history, all the commanding officers at MWTC and their staffs have been very helpful by providing photographs and meeting the authors requests for copies of written documents. In this regard, the assistance rendered by Colonel Norman L. Cooling, who commanded MWTC from 2008 to June 2010 was particularly noteworthy.

Others who gave personal accounts of their experiences at MWTC as either instructors or students were: Lieutenant General Ernest C. Cheatham, Jr.; Colonel Warren H. Wiedhahn, Jr.; Colonel Gerald H. Turley; Colonel James "Jim" Knapp; Sergeant-Major William J. Conley, and former Marine Corporal John Schneider. One unforgettable telephone interview was conducted in 2003. It was with the late General Robert H. Barrow, 27th Commandant of the Marine Corps, who patiently explained the reasoning behind his critical decision in 1981 to not only keep MWTC open, but to commit substantial Marine Corps resources to ensure its future and its usefulness for decades to come.

Our thanks also go to General Carl E. Mundy Jr., 30th Commandant of the Marine Corps, Major General Harry Jenkins, Jr., Colonel Richard Johnson, Major Anthony F. Milavic, Gunnery Sergeant Hank Vozka, Gunnery Sergeant Coy D. Ziglar, Colonel William H. "Bill" Osgood, Colonel John F. Stennick, Mr. Bob Peters, Colonel Jeffery W. Bearor and Chief Historian Charles D. "Chuck" Melson for taking the time to read over drafts of the chapters as they unfolded and for making valuable suggestions for change.

When conducting research in Washington D.C., and Quantico, I frequently enjoyed the hospitality of my longstanding friend and a former Assistant Secretary of Defense for six years, the Honorable Stephen M. Duncan. Steve not only provided me lodging from time to time during my trips east, but also managed to stiffen my backbone to ensure I stayed with this project to its bitter end.

Writing this history has taken far longer than I ever anticipated at the outset. Although during the first year I made reasonably good progress, following the attacks of 11 September, I became increasingly engaged in doing consulting work for the Department of Homeland Security and other government agencies. By mid-year 2008, drafts had only been written through Chapter 8. I was grateful therefore, when during the summer of that year Chuck Melson contacted me with the very welcome news that a Reserve Lieutenant Colonel by the name of Michael I. "Mike" Moffett had been assigned to the staff at the History Division (which by now had moved to Quantico) and was interested in working on the MWTC project. Chuck was well aware that I had been seeking a collaborator from the Reserves for over three years. Thus after learning Colonel Moffett's background and his many other professional qualifications, I immediately said yes. That September, Mike Moffett and I were able to spend a day together in New England going over the draft manuscript. Thereafter, the two of us devised a plan for a division of labor, which would take advantage of our respective strengths and knowledge on the subject matter. Mike, we decided, would edit all of the earlier drafts and write the final chapter detailing the 1990s, plus the Epilogue; meanwhile I would concentrate on completing Chapters 10 and 11. I cannot sing the praises of Mike's skill and commitment to this project loudly enough. It has been a joy for me to work side-by side with him over the past several years and to have his steadfast support and have the benefit of his keen eye for clarity. I would also be remiss not to add that had he not appeared on the scene when he did, it is very questionable whether this particular monograph would have ever seen the light of day.

Finally, both my co-author and I wish to thank Colonel Rod Andrews, and a History Division colleague who from February through May 2010, served as pinch hitter for Mike Moffett while he was performing duty in Afghanistan. When not in uniform, Rod is a Professor of History at Clemson University and is a published author of several historical books pertaining to the American civil war. As a certified "historian," Rod not only managed to keep this project on track during Mike's absence, but rendered invaluable professional assistance by polishing the manuscript, clarifying its endnotes and serving as this monograph's chief editor.

This monograph is dedicated to all the Marine, Navy, and civilian personnel and their families who have served at the Marine Corps Mountain Warfare Training Center, whose legacy for training excellence has lasted for six decades. For their extraordinary resolve and commitment to molding Marine Corps MWTC into one of the foremost and highly valued combat training centers of our Corps. Especially to the memory of:

Brigadier General Donald M. "Buck" Schmuck (1915-2004)
Lieutenant Colonel Gerald P. Averill (1919-1994)
Lieutenant Colonel Stanley Wawrzyniak (1927-1995)
Captain Charles H. Clipper (1917-2004)
Sergeant Major Richard R. "Big Red" Ebert (1922-2002)
Master Gunnery Sergeant John Marjanov (1923-2002)
Lieutenant Colonel Edward J. Robeson IV (1947-1990)
Lieutenant Colonel Rodney C. Richardson (1952-2006)
Colonel John W. Guy (1933-2008)
Colonel William H. Osgood (1938-2011).

Orlo K. Steele
Major General, U.S. Marine Corps (Retired)

Introduction

This is the story of the Marine Corps Mountain Warfare Training Center. MCMWTC was established due to lessons learned from the legendary Chosin Reservoir Campaign in North Korea during the winter of 1950-1951. Experiences there showed a pressing need for a training program to prepare Marines for the rigors of harsh winter combat. What started as a basic cold-weather indoctrination program for the replacement drafts bound for Korea evolved over time into a year-round training facility that is one-of-a-kind for the entire Department of Defense. During its 60-year history the MWTC evolved into what is today the best venue for the USMC to develop individual confidence and leadership skills for the Marines that train there. I was stationed there as an instructor-guide in the early 1960s, and would returned as a regimental commander and later as the Commanding General, 4th Marine Expeditionary Brigade.

The reason for MWTC's extraordinary reputation is its physical environment. The base camp is situated in Pickel Meadow, at an elevation of 6,800 feet on the eastern slope of California's Sierra Nevada Range. The training area includes peaks that rise from 9,000 to over 11,000 feet in elevation. During the winter months snow depths can exceed 10 feet in the canyons and can be as deep as 25 feet in the Sonora Pass. All mountain passes remain closed until late spring, which limits the base camp to only one access road. Temperatures vary from bitter cold in the in the winter months to warm during the day and freezing at night in the spring. During the spring thaw the West Walker River can be raging torrent and a deadly threat to Marines attempting to cross it.

Training at the MWTC can be a high risk endeavor that requires all personnel to be thoroughly schooled in mountaineering skills, tactics and survival techniques. A long list of superb mountain leaders, many in the mold of stalwarts like Lieutenant Colonel Gerald P. Averill, Captain Stanley Wawrzyniak and Lieutenant Vincent R. Lee, provided a talented instructor cadre that was extremely demanding. High altitude, cross-compartment maneuvering with standard loads requires maximum efforts from Marines. The end result of this training is a high level of self-confidence to operate in a challenging climate or rough terrain. There is no other USMC training environment that requires so much endurance and perseverance.

MWTC's continued existence can be attributed to the foresight and perseverance of several legendary Marines who recognized its potential and who refused to let it be closed. Generals Oliver P. Smith, Lemuel C. Shepherd, Jr., Louis H. Wilson Jr., Robert H. Barrow, and other great leaders all knew the value of MWTC and supported it despite the difficulties associated with maintaining the remote facilities. It was through their leadership that the MWTC survived over the years, despite being in a cadre status during the Vietnam War. In the ensuing years MWTC's training syllabus would evolve and feature many new options for units and individuals. Studies were conducted at Headquarters Marine Corps to determine the optimum size of the permanent staff as well as an adequate infrastructure. Continuous improvements enabled MWTC to meet new Cold War requirements, including contingencies on NATO's northern flank.

The 4th Marine Amphibious Brigade (4th MAB) began to focus on exercises in Norway in the late 1970s. These exercises identified major deficiencies in USMC Arctic capabilities. Much had to be learned if the Marine units were to be able to live and fight in that part of the world on a proficiency level comparable to that of Royal Marine, Canadian and Norwegian counterparts. The issue was not the desire of the individual Marine, but the fact that he had not been properly trained or equipped to operate 24-hours a day in the harsh winter climate found in the mountains of northern Norway. Attempts were made to improve winter training at places like Fort Drum in New York or Camp Ripley in Minnesota, where cold temperatures and snow could be found during the winter months. The problem in both places was that neither replicated the mountainous environment found in Norway above the Arctic Circle.

The 4th Marine Amphibious Brigade continued to participate in winter exercises in northern Norway throughout the 1980s. However, many of the same problems regarding training and equipment continued to persist. It was not until 1984 that the training workup began to change in preparation for regular winter exercises on NATO's northern flank. The key to that change was the requirement to get the assigned infantry battalion, the attachments and the regimental headquarters (2d Marines) to MWTC for a specifically designed 30 day winter warfare training package in January of the exercise year. This was followed be a MAGTF exercise where all elements came together at either Fort Drum in New York or Fort McCoy in Wisconsin. Following that the 4th MAB would deploy to Norway for exercises with its NATO counterparts. The fundamental training package at MWTC, carried out by its instructors along with liaison officers from 3 Commando Brigade, Royal Marines and the Norwegian Army, was what finally resolved the training issues. By the time that a MAGTF arrived in Norway for the 1985 pre-exercise workup, the Marines had spent more time in the field then their Norwegian counterparts, and were maneuvering over the snow on skis during all hours of the day and night. That, coupled with the exceptional aviation capabilities of Marine helicopter units in the mountains and fjords, provided mobility that no one else could match. The key to this success in the years that followed was the training that continued to be received at the Mountain Warfare Training Center.

It was during this period that significant improvements were made in the clothing and equipment that was issued to units getting ready for the annual winter exercises in Norway. In a visit to the units in the field during Cold Winter 85 the Commandant, General Paul X. Kelley, was quick to see many of the equipment problems that the Marines were dealing with in the Arctic. Upon his return to Washington, steps were taken to rapidly replace much of the Korean War vintage clothing and equipment that had been around for years. Subsequent deployments to the MWTC and Norway saw Marine units with some of the best gear that was available. Much of it had been tested and evaluated in exercises at Pickel Meadow.

With the end of the Cold War there was less emphasis on cold-weather training and exercises as new contingencies developed that changed the focus of the Marine Corps. Operations in Southwest Asia during the 1990s and through the first decade of the 21st century have required a different emphasis on tactics and techniques that has carried over into current operations in Afghanistan. During this period the Mountain Warfare Training Center has shifted its training packages to meet new requirements. Very difficult and challenging training in the mountainous environment is now coupled with relevant, contemporary counterinsurgency scenarios.

Marines are still required to give their all in order to be successful in the mountains. Individuals and units that complete MWTC training acquire the same confidence and ability as previous generations of Marines. It is a tribute to the professionalism of the Marines stationed at this superb facility that they continue to demand the most out of those who train in that environment.

Harry W. Jenkins, Jr.
Major General, U.S. Marine Corps (Retired)

Table of Contents

Foreword..iii

Preface..v

Introduction ix

Table of Contents xi

Chapter 1: The Sierra Nevada Range 1

    The Mountains 1

    The Indians 2

    Colonizers and Trappers 3

    Fremont and the Lost Cannon 4

    Emigrants and Argonauts 6

Chapter 2: U.S. Marine Corps Cold Weather Experience and Doctrine Prior to 1950....................11

    Introduction..11

    Special Duty in the Bering Sea 11

    Expedition to Iceland 12

    Between World War II and Korea..16

Chapter 3: The Marines Arrive 19

    Korean War Backdrop 19

    "All personnel . . . would be thoroughly indoctrinated"..19

    "Take what action is necessary to establish a suitable training site"....................23

    Activation of the Cold Weather Battalion 26

Chapter 4: Cold Weather Battalion's First Year 29

    "We've got to get 'em tougher to survive" 29

    The Winter of 1951-1952 32

Chapter 5: Making Improvements, 1952-1956 37

    Introduction..37

    Facilities..37

    Organization for Training 38

    Cold-Weather Clothing Equipment 38

    Command Relationships 39

    Building a Camp, 1952 40

    Cease-Fire in Korea 43

Chapter 6: Expanding the Mission, 1957-1958..47

    Introduction..47

    Changes to Command Relationships 48

    Organization for Meeting the New Training Mission..51

    Evasion, Escape, and Survival Course 52

    Mountain Leadership Course 52

    Unit Training 56

Chapter 7: Winners Never Quit, 1958-1961 61

    Introduction..61

"Zum Gipfel" 61

1960 Winter Olympic Games 66

A Change in the Watch 67

Chapter 8: Mountain Men, 1962-1965 71

Marines Who Proved a Match for the Mountains 71

Shifts in the Wind 76

Chapter 9: In the Doldrums, 1966-1979 85

Vietnam War Backdrop...85

MWTC on the Slippery Slope...85

Deactivation and Caretaker Status 88

Use it or Lose it! 89

Reactivation of the Mountain Warfare Training Center 94

Chapter 10: NATO's Northern Flank: A New Imperative, 1979-1983 97

Strategic Background: From Benign Neglect to Heightened Awareness.............97

Costs and Risks of the New Initiative 98

1981: Year of Decision...100

Laying the Foundation for Improvements...105

Chapter 11: Ascending New Heights, 1984-1990...107

Rebuilding MWTC and Expanding its Capabilities 107

Improvements in Cold-Weather Clothing and Equipment 113

Land Prepositioning in Norway 117

Picking up the Pace in Operations and Modernization of the Training Center 118

Reaching the High Water Mark 123

Chapter 12: The 1990s: A Post-Cold War World 127

Introduction..127

Continuing Operations while dealing with Future Uncertainties....................127

Demonstrating MWTC value During Peacetime 133

Golden Anniversary 135

Epilogue...135

Strategic Backdrop...137

Mountain Warfare Training Center Shifts with the Tides of War 137

Debates over Deployment...138

A Strategic Vision for Mountain Warfare Training Center's Second Half-Century............................140

Notes 143

Appendix A: Lineage and Honors, 1951-2001 149

Appendix B: List of Commanding Officers, 1951 to Present..................................151

Appendix C: List of Sergeant Majors, 1958 to Present...153

Appendix D: Department of Agriculture and Navy Joint Policy..............................155

Index 162

Chapter 1

The Sierra Nevada Range

Bring me men to match my mountains,
Bring me men to match my plains,
Men with empires in their purpose,
And new eras in their brains.
-Sam Foss

The Mountains

The Sierra Nevada is one of the great mountain ranges of the world. Its land mass almost equals that of the Swiss, French, and Italian Alps combined. Its southern boundary rises out of California's Mojave Desert. From there, it extends 400 miles in a general northwesterly direction to a point near the 40th Parallel. The highest peaks are located in the southern portion. Popularly known as the "High Sierras," geologists believe this part of the range is still undergoing growth and further uplifting even today.[1] From its crowning peak, Mount Whitney (14,496 feet), the highest mountain within the borders of the continental United States, the chain gradually slopes downward as it proceeds north. Sixty miles beyond the Lake Tahoe Basin, the elevation at the crest is only 8,000 feet. Standing at this vantage point, one can see the Sierras begin to fade away and merge with the volcanic lava flows of Mount Lassen and the Cascade Range.

The width of the range varies from 50 to 80 miles. Because of the barrier created by this formidable mass of land, much of the rain and snow falls on the western side, leaving the eastern face relatively dry and the land beyond it a desert. This eastern side of the Sierra rises sharply out of the Owens River valley and Nevada's Great Basin at a gradient in excess of 25 degrees. Near the summit, the face becomes even more precipitous, until it reaches an escarpment of peaks that are almost vertical. Therefore, eastern vistas of the range can be strikingly alpine. In contrast, the western side of the divide appears deceptively gentle. It has an average tilt of only two or three degrees. Yet it is that long, largely tree-covered western side, deeply packed with winter snow and carved by a series of deep rivers that forms the vast watershed making California's central valley the giant agricultural producer that it is.

How was the Sierra Nevada formed, and why did it develop here? In the words of Mary Hill, a senior geologist with the California Division of Mines and Geology, "No one as yet knows."[2] The range is too complex and the forces of nature too turbulent to go beyond the realm of theoretical speculation, despite 150 years of scientific study. Nevertheless, through analysis of rock formations, geologists are able to provide a general reconstruction of the phenomenon that first created these mountains, as well as a description of the likely forces that altered them many times over throughout their geologic history.

Told briefly, the Sierra chronology begins some 210 million years ago when the entire area lay beneath the sea. During the ensuing 130 million years of the Mesozoic Era, bodies of molten granite, deep within the earth, began to cool into rock. As the last of the granite cooled, gold and other metals were left in veins and fissures. Meanwhile, the oceanic Farallon plate moved north, dipping under the lighter North American plate, and was simultaneously crushed and obliterated by the enormous Pacific plate to the west. It was this geological convulsion that uplifted the Sierra Nevada above the waters of the sea. Over the next 50 million years (first half of the Tertiary Period) the sea receded; the climate became almost tropical, and lagoons and rain forests covered the lands to the west. Although the range was still being uplifted, the forces of erosion began tearing the rock from the mountainsides depositing the debris into the sea and forming the foundation of what was to become the great central valley of California. Altogether, geologists estimate that more than nine vertical miles of rock was worn away in the space of 25 million years, leaving the crest at not much more than 3,000 feet high. The last half of the Tertiary period was marked by "the days of fire." Beginning about 30 million years ago, the shifting tectonic plates spawned repeated episodes of volcanism, throwing a blanket of hot ash over the northern Sierra and obliterating the rest of the range with mudflows of lava. Sometime after that, probably in the last 15 million years, the Sierra was uplifted to about its present height and tilted decidedly to the west. Just how rapid was this rise and whether it is continuing today, is still a matter of scientific debate.[3] Sometime thereafter, the earth grew colder, causing great glaciers to descend over much of North America. Within the Sierra, local glaciers waxed and waned several times during this great ice age, sculpturing its peaks and gouging out new valleys and waterways. Then, about 25,000 years ago, the earth's climate began to warm again. The great ice cap receded and the seas rose. But before Asia and America could become completely severed, man began to cross to the New World over the Siberian bridge to what we now call Alaska. Much later, some of these nomadic people would move south to permanently settle under the shadow of the Sierras.

The Indians

The ancestors of our Native Americans probably wandered into the Sierra region several thousand years BC. By the time of Columbus, these aboriginal hunters and gatherers had become increasingly more clannish. As a result, distinct differences in culture, religion, and language developed between the various tribal groups. It is estimated that at between 100 and 135 separate tribes lived in what is now California prior to European settlement.[4] Chiefs usually headed these groups, and the culture was largely shaped by the means and methods of gathering food.

Two historic Indian cultures populated the western slopes of the Sierra divide. In the northern sector were the Maidu; to the south and west of the Yosemite Valley, lived the Miwok.[5] Later, white men would simply lump these two groups and their neighbors into a non-existent "tribe" they called "Digger." This unfortunate name came from the fact these native people used digging sticks to harvest bulbs and tubers.

Likewise, the eastern foot of the range was also inhabited by two distinctly different Indian cultures. The smaller of the two were the Washo.* Probably numbering no more than 5,000, the Washo laid claim to the land from Honey Lake in the north, to the Walker River in the south. Also inhabiting the Great Basin to the east and south of the Washo, were the neighboring tribes of the people called Paiutes, meaning those who lived on desert land, but always near water.[6]

Each of these tribes tended to follow strict codes of behavior in order to keep their separate cultural identities. Although normally not aggressive, wars, or punitive raids were common when a perceived offence was committed, or when a neighbor encroached on ancestral lands. Despite these occasional disputes, one common trait tended to link all of these people together: their nomadic character forced them to harmonize their lives with the pulses and rhythms of the seasons. This was vital to their survival.

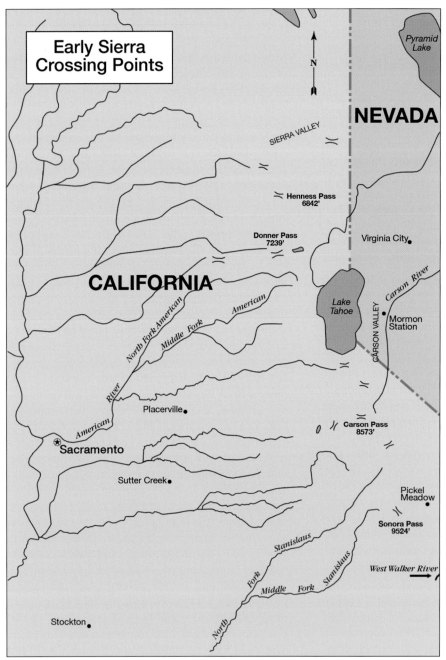

Early Sierra Crossing Points (map showing CALIFORNIA and NEVADA, with Pyramid Lake, Sierra Valley, Henness Pass 6842', Donner Pass 7239', Virginia City, Lake Tahoe, Carson River, Carson Valley, Mormon Station, Carson Pass 8573', Placerville, Sacramento, Sutter Creek, Pickel Meadow, Sonora Pass 9524', Stockton, West Walker River, and various rivers including North Fork American, Middle Fork American, American River, Stanislaus)

---
* This is the historic name of this tribe; the modern name is "Washoe."

In the late spring, as winter stores came close to exhaustion and with the danger of starvation a real possibility, individual tribal families or villages would start to forage upslope from both east and west. There was nothing casual or unplanned about these movements. Indeed, exploiting the environment to its fullest required careful planning and an extraordinary knowledge of the plants, animals, climate, and soils of the area. This annual event resulted in the creation of a well-defined network of east-west trails that crisscrossed their way to the various encampment sites. The summer months were spent at the higher elevations, taking advantage of not only the cooler climate, but also the abundance of fish and game. Summer and early fall also provided the opportunity to barter with tribes from the opposite side of the divide.* Western tribes, for example, hauled extra supplies of acorns or tubers for this purpose, while those from the east brought highly prized flint and obsidian that lay in considerable quantities on the eastern slope. When the aspen leaves started to turn from green to yellow, it was the signal to start the long descent back to the lower elevations. En route, the men continued to hunt while the women harvested the pine nuts needed for winter stores and grasses and used in the weaving of fine baskets. Winter was the season for improving shelters, mending clothes, fashioning new weapons, and preparing for the cycle to begin anew as soon as the snow left the ground. Such was the pastoral existence that the tribes of the Sierras knew and followed for thousands of years in almost complete isolation, until their customary life was abruptly disrupted in the middle of the 19th century.

Colonizers and Trappers

In 1540, the Spanish navigator Hernando de Alacron became the first European explorer to set foot in what is today California. Two years later, Juan Rodriguez Cabrillo, commanding two vessels, put in at San Diego Bay and claimed *Alta* (Upper) California for the Spanish Crown. However, it would take another 230 years before the next European would gaze upon the Sierra Nevada. The first tentative steps toward unlocking the mysteries of the California interior did not begin until 1769. On 1 July of that year, Don Gaspar de Portolá and Father Junipero Serra arrived in San Diego Bay to implement the Viceroy of Mexico's plan to colonize

Upper California. Their commission directed them to build a series of missions and pueblos, supported by several military garrisons, (*presidios*) along the California coastline.* Over the next half century, a total of 21 missions would eventually be established, with one of the last being located a few miles north of San Francisco Bay.[7]

In 1772, one of Father Serra's missionaries, Fray Juan Crespi, climbed to a viewpoint near the recently discovered bay. Looking toward the eastern horizon, Crespi recorded in his diary: "We made out that these three arms or three large rivers were formed by a very large river, a league in width at least, which descended from some high mountains to the southeast, very far distant."[8] Four years later, the Franciscan missionary, Pedro Font, also gazed upon these same "high mountains" and recorded it in his journal and, a year later, on a map he had drawn. Fray Font awarded them the simple Spanish name: "Sierra Nevada," or "snow covered mountains." It was a name that would endure.

During the ensuing half-century, however, these lofty peaks in the distance were practically ignored. Unlike their conquistador ancestors, the latter-day colonizers seemed perfectly content to stay close to the coastal plain. With the exception of one minor foray led by Ensign Gabriel Moraga to the lower reaches of the Merced River in 1806, the early Californians made no serious effort either to explore the Sierra Nevada, or determine what treasures might lay beyond. Consequently, the first recorded penetration of the range by white men was conducted by a party of American trappers under the leadership of Jedediah S. Smith.

Coming from the Mississippi River to California in 1826, Smith and his party bypassed the Sierra completely on the way west, entering Alta California by a southern route through the Mojave Desert. Four years earlier, Mexico had successfully achieved its independence from Spanish rule. The Mexican Governor at San Diego, apparently suspicious of Smith's intentions, ordered him and his party to return forthwith to U.S. territory. In order to take the most direct route back to his base of operations at the Great Salt Lake, Smith then led his party up the central valley for several hundred miles. In May of 1827, the party made two attempts to cross what Smith referred to as "Mount Joseph." But deep snow in the high passes beat back both of these efforts. On the third try, probably following a water-

---

* Numerous petroglyphs carved into the granite rocks can be found throughout the Sierra at the higher elevations. Anthropologists believe these carvings may have marked boundaries, or perhaps indicated sites where the various tribal groups might have come together to trade goods.

* These settlements were to thwart any encroachment by the Russian and English fur trading companies that had established posts in Alaska and the Pacific Northwest; the Russians and English may have been contemplating others posts further south.

course that was later to be named the Stanislaus River, the party finally succeeded in reaching the crest after eight days of tough trail breaking through snowdrifts of four to six feet. Just exactly where this party may have made its eastern descent into the Great Basin has never been established. However, based on later accounts, presumably they emerged somewhere in the vicinity of the present day Bridgeport Valley.[9]

The next group to test its mettle against the Sierra, and the first to cross from east to west, was led by another well-known American trapper and mountain man. His name is Joseph R. Walker. Leading a contingent of 50 mounted men in search of beaver, the Walker party bivouacked on 10 October, 1833 at the edge of a lake that had a high saline content. The Paiute Indians, living near these waters, called this lake and the surrounding region *Mono,* which in their language meant "beautiful." As the party was very low on supplies, Walker decided to cross the mountains and reprovision in California, rather than to retrace his route back along the Humboldt River where he had encountered many hostile Indians. Ascending the east branch of a river that was later to take his name, Walker and his party slowly started up the rocky mountainside, somewhere near today's town of Bridgeport.* Unknowingly, three weeks of tough, arduous travel, early winter storms, near starvation and outbreaks of mutiny lay ahead of them before the party would finally descend to the western foothills and the warmer climates. Fortunately, Zenas Leonard, who was a clerk and a member of the party, has left us with an excellent journal that provides graphic details of this grim crossing. From its accurate descriptions of the terrain, it is not only possible to track the route of the Walker party, but also reasonably conclude that they were probably the first white men to lay eyes on two of nature''s great wonders: the giant sequoia trees and Yosemite Valley.[10]

Fremont and the Lost Cannon

In spite of all the tests and trials that each of these first two trans-Sierra expeditions encountered, neither one can begin to compare with the appalling conditions experienced by the so-called Party of Exploration in the winter of 1844. The leader of this expedition was the flamboyant John C. Fremont, a lieutenant in the United States Topographical Engineers and son-in-law of the influential Missouri Senator Thomas H. Benton. Having already been extolled in the American press as the "Pathfinder," Fremont

Courtesy of Fort Jackson, Savannah, Georgia

A mountain howitzer and carriage of the type left by Fremont's party in the Sierra Nevada. Iron work from the carriage has been located by the National Park Service.

was on his second mapping survey of the western frontier. His 39-man detachment included a second topographical engineer named Charles Pruess, two Delaware Indians and the three famous scouts: Thomas "Broken Hand" Fitzpatrick, Alexis Godey, and Christopher "Kit" Carson. Also included in the detachment were three artillerists and a brass, 12 pound mountain field howitzer, dragged behind two mules. Designed by the French for their colonial war in the Atlas Mountains of Algeria, Fremont later praised the piece for being "well adapted to its purpose."[11*]

Departing Saint Louis in May of 1843, the exploring party spent the remainder of the year carrying out its primary task of mapping all of the Oregon Trail and much of the Great Salt Lake. Then, for reasons that are still unclear, Fremont decided to head south from Oregon into the Great Basin. On 14 January 1844, he camped on the shore of a body of water that he named Pyramid Lake. Here his tired men rested and gorged themselves on native cutthroat trout. After exploring southward for another 10 days in search of the fabled Buenaventura River (probably while on the eastern slope of the Sweetwater Mountains), Fremont suddenly announced to his now flagging troops that it was his intention to cross the snow-covered mountains, and resupply at Sutter's Fort in the Sacramento Valley.

From those who have carefully studied Fremont's journal and the diaries kept by others in the party, most agree on the general trace of the expedition as it moved next through the Bridgeport Valley,** then

---

* Author Frank Wedertz believes Walker may have ascended either Bloody Canyon or Virginia Canyon following established Indian trails.

* Fremont requisitioned this howitzer from the post ordnance officer at Jefferson Barracks, Missouri. What may have motivated him to add artillery to an exploration party, supposedly engaged in scientific study, is still open to speculation by historians; some assert that it was probably the result of an impulsive decision.
** At the time this valley was simply referred to as "Big Meadow."

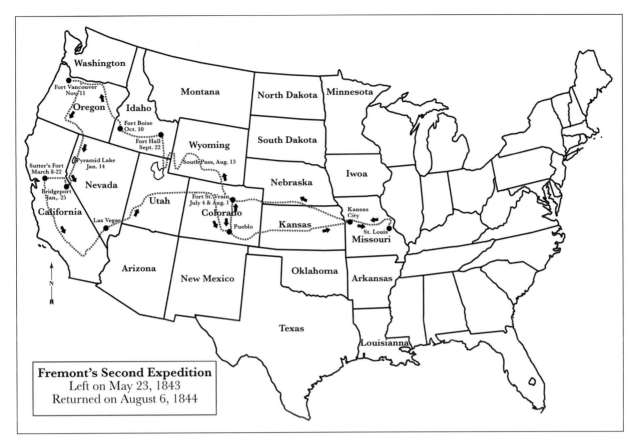

Fremont's Second Expedition
Left on May 23, 1843
Returned on August 6, 1844

north above Devil's Gate Pass and down the eastern side of the canyon, eventually crossing the present day West Walker River. However, during the three days it took to make this difficult traverse, (27-29 January,) it appears that Fremont was lost. Moreover, because of the steep terrain and miserable weather, the expedition was frequently divided into three echelons: Fremont and Fitzpatrick scouting ahead, a main body under Pruess, and the heavier, slower trains pulling up the rear. Consequently, there are a number of different theories as to the likely location of each of these divisions when Fremont was finally notified on the morning of the 29th that the howitzer was at an impasse on a very steep hill and could not be moved. Later, Fremont wrote:

> The other division of the party did not come in to-night, but encamped in the upper meadow, and arrived the next morning. They had not succeeded in getting the howitzer beyond the place mentioned, and where it had been left by Mr. Preuss, in obedience to my orders; and, in anticipation of the snowbanks and snowfields still ahead, foreseeing the inevitable detention to which it would subject us, I reluctantly determined to leave it there for the time. We left it to the great sorrow of the whole party.[12]

Where this cannon, along with its 500 pounds of powder and shot may have been abandoned, or per-

haps even disassembled and cached, is a mystery that has tantalized searchers to this day. Most believe the howitzer's' final resting place is somewhere on the east side of the West Walker River on the high ground to the north of Burcham Flat. Others are convinced that its location is on the river's' west side, most likely in the vicinity of Mill Creek Canyon, or higher up in Grouse Meadow. A few even claim its location to be closer to Sonora Pass, but buried under tons of talus rock. To be sure, there have been the usual rumors and claims of past sightings by Indians and others. Hence, one would think these leads would have given some identifiable clue as to the location of the piece. Yet, for over a century and a half, this legendary lost howitzer has continued to defy numerous recovery efforts made by amateur and professional treasurer -hunters alike. According to, author Ernest Lewis's assertion that the Fremont cannon represents "one of the last unfound artifacts of the early western history of the United States," holds true to this day.[13]*

While Fremont may have lamented the loss of the

---

* According to Mr. Eric M. Williams, Archaeologist at the Bridgeport Ranger District Office, an assemblage of forged iron parts (trunnion plate) and three iron tires were recovered by a team under the direction of the U.S. Forest Service "within 50 miles of Bridgeport" in 2006. These artifacts are on display at the Bridgeport 'District Ranger' Office and are believed to be the remains of the gun carriage of the Fremont Cannon. Search efforts to locate the yet unfound barrel continue as of June 2010.

howitzer, it is unlikely that anyone else in the party truly felt the "great sorrow" that he would have his readers believe, especially the three artillerymen who had already manhandled the piece through 3,900 miles of trackless terrain. Just getting themselves and their animals across 70 miles of snow-packed peaks in freezing weather must have seemed daunting enough, even without the burdensome task of hauling half a ton of cannon, carriage and ammunition. But despite any fears or misgivings the men must have had about the ordeal that lay ahead of them, when Fremont boldly began his ascent up the east wall on 2 February, not a man failed to follow him. Later, coming upon several friendly Indians, the older of the two braves tried to dissuade Fremont from attempting such a hopeless enterprise: "Rock upon rock–snow upon snow" the Indian warned; "even if you get over the snow, you will not be able to get down from the mountain."[14] But the intrepid Pathfinder was not to be deterred, so on they pressed. Scouting ahead on snowshoes, Fremont, Carson and Fitzpatrick managed to reach a summit peak on 14 February. From there, they could look down into the Sacramento Valley and see Mount Diablo in the far distance.[*] While this sight must have been encouraging to the entire party, two more brutal weeks of freezing nights and hazardous trail breaking through deep snowdrifts still lay ahead of them. Miraculously, the perilous descent down treacherous canyons and icy slopes cost no loss of life to either men or animals, except for the mules that were killed for subsistence. Finally, the exhausted and starving party reached the valley floor. Having faced the insurmountable odds that were against them, they had won. Thereafter, and

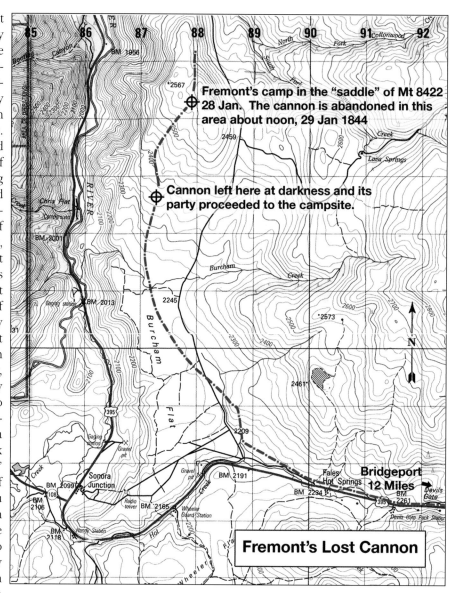

Fremont's camp in the "saddle" of Mt 8422 28 Jan. The cannon is abandoned in this area about noon, 29 Jan 1844

Cannon left here at darkness and its party proceeded to the campsite.

Bridgeport 12 Miles

Fremont's Lost Cannon

---

[*] On 14 February from a similar vantage point, both Fremont and Pruess were able to look down on a large mountain lake, which Fremont named "Lake Bonpland" in honor of the French botanist. To the Washoe Indians it was "Lake of the Sky." Later it would take the name "Tahoe."

exactly one month from the day that he began his ascent up the eastern ridge, the indomitable Fremont was able to lead his tattered detachment of iron men through the gates of Sutter's Fort, and into the pages of history.[15]

Emigrants and Argonauts

Not far behind these trappers and explorers came the emigrants. In the early 1840s, most of these pioneer families directed their trains toward the Oregon Territory. A few parties, however, either by design or through ignorance, struck out directly for California. An example of the latter is the Bidwell-Bartleson party. Having followed different routes from Kansas Territory through the Humboldt Sink, the two parties eventually came together at the eastern base of the Sierra along the Walker River. By this time both parties had already abandoned their wagons and were carrying what food and possessions they had left on pack mules. Fortunately, it was still early autumn of 1841. This meant snow in the high passes would be at its lowest level. Taking advantage of the fair weather, the two groups lost no time in hauling and pushing their animals and themselves up the mountain slopes, staying on the north side of the Walker River. Once on the summit, they followed a stream running west, which proved to be the headwaters of the Stanislaus River. But even the western side of the divide proved extremely rough going. In forcing passages up and down the steep canyons the last of their few oxen either died, or had to be slaughtered along the way. Despite all the hardship they encountered daily, these half-clad, shoeless, yet undaunted pioneers managed to straggle out of the wilderness and into the central valley on 1 November 1841. Thus, with no map or early trailblazer to guide them, this group became the first American emigrants to travel overland and cross the Sierra Nevada into California.[16] That everyone in the party had survived was something of a miracle.

What began as a dribble of emigrant trains to California in the early 1840s, soon developed into a steady stream over the next decade. Frequently, former trappers and mountain men guided these caravans through the western expanse. In the process, many different crossing sites over the Sierra were investigated and tried. Improvisation while negotiating granite headwalls was often the key to success. Of special interest to this history is the route pioneered by the Trahern Party.* Moving west in the spring of 1853, the party attacked the Sierra from Leavitt Meadows and formed the first oxen train over Sonora Pass. According to one account: "The ascent to the crest was torture." Wagons were pushed, pulled, lifted with rope and block and tackle anchored to trees and rock up and down the steep granite crest. As many as six oxen were hitched behind wagons to act as brakes".[17] Eventually, some of these routes became established over time, while others proved too hazardous and were given up. Even passes traversed with relative ease by a succession of trains could still

be deadly fatal if the party was not sufficiently strong, or had miscalculated the affects of weather. Such was the calamity that befell the tragic Donner Party in the winter of 1846.

After the two-year war with Mexico ended with the 1848 Treaty of Guadalupe Hidalgo, which ceded to the United States the vast expanse of land west from Texas and north to Oregon, the number of emigrants heading west increased significantly. Initially, the responsibility for administering these new territories was placed in the hands of the U.S. Army. But just about the time the Army was coming to grips with its new responsibilities, as well as protecting the rising flow of emigrants, word began to circulate about a gold strike in the North Fork of the American River. Colonel Richard B. Mason, Commander of the California Department, accompanied by his Adjutant, Lieutenant William T. Sherman, then traveled to Sutter's Fort to see for themselves whether the rumors were true. After witnessing operations in the gold fields and being impressed by what he saw, Colonel Mason lost no time in filing an official report of his findings to President James K. Polk. Furthermore, he sent along 230 ounces of gold to Secretary of War James Buchanan, just to verify the astonishing events that were taking place in California. In giving his own judgment as to the potential size of the discovery,

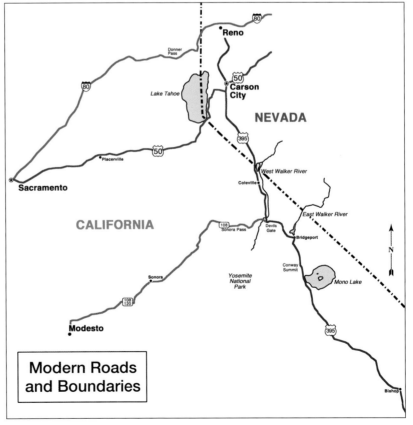

Modern Roads and Boundaries

---

* Some sources also refer to this group as the "Cherokee," and the Trahern-Duckwell Party.

John C. Fremont, American general and explorer.

Mason reported: "I have no hesitation in saying there is more gold in the country drained by the Sacramento and San Joaquin rivers than will pay the cost of the war with Mexico a hundred times over."[18] The Mason report in turn became the essence of the message that President Polk delivered to the second session of the 30th Congress on 5 December 1848. The President's official endorsement of the discovery of a rich bonanza in California was received with unrestrained enthusiasm wherever it was published. In effect, this message became the starting pistol that set in motion the largest migration of people ever to take place on the continent of North America.

How many people participated in this rush to California for riches? The exact numbers can never be known. But author Irving Stone estimates that during 1849 and 1850, more than 100,000 people traveled the overland route alone, while tens of thousands more had come via the sea.[19] By 1852, upwards of 90,000 prospectors could be found concentrated in a rectangle 20 miles wide and 60 miles long, while many more thousands fanned out over the entire western slope in search of new claims. In the process, these modern Jasons gutted the mountains of their golden wealth, denuded the forests, and almost exterminated the wild things of the land and the air. The Indians were simply overwhelmed by this chaotic surge of humanity on their

land. Either they adapted to this new reality, or were pushed aside as their ancient trails were rapidly transformed into permanent routes used by packers and teamsters to bring supplies to the growing number of remote mining camps. Also, it was not uncommon for some of these camps to change practically overnight into cities in excess of 5,000 inhabitants whenever word got out about the discovery of a new, rich ore body. Usually, this explosion of people would drive the cost of food and equipment to astronomical levels. But once the "pay dirt" was gone, or if some new bonanza was discovered elsewhere, the town might just as quickly become deserted and left to slip back to its previous obscurity.

Then in 1859, about the time the placer mining on the western slope was coming to an end,* vast deposits of gold and silver were discovered on the eastern side of the Sierra in the vicinity of what is today Virginia City, Nevada. Later, this body of ore was to take the name Comstock Lode. As the news of this discovery spread, miners who had been working the western streams quickly packed their equipment and began an exodus in reverse of the way many had come when traveling west in the 1850. In some cases, new passes were opened and old routes improved as thousands came over the mountains to prospect for gold in the dry diggings located along the eastern base of the Sierra. Dan De Quille, who became famous as a journalist with the *Territorial Enterprise* in Virginia City, describes this latest migration best:

> Miners and men of all classes and trades and professions flocked over the Sierras, in the spring of 1860. At first they came on foot, driving donkeys or other pack-animals before them, or on horseback, riding where they could and leading their horses where the snow was soft; but soon sleighs and stages were started and in some shape floundered through with their passengers. Saddle trains for passengers were started, however, before vehicles of any kind began to run, and the snow passed over was in many places from 30 to 60 feet in depth.[20]

Although most of the excitement centered on the Washoe, Eagle, and Carson Valleys, a small number of miners began to stake claims further south in the region of the Walker River and Mono Lake. It was

---
* Placer mining was the search for granulated gold, or nuggets that were found in the streams and ancient alluvial rivers. This method usually employed simple equipment such as pans, sluices, and crude cradles. Hard-rock mining for lode gold and hydraulic operations continued well into the next century.

not long thereafter that two small settlements sprang up: Dogtown and Monoville. Within a year, rich gold and silver deposits were also located in the outlying areas, resulting in the establishment of towns at Bodie, Masonic, and Aurora.[21] The rising population on the east side of the Sierra divide meant that two imperatives had to be met if these new communities were to prosper: The first need was for wagon routes over the mountains that could bring enough food products from the central valley to sustain people through the winter months; the second called for a political entity that would protect the claims of the miners and bring law and order to the newfound settlements. The latter goal was to be fulfilled first.

On 24 April 1861, the creation of Mono County, made up from portions of its several neighboring counties, was approved by an act of the California Legislature and was enacted into law on 10 May of the same year. The seat of justice was set at Aurora. But on 2 March, 1861, an Act of Congress established the Territory of Nevada. Moving swifter than his California counterpart, the new territorial governor, James W. Nye, also claimed Aurora as one of the election districts, and Esmeralda as one of nine counties making up the Territory. The ensuing dispute over the county seat of government and the state in which it was located was not resolved for three years. Finally, the matter was settled when a new survey of the state borders found Aurora to be just inside the Nevada line. As a consequence, in 1864, the magistrate and other county officials moved the seat of government to Bridgeport, in Mono County, taking the county records with them.[22]

The second goal of establishing trans-Sierra wagon routes would take a bit longer, but not much. By the early 1860, three separate wagon and stagecoach routes were in operation. The northern route came out of Nevada City on the western slope and crossed the Sierra at Henness Pass. The central route originated at Hangtown,* crossed the Sierra in the vicinity of Carson Pass, and dropped into the eastern basin at the old Mormon Station of Genoa. The southern route connected the town of Sonora in the west to Aurora in the east. This route generally followed the trace of the former Indian and emigrant trails along the course of the Stanislaus River to Kennedy Meadows and over Sonora Pass. Eventually, stage stops along this route would be established at Strawberry Flat on the western slope and at Leavitt Meadows and Fales Hot Springs on the eastern side. It goes without saying that winter

_____
* This historic mining camp later changed its name to Placerville.

travel over all three routes could be problematic, and therefore was either limited to animal or man packing, or closed down altogether. Most of the roads were constructed under state franchises, and developed by stock companies that were allowed to charge tolls to recoup their construction and maintenance costs. During boom times the road companies and teamsters prospered. But once the ore bodies withered and the mines began to fail, these ventures too, would become busted.

Thus, about the same time that the opening battles of the American civil war were being waged in the east, the Sierra Nevada was gradually being tamed. Towns and industries were springing up daily on both its slopes. The land was coming under cultivation, or being turned into cattle and sheep ranches to feed the growing number of miners, teamsters, loggers, mill workers, and their families. More and more wagon and stage routes were under construction to connect these new towns and centers of activity. Moreover, outside the towns of Omaha, in the Nebraska Territory, and Sacramento, California, the Union Pacific and the Central Pacific were also beginning to lay track for what was to become the first transcontinental railroad. Within a decade the two rail lines would be joined, thereby cutting the normal travel time to California from five months to 10 days. Not unlike Jonathan Swift's mythical Gulliver, the ties of civilization were slowly, but similarly, binding up the mighty Sierra Nevada Range.

According to Mono County records, a German immigrant by the name of Francis (Frank) Pickle arrived in the county from San Francisco and purchased several mining properties in late 1862.[23] In the following year (1863) Pickle took possession of 160-360 acres of land 18 miles north of Bridgeport, situated between Leavitt Meadows and the Hot Springs where Samuel Fales would soon come to operate his stage station. Here, on the north side of the West Walker River, just above the flood plain along Silver Creek, he built a cabin, made other improvements and started to mine and run livestock consisting of two horses, 21 cows and six hogs.[24] In late 1870, Frank Pickle was found shot dead in his cabin. Although Mr. Kent Stoddard, president and curator of the Mono County Historical Society Museum, believes that the local authorities had a strong suspicion of who had committed the crime, Pickle's assailant was never brought to trial. Nevertheless, as things turned out, this luckless prospector and pioneer stockman would not be forgotten completely. For it wasn't long after his death that people started referring to the valley as either: Pickle or Pickel Meadow. The latter spelling seemed to stick, at least long enough for the next mapmaker to come along and bless the location officially. Ironically, because of a war that would break out on the Asian continent 80 years later, the same Pickel Meadow would also become a very familiar name and place to thousands of U.S. Marines.

Chapter 2

U.S. Marine Corps Cold Weather Experience and Doctrine Prior to 1950

Again in nineteen forty-one,
We sailed a north'ard course,
And found beneath the midnight sun,
The Viking and the Norse.
The Iceland girls were slim and fair,
And fair the Iceland scenes,
And the Army found in landing there,
The United States Marines.
-Unofficial verse of the Marines' Hymn, circa 1942

Introduction

"To the average Marine officer the problems and experiences of field operations in very cold climes is purely hearsay. Marines are, by and large, warm weather fighters. In all our battles since World War I, khaki or cotton dungarees have been satisfactory uniforms and the problems of keeping warm and dry while living in the field have not been very great. Now we can no longer base our thinking or planning on the assumption that we will carry on future operations under warm suns in tropical or semi-tropical areas." So wrote Major Michael S. Hall in his article "Cold Weather Combat Clothing," which appeared in the May 1948 issue of the *Marine Corps Gazette*. In his article, Major Hall was making the point that, if it became necessary to fight in a cold climate, commanders were going to face unique problems that only a handful of Marines had encountered in the past three decades. Therefore, he argued that "all our troops need to be thoroughly indoctrinated in the wear and maintenance of the present kit of cold-weather clothing," and also become aware of its shortcomings.[25]

Major Hall's prescient comments were close to the mark. For the previous 30 years the vast majority of U.S. Marine expeditionary forces had been committed to the tropical zones of either the Caribbean or the Pacific Ocean areas. True, during the middle of World War II, Marine planners had looked to an invasion of Japan and the conduct of field operations in colder temperate areas. In anticipation of this requirement, the Quartermaster General of the Marine Corps had developed the M1943 cold-weather uniform. But the war had ended before either this clothing or the Marines themselves could be put to the test of a large-scale combat field operation in a northern climate. Therefore, compared to the U.S. Army, which had conducted recent winter campaigns in the Aleu-tians and in northern Europe, Marine Corps doctrine and the experience level of its troops for operating in cold-weather was indeed limited. Nevertheless, there had been a few episodes in its history from which the Corps could claim practical lessons learned for maintaining its fighting efficiency in cold climates.

Special Duty in the Bering Sea

The first instance of any sizable number of Marines being dispatched to "far off northern lands" occurred in the last decade of the 19th century. During the late 1880s and early 1890s the question of sealing rights in the Bering Sea became a significant diplomatic problem between Great Britain and the United States. In June 1891, as a first step toward resolving this dispute, both governments agreed to a suspension of all commercial sealing in those waters for a period of one year. Immediately after the parties signed the agreement, a joint Anglo-American naval force was hurriedly dispatched to the Aleutian Islands to prevent the compact from being violated.

A combined force of U.S. Marines consisting of five officers and 113 enlisted men supported the efforts of the American naval squadron. By today's standards this number would hardly be called "sizable," but in 1891 that figure represented over five percent of the Corps' entire strength. The majority of Marines who participated in the operation served with ships' detachments on board the four American ships making up the squadron. In addition, a separate guard detachment of three Marine officers and 40 enlisted from the Mare Island Navy Yard was also embarked aboard the *SS Alki*, a merchantman that had been converted to support the combined fleet as a prison and depot ship. Both this ship and its Marine guard detachment steamed out of San Francisco Bay having only three days and nights to prepare for the expedition. Commanding the Marine guard force (and the senior Marine officer present) was the veteran Captain Henry C. Cochrane.

The joint force cruised the foggy Aleutian Islands from June through October, searching the sloops of the Canadian and American sealers, seizing those that failed to heed the joint proclamation to "depart these waters." Meanwhile, the *SS Alki* was either on station at the almost barren anchorage across from Dutch Harbor on Unalaska Island, or it was engaged in transporting captured sloops and their crews to the

U.S. magistrate located at the territorial seat of government in Sitka.

Although this joint operation was largely conducted during the months of summer, weather conditions were far from ideal. Indeed, old hands who have lived in the Aleutians like to remark that "it's a good year when summer falls on a Sunday."[26] But despite the cold and frequent gale winds, Cochrane would brook no idleness from his Marines. To him there was always work to be done and new skills to be learned. Thus marksmanship, signaling, bayonet drill, and crewing small boats were all part of the daily routine, no matter how inclement the weather. Besides, prior to departing from Mare Island, the strict commander had been granted authority by the Commandant himself to purchase special sets of foul weather clothing for his men. This purchase alone cost $56.50. To not put this special gear to use in bad weather would have been a waste, and for the thrifty Cochrane, "waste" was a sin that was second only to idleness. "Throughout our absence," he later wrote in his report to the Commandant, "drills and instructions were unremitting. I am thankful to report the detachment at full strength and all well, and to be able to say, that its conduct has been most creditable."[27]

Expedition to Iceland

A half-century later in the late spring of 1941, Britain stood alone in preventing a Nazi conquest of all Western Europe. Seriously concerned for the defense of the Western Hemisphere, especially if Great Britain was invaded or suddenly collapsed, U.S. Army and Navy planners began to hastily draft a number of contingency plans. Among them was a plan to employ U.S. Army and Marine forces for the purpose of seizing and defending the Azores, the Vichy French colony of Martinique, or both. To give added strength to General Holland M. Smith's 1st Marine Division, based on the east coast, Headquarters Marine Corps ordered the 6th Marine Regiment to be detached from its parent and newly formed 2d Marine Division, and proceed by naval transport to the eastern seaboard. On 31 May 1941, the convoy with the 6th Marines (Reinforced) got underway from San Diego harbor and headed for the Panama Canal.

While the convoy bearing the embarked 6th Regiment steamed south, the war situation in the North Atlantic began to look more threatening.* As a result,

President Franklin D. Roosevelt decided to accede to Prime Minister Winston Churchill's earlier request for sending American troops to Iceland to free up some of the British forces garrisoned there, provided the Icelanders invited an American occupation force to their island. The Army-Navy Board then quickly put together a plan that called for the immediate formation of a provisional Marine brigade as the lead element of a larger U.S. commitment. Using the reinforced 6th Marine Regiment as its nucleus, augmented by the 5th Defense Battalion from Parris Island, South Carolina, and a sprinkling of combat support units from the east coast, the brigade formed at the Charleston Navy Yard. Thereafter, or as soon as the U.S. Army was able to organize an infantry division of regulars, it too would follow on to Iceland and relieve the Marines in place.

President Roosevelt approved the plan on 5 June and directed his Chief of Naval Operations, Admiral Harold R. Stark, to have the brigade ready to sail in 15 days' time. On 15 June, the 6th Marines (Reinforced) arrived in Charleston Harbor. On the following day the 1st Marine Brigade (Provisional) was formally activated under Brigadier General John Marston. Following five days of hectic dockside loading, on 22 June 1941, the new brigade consisting of 4,095 Marines, steamed out of Charleston harbor to join the impressive array of warships that were there to escort them to the North Atlantic.[28] Oddly enough, it had been exactly 50 years to the day since Cochrane and his Marines had shoved off from San Francisco Bay aboard the *SS Alki*, similarly bound for expeditionary duty near the Arctic Circle and likewise, severely strained by the short-notice orders.*

On 1 July 1941, Iceland finally accepted the agreement proposed by the British government that formally invited U.S. troops to occupy and defend its national boundaries. Under the terms agreed upon, the United States pledged to withdraw its troops promptly on the coming of peace, to recognize the complete independence and sovereignty of the Icelanders, and not to interfere in the internal affairs of the island.[29] On 7 July, following a brief layover in Newfoundland awaiting the Icelanders' invitation, the convoy arrived at Iceland and anchored in Reykjavik Harbor. Within a week the Marines had off-loaded their supplies and equipment, largely by man-handling from small craft over a narrow beach, and had moved into the dispersed camps of Nissen huts that the British forces had turned over to them.

---

* The German battleship *Bismarck* and cruiser *Prinz Eugen* had two weeks earlier been raiding in the shipping lanes around Iceland, before a British naval force was able to corner *Bismarck* and sink her on 27 May. Also, the sinking of the American merchantman *Robin Moor* by a German U-boat on 21 May angered the president and probably strengthened his view of the strategic importance of keeping Iceland out of German hands.

---

* 22 June 1941 was also the day Hitler launched his invasion against the Soviet Union.

The 1st Provisional Marine Brigade passes in review before British Prime Minister Winston S. Churchill in Iceland on 16 August 1941.

Command relations between Major General Henry O. Curtis, the senior British commander, and General Marston were cordial from the outset. On paper, General Marston's designated superior was the Chief of Naval Operations in Washington, D.C. But his standing orders did authorize him to coordinate his operations with the British "by the method of mutual cooperation."[30] By agreement, the 6th Marines were given the mission as the garrisons' mobile defense column. This was considered an important task, for it was assumed that any attempt by the Germans to seize the island would likely be pre-

Marine standing in front of Nissen huts in Iceland, 1941. Note the fur cap with Marine Corps emblem and the "Polar Bear" shoulder insignia which had been adopted from the British 79th Division by the 1st Provisional Marine Brigade.

ceded by a thrust of airborne forces. When General Curtis suggested that the Marines wear the British 79th Division "Polar Bear" shoulder patch, General Marston readily agreed. "The British complied with our requests and we complied with theirs. It was as simple as that," wrote General Marston in his first report back to Major General Commandant Thomas Holcomb.[31]

First priority of work for the Marines went to building, or improving field fortifications and defensive positions within their assigned sectors of defense. The long daylight hours and fair weather also gave commanders the opportunity to devote time toward the second priority of conducting conditioning marches, small arms firing, and tactical field exercises over the rugged Icelandic terrain. But as the summer waned and the available daylight hours began to diminish, more of the brigade's time was given over to preparing for winter. Moreover on 22 September, in compliance with an executive order signed by President Roosevelt, the chain-of-command of the 1st Provisional Marine Brigade shifted formally from the naval establishment to that of the U.S. Army and the War Department. Thereafter, General Marston reported to Major General Charles H. Bonesteel, USA, who had just arrived and was

now the senior U.S. officer present. Under General Bonesteel's orders, the Leathernecks assumed the additional task of erecting Nissen huts, in anticipation of a U.S. Army division that was under orders to deploy to Iceland in the spring.

Back in May, when the 6th Marine Regiment (Reinforced) was at Camp Elliot and received its orders from Headquarters Marine Corps to proceed to the eastern United States, the message gave no hint as to the regiment's mission or its destination. Most of the officers thought the destination would be either Guantanamo or Martinique; a few believed it might be the Azores. Consequently, the commanding officer of the regiment, Colonel Leo D. Hermle, was in a quandary about what uniforms he should order his men to bring. Ultimately, he decided that each Marine would take his complete kit of summer and winter uniforms. As arctic winds began to blow over Iceland in 1941, Colonel Hermle's men were likely quite grateful for his having made that decision. Although the green kersey dress uniform was tailored too tight to permit a true layering system, nevertheless it, along with the winter overcoat, provided reasonably good protection up through the month of October, until the arctic winds began to increase in velocity. With temperatures falling, Ma-

Colonel Leo D. Hermle, commanding officer of 6th Marine Regiment, Iceland, 1941-1942.

Courtesy of Col James A. Donovan

Courtesy of Col James A. Donovan

A squad of Marines from 6th Marine Regiment training in Iceland, during the winter of 1941-1942.

rine officers in Iceland soon learned that it was possible to fare a bit better than their men, as they had access to the British Quartermaster stores where they could buy quality trench coats, boots, wool shirts, and other items.

Until 1943, the Marine Corps had no winter field service combat uniform other than its winter service greens, including the overcoat in the same heavy wool worn since World War I. According to Colonel James A. Donovan, Jr., who served with the 1st Provisional Brigade, the one distinctive item of Marine Corps uniform issue, which was also the most popular with the troops, was the fur cap with the Marine emblem on the front. The cap had a green crown and thick, brown fur trim and earflaps that provided good protection as the winds rose and the chill factor dropped. Its origins had come from Marines who had served in North China.[32] In addition, prior to sailing from Charleston, the brigade staff had scoured the Marine Corps supply system for whatever special winter clothing it had on hand and could be furnished. Therefore as winter deepened, Marines were issued a variety of items, including 20-year old-mustard-colored wool shirts, which had been in use during the "banana wars"; woolen underwear; heavy-wool socks; rubber galoshes; and even some sheepskin-lined canvas coats that had been purchased from Sears Roebuck and Company and other civilian sources just before the brigade sailed.

Second Lieutenant William K. Jones served as a company officer with the 1st Battalion, 6th Marine on Iceland. With the onset of winter, he later recalled: "Daylight slowly diminished from almost 24 hours a day to about six. The wind seemed to blow constantly, with gusts up to 70 and 100 miles an hour, necessitating lifelines between huts and mess halls."[33] Under these extreme cold conditions, the bits and pieces of field-combat clothing that were issued to the Marines for service in Iceland were deemed far from satisfactory. Even at the squad level there was no standard uniform for outside wear. Often, when the wind chill dropped near zero, outdoor troop activities had to be restricted to essential security and maintenance duties.

So the Iceland Marines carried on, warm enough, and without experiencing any serious trench foot or frostbite problems. But mainly that was because the bulk of the German Army was already bogged down in one winter campaign in the Soviet Union and German commanders were likely reticent about a second, cold-weather front. Had Adolf Hitler not turned east in 1941 and the Marine brigade been called upon to fight and live in the field for an extended period in that cold bleak place, the number of casualties from cold injuries alone would have likely been very high. The Marine leadership did not fail to recognize this obvious lesson. As relieving U.S. Army units began to arrive in late February, the cold-weather combat clothing that had been issued to the soldiers impressed the Marines, especially the olive-drab parkas with the alpaca linings.

Courtesy of Col James A. Donovan

A 6th Marine platoon in Iceland in late 1941. Most of these Marines display the Polar Bear patch insignia with Nissen huts are in background.

In his after-action report, General Marston urged that the Marine Corps also adopt a similar uniform suitable for combat in cold climates.

During February and March, the Marine brigade was incrementally relieved in place and returned to the United States and its former duty stations. From there, its Marines either shipped out to the South Pacific or remained stateside as cadres for the new units being formed. The brigade headquarters landed at New York on 25 March at which time the 1st Marine Brigade (Provisional), was officially disbanded. How much strategic value this Marine deployment remains questionable.* But that is not of import to this particular history. What is significant is the fact that a number of the Corps' future leaders likely benefited from the unique experience of learning first hand the challenges associated with operations in a cold, unforgiving climate. Among that group was the commanding officer of the 1st Battalion, 6th Marines, Lieutenant Colonel Oliver P. Smith. Nine years later, this same officer would be commanding the 1st Marine Division in North

---

* Col Robert D. Heinl believed that "the 1st Provisional Marine Brigade's arrival tipped the scales and saved Iceland" (See Heinl, *Soldiers of the Sea: The United States Marine Corps, 1775-1962,* 2d ed. (Baltimore, MD.: Nautical and Aviation Publishing Co., 1991), p. 312.

Korea under very similar conditions of extreme cold.

Between World War II and Korea

Between 1945 and 1950, the Marine Corps' exposure to the conduct of operations in cold climates turned out to be few and far between. The III Marine Amphibious Corps (largely constituted by the 1st and 6th Marine Divisions) did gain some practical experience during the winter of 1945–1946 when it served as a buffer between Chiang-Kai-shek's National forces and the Chinese Communist Army in Manchuria. However, most of the force was garrisoned in population and communication centers where it could carry out its primary mission of keeping the road, rail, and port facilities open to commerce. Inasmuch as the Communist armies chose not to interfere at this time, the Marines did little in the way of large-scale field maneuvers or combat operations. Therefore, the M1943 cold-weather uniforms that were issued to the Marines received only a partial test of their adequacy and serviceability. By 1947, the number of Marines serving in North China had been scaled down to less than 3,000, most of whom were stationed at Tsing-tao. Two years later, the last Marine unit was withdrawn from the Chinese mainland.

Other duty stations where Marines found themselves contending with the rigors of a frigid climate in the post World War II years included the Corps' security forces in the Territory of Alaska. In 1939, the U.S. Navy established a naval air station along the northeastern shores of Kodiak Island. Soon thereafter, a Marine barracks was activated to provide security and form the nucleus of a ground defense force. After the Japanese attack on Pearl Harbor, Marine strength of the outpost grew to six officers and 265 enlisted men, but by the end of the war the barracks had returned to its normal staffing of four officers and 100 enlisted Marines. Although located in the so-called "Banana Belt" of Alaska, temperatures of 10 degrees below zero were not uncommon during the winter months. The annual training syllabus for the Marines in those years traditionally included a weeklong field maneuver on Afognak Island. Small groups of Marines also trained with the U.S. Army Arctic Survival School in Fairbanks. Thus Marines who had completed a two-year Alaskan tour of duty at this northern outpost could therefore rightly claim a degree of proficiency in winter survival and cold-weather warfighting techniques.

Another security detachment where a Marine could gain an appreciation for the challenges of cold-weather operations was at the Marine Barracks, Adak. Located in the remote western half of the Aleutian chain at the U.S. Naval Station, the Marine Corps established its first security detachment there in 1943. During the post-war years the Marine guard force normally numbered five officers and about 125 enlisted Marines. Basic missions included providing security for the naval station and becoming the backbone of the base ground defense force during emergencies or high threat alerts. The island's fierce winds, damp climate, treeless terrain, and frequent earthquakes were conducive toward instilling confidence in the individual Marine that he could not only survive in such a harsh climate, but with knowledge and extra effort, remain combat effective.

As relations between the Soviet Union and the United States deteriorated in the late 1940s, both the U.S. Navy and its Marine land arm began to take closer looks at their collective capabilities for conducting combat operations in a northern zone. During November and December 1948, the latest version of the Marine Corps' landing vehicle track (LVT), underwent a major operational evaluation at the U.S. Navy Arctic Test Station, Point Barrow, Alaska. Marine Corps Headquarters also initiated ex-

Officers of 1st Battalion, 6th Marines, 1941. Lieutenant Colonel Oliver P. Smith is seated in the front row, fifth from left, and Second Lieutenant William K. Jones is standing in second row, far right, both became Marine general officers.

Courtesy of Col James A. Donovan

perimental testing of the helicopter in cold-weather operations off Newfoundland about this time. Then, in February 1949, Commander-in-Chief, Pacific Fleet (CinCPacFlt) conducted a 10-day fleet amphibious exercise on Kodiak Island named MICOWEX 49A. Regimental Landing Team 7 (RLT 7) from the 1st Marine Division at Camp Pendleton, California, formed the nucleus of the 3d Marine Brigade. The commander landing force (CLF) and commander of the brigade was Brigadier General Harry B. "Harry the Horse" Liversedge.[34]

One of the landing force objectives was to evaluate the adequacy of the M1943 cold-weather uniform, under field conditions with temperatures in the +10 to –10 degree range. The M1943 winter uniform closely resembled the U.S. Army pattern and was based on the same "layering" principle, with a variety of garments worn one over the other. This included a jacket, trousers, pile cap, gloves, and the leather and rubber shoe-pacs. The latter had a rubber sole, 7/8 inch heel, a steel shank, leather top, and felt insoles and was worn with two pairs of heavy wool socks. A second objective was to test a new backpack system for the winter uniform that was then under development by the Quartermaster General of the Marine Corps. Because of the weight and bulk of the cold-weather kit, this consisted of a large waterproofed bag (popularly referred to as a "willie peter" bag), which could then be affixed to a wooden pack board.

In the 3d Marine Brigade post-exercise report, General Liversedge confirmed what a number of organizations and units had been reporting for several years: The M1943 cold-weather uniform had several problems that needed to be remedied. First and foremost were the serious deficiencies found with the shoe-pacs footwear. Many troops complained that the shoe-pacs lack of ankle support made marching difficult. This footwear also caused feet to sweat, which allowed the moisture to freeze inside during periods of inactivity. Thus it was concluded that a combat boot that could prevent frozen feet and trench foot should be developed. Other reported shortcomings of the winter uniform included the weight of the cold-weather combat load (110

pounds); the bulky parka that tended to restrict movement of the combat Marine; and the issued glove, which offered only fair protection. In the latter case, the addition of a mitten shell with a trigger finger was recommended.[35] For man packing the heavier loads during operations ashore, the combination pack board and willie peter (WP) bag proved to be superior to the 1941 Marine Corps pack system. However, its lack of belt suspenders and its bulkiness made it unsatisfactory for climbing up and down cargo nets during the ship-to-shore phase.

In terms of doctrine, the Marine Corps had issued no special publications, handbooks, or standing operating procedures pertaining to cold-weather operations prior to 1950.[*] Instead, except for operations involving the amphibian tractor, it relied on the technical and field manuals published by the U.S. Army. Fortunately, these were of good quality and covered a range of climatic conditions from the cold/wet to the arctic. More importantly, they were current. Basic principles were based on the practical experiences and bitter lessons that soldiers had learned during months of tough winter campaigning in the Aleutians and northern Europe less than five years before. Also, a major contributor to the U.S. Army's level of experience and doctrinal publications came directly from its 10th Mountain Division. This highly acclaimed division had trained intensively for two years at Camp Hale, Colorado. Moreover, it had participated in the Aleutians campaign with one regimental combat team, and had undergone almost a year of combat operations in the mountains of northern Italy before the Nazi government of Germany collapsed in May of 1945.

With the total active duty strength of the U.S. Marine Corps falling to 75,000, this is where things stood regarding USMC cold-weather operations on 25 June 1950 when the North Korean People's Army crossed the 38th Parallel and invaded South Korea.

---

[*] Indeed, the *Guidebook for Marines* did not mention the topic of cold-weather indoctrination and training until it was published in the 1954 printing.

Chapter 3

The Marines Arrive

I am enthusiastic about the location selected for your cold-weather training and am confident that our replacements will be well fitted for a winter campaign, if they have to fight one.
-Commandant Clifton B. Cates to Major General O.P. Smith, 25 September 1951

Korean War Backdrop

The strategic situation on the Korean Peninsula during the first six months of the war was dynamic and dramatic. From 25 June through 31 December 1950, the military fortunes of the U.N. and communist forces shifted widely back and forth, with each side enjoying stunning victories as well as catastrophic defeats. Scores of histories and chronicles have since been published that document in minute detail, and at every level of command, just how those battles ebbed and flowed. Therefore, it is unnecessary to review them in detail here.

It should be recalled, however, that on 5 October, after the successful amphibious assault at Inchon, several weeks of hard fighting followed for the recapture of Seoul. The 1st Marine Division, supported by the 1st Marine Aircraft Wing, then re-embarked for a second amphibious assault on Korea's northeast coast. The designated amphibious objective area was Wonsan Harbor. The objective of this second sea-borne assault was to cut off the North Korean land forces that were in headlong retreat north along the coast. But the Marine landing at Wonsan was delayed for several weeks when the advance force discovered communist mines blocking the harbor entrance. Although Major General Oliver P. Smith fumed offshore, there was nothing that he or his division staff could do to speed up the mine clearing operation.* Thus, it was not until 26 October that commander, Amphibious Task Force finally gave the signal to "Land the Landing Force." By this time, the Republic of Korea's 3d and Capital Divisions had already occupied Wonsan, thereby permitting the Marines to come ashore unopposed.

On 24 October, General Douglas MacArthur issued the directive that removed all remaining restrictions on the movement of American troops toward the Yalu River. Eighth Army and X Corps were therefore "authorized to use any and all

---

* Five U.S. Navy minesweepers were lost or damaged during these clearing operations.

Major General Oliver P. Smith (in helmet), Commanding General, 1st Marine Division talking with Major General Edward D. Almond, X Corps commander, in Korea, 1950.

ground forces as necessary to secure all of North Korea."[36] Thus, in spite of the crisp fall weather that had descended over the northern peninsula, there was still a sense of optimism in the air as the 1st Marine Division and the 7th U.S. Army Division, the two major components of Major General Edward M. Almond's X Corps, made preparations for what everyone hoped would be the final knockout blow. Then, on 3 November, northeast of the port of Hungnam, the 1st Marine Division encountered its first opposition from Chinese Communist Forces. Several days of fierce fighting in the vicinity of Sudong ensued. On the fourth day, what was left of the *124th Division*, Chinese People's Army, suddenly broke contact and disappeared into the mountains.[37] Following this encounter, sets of M1943 cold-weather clothing were quickly issued to Colonel Homer L. Litzenberg's 7th Marine Regiment, as it resumed the lead of the 1st Marine Division's final northwestern push to the Chosin Reservoir and to the banks of the Yalu River.

"All personnel ... would be thoroughly indoctrinated ..."

About the same time that cold-weather clothing and equipment was being issued to the 1st Marine Division in North Korea, the Commandant of the

Marine Corps History Division

As commanding general of Training and Replacement Command, Brigadier General Merrill Twining was responsible for conduct of training and preparing of all Marine replacement troops headed to Korea, 1950-1951.

Marine Corps General Clifton B. Cates sent a letter on the subject of guidance for cold-weather training to the Commanding General, Marine Barracks* Camp Pendleton, California. This directive, dated 9 November 1950, established the requirement "that all personnel scheduled to arrive in the Korean area prior to 1 May 1951 would be thoroughly indoctrinated in the measures of living and operating in snow and extreme cold prior to overseas movement." Further, "a minimum of eight (8) hours would be allotted to this training and that a schedule of cold-weather training would be submitted to Headquarters Marine Corps prior to 25 November 1950 for approval."[38]

The tasking letter must have been immediately passed for action to Brigadier General Merrill B. Twining, the Commanding General, Training and Replacement Command, then a subordinate command under Camp Pendleton. For on 12 November, it was this officer who responded to General Cates by submitting a proposal for a cold-weather training syllabus which included a three and one-half day practical field exercise. "This training," General Twining went on to say, "would be conducted in

_____

* Marine Corps Base, Camp Pendleton was designated as a "Barracks" from its activation date on 25 September 1942, until it was re-designated as a Marine Corps Base on 1 September 1953.

the Big Bear Region of the San Bernadino Range, about 75 miles from Camp Pendleton."[39] On 11 December, the same day the rear guard of the 1st Marine Division was fighting its way back into the perimeter at Hungnam, the Commandant approved the proposed training syllabus, including the three and one-half day field exercise.

In theory, establishing a syllabus for a Cold-Weather Indoctrination-Training Program should not have been difficult in 1950. The planners had only to refer to the appropriate U.S. Army Field Manual on cold-weather operations, select those subjects that they believed were essential, and staying within the limits of the time allowed, organize the subjects into a coherent program of instruction. But the field manual assumed that all the necessary resources would be on hand and readily available for use by the trainers. Unfortunately, this was not the case. The Staging and Replacement Command soon found that many of the basic requirements needed to put the program into being were in scarce supply. As a result, those first few hectic months of providing cold-weather indoctrination to the mix of units and replacements bound for Korea proved to be a more challenging task than anyone anticipated. This was especially true for the cadre of relatively inexperienced instructors who were called upon to implement the plan. One can infer from their reports that the trainers continually struggled with all the unforeseen problems that typically befall an untested training program that has been hastily conceived.

The scarcity of qualified instructors was a challenge during that first year. Another problem was related to the Big Bear training site itself. Soon after the program got underway, General Twining paid an unexpected visit to the former Big Bear Civilian Conservation Corps facility where the training unit had set up its base camp. It was a Sunday morning and Twining knew an 800-man training increment was scheduled to arrive that afternoon. What he saw did not please him. The camp was a shambles. Also, the instructors he talked to were disorganized and, in his mind, utterly unready to receive the training unit that would soon be arriving. Furthermore, no one could locate the Reserve officer-in-charge, or any of his officers. Apparently, they had gone off on liberty the day before and had yet to return. Unquestionably, the unprofessional scene that was before him and the base camp's proximity to the holiday atmosphere of the Big Bear winter resort area did not please him. This was not what General Twining had envisaged when he had told his superiors that this training would approximate conditions similar to those found in North Korea.

Immediately, he directed his aide to call Captain Walter Moore at his Camp Pendleton quarters and inform him that a staff car would soon arrive to pick him up and deliver him to Big Bear. As of that moment, Captain Moore was now the officer-in-charge of the field-training portion of the cold-weather indoctrination program.[40] Known to his friends as "Mu Mu," this veteran Marine of 10 years, who had earned a battlefield commission during World War II, would prove to be the right man for the job.

Before receiving these unexpected orders, Captain Moore had been assigned to the 6th Replacement Draft at the Training and Replacement Command. The 6th Draft was then undergoing its final staging preparations before shipping out to Korea. Apparently, however, the commanding general was aware of Captain Moore's unique past experience and qualifications for winter warfare. In 1947-1948, Moore had served as an exchange officer with the U.S. Army at Fort Carson and at Camp Hale, Colorado. Here he was assigned to the 1st Battalion, 38th Infantry Regiment, the last remaining remnant of the U.S. Army's famed 10th Mountain Division. After going through the summer rock climbing and winter ski courses at Camp Hale, Captain Moore proved to be such an apt military mountaineer that his battalion commander entrusted him with command of Company A for the balance of his 16-month exchange tour. Therefore, General Twining must have reasoned, Captain Moore was the only officer within his immediate reach who possessed the experience and skills to put his floundering Cold Weather Indoctrination Program back on track. Consequently, the captain's name was removed from the rolls of the 6th Replacement Draft and he was informed that his orders to Korea would be delayed until late in the next spring.

After that first increment of troops had completed its field training, the new officer-in-charge scouted around other nearby forest reserves in search of an alternate site to the one at Big Bear. Eventually, he settled on a more remote location known as Black Mountain in the San Jacinto Mountains, five miles above the town of Idyllwild. Meanwhile, after ridding himself of most of the incompetent members of the training group and replacing them with known leaders, some with whom had served with him in the 3d Raider Battalion in the Pacific, Captain Moore gradually managed to improve the quality of the instruction and the practicality of the training to the point where the Black Mountain field exercises did, in fact, closely resemble conditions that one could expect to fight and live under in Korea.[41] By early spring, however, even the San Jacinto site became less satisfactory

Captain Walter "Mu Mu" Moore, circa 1950. Moore, a World War II veteran, became the first officer-in-charge of the field training portion of the cold weather indoctrination program. He organized the Marine Corps' earliest cold-weather training programs at Big Bear and later in the San Jacinto Mountains, California, in the winter of 1950-1951.

due to the lack of deep snow and cold temperatures at the lower elevations. By late March, troop indoctrination in cold-weather operations was limited to the basic eight hours of classroom instruction, followed by a five-day field exercise in the Case Springs maneuver area at Camp Pendleton.

As the first winter training season came to a close, the planners and trainers met at Camp Pendleton to take stock of what had and what had not been accomplished. Even with all its shortcomings, this first effort was not viewed as a total failure. Thousands of Marines who were now serving at the frontlines in Korea had at least been provided a sense of the climatic conditions in which they were now living and fighting. Moreover, in the process of overcoming the many problems that surfaced, valuable lessons had been learned by the staff of instructors. Nevertheless, they agreed, a number of the features of the program still had to be remedied before the Cold Weather Indoctrination Program resumed in the following fall.[42]

Whether the program would or should continue was never discussed. The leadership at both Headquarters U.S. Marine Corps and at Camp Pendleton had acknowledged the need for cold-weather training. First, the war in Korea was beginning to look more like a long-term military commitment. Second, and perhaps even the greater imperative, were the

A Marine rifleman undergoing training at the San Jacinto Mountains site.

casualty figures that had been reported after the Chosin Reservoir breakout. Of the 7,313 non-battle casualties reported by the 1st Marine Division during the period of 26 October to 15 December 1950, most had been attributed to frostbite and other types of cold injuries suffered in the 0 to –35 degree weather.[43] This was a discomfiting revelation for an organization that boasted of its readiness and ability to fight in every "clime and place." Clearly, the need for a Cold Weather Indoctrination Program would be around for some time to come. Therefore, long-term solutions were needed.

Proponents for enhancing the practical field application phase of the program received a boost on 12 May, when the Marine Corps transferred Major General Oliver P. Smith from command of the 1st Marine Division in Korea to serve as Commanding General of Camp Pendleton, as well as Commanding General, Fleet Marine Force, Pacific Troops. No general officer serving in the Marine Corps at the time could claim a greater appreciation for the adverse effects that extreme cold could have on combat operations. General Smith's personal interest in strengthening the program was soon to prove beneficial.

Radio jeeps at the San Jacinto training site, early spring 1951. There was a relative lack of snow for cold-weather training purposes.

"Take what action is necessary to establish a suitable training site"

During the late spring and early summer of 1951, General Twining, with the full support of General Smith, dispatched reconnaissance parties to locate a new winter training site that might be used by the Marine Corps on either a temporary or long-term basis. The two generals sought a site that would provide isolation, mountainous terrain with suitable maneuver areas, low winter temperatures with sufficient snow levels to enable the proper indoctrination of troops to living under cold-weather field conditions, and a suitable campsite for the logistic and administrative support of both the permanent personnel and those who would be undergoing instruction.

In mid-June the reconnaissance parties returned to Camp Pendleton and reported their findings. Several locations were identified as meeting most of the General Twining's criteria for suitability. On 15 June 1951, General Twining sent a letter to Headquarters U.S. Marine Corps in which he outlined his plan for the conduct of cold-weather training for replacements during 1951 and 1952.[44] He proposed three new site locations for the conduct of this training. Responding with a speed letter to the Commanding General, Camp Pendleton, dated 7 July, the Commandant approved the recommendations that had been submitted on 15 June and directed the following:

> a. Commence extended cold-weather training for a period of a week to 10 days in the early fall of 1951 as soon as weather conditions permit.
> b. Take what action is necessary to establish a suitable training site in one of the locations suggested by CG Tra&Repl Comd ltr of 15 June 1951. This Headquarters will render any assistance required.[45]

In a subsequent letter addressed to the Commandant dated 31 July 1951, General Twining notified Headquarters U.S. Marine Corps that that he was recommending the Wheeler area in northern California as the new cold-weather-training site.[*] The Wheeler Guard Station and Wheeler Mountain are located about six miles to the Southeast of Pickel Meadow on Highway 395. Further, he expected training to commence with the 14th Replacement Draft on, or about 18 September, with an estimated monthly training load of 2,800 trainees.[46] Then, in mid-August, the Commanding General of the Training and Replacement Command sent a follow-up to his previous letter to the Commandant. In this letter he referred to the new training site at a place called "Pickel Meadow."[*] He described an area located about 90 miles southwest of Reno, Nevada, and better than 400 miles north of Camp Pendleton, and explained that it offered the type of terrain and the weather conditions for the desired training. What he might have added was that the site was also located at the 38th Parallel, exactly the same latitude where the U.N. forces were then locked in combat with the Communists on the Korean Peninsula.

According to one eyewitness account, it was sometime in early June 1951 when the Pickel Meadow area was first surveyed as a potential site for Marine cold-weather training. The leader of the reconnaissance party was Lieutenant Colonel Donald B. Hubbard, who for the previous year had been serving in the G-3 Section of the Staging and Replacement Command. This officer was intimately familiar with the program that had been established by Captain Moore the previous year and therefore had a keen appreciation for the type of terrain and cold-weather environment needed to make the field application phase realistic and meaningful. Accompanying Colonel Hubbard was First Lieutenant Richard M. Johnson. Lieutenant Johnson had served in Korea as a rifle platoon commander in Company D of Lieutenant Colonel Harold S. Roise's 2d Battalion, 5th Marines, during the Chosin Reservoir campaign. During mid-morning of 27 November, Lieutenant Johnson's platoon was in the point, and he was wounded at Yudam Ni when the Chinese began their first major offensive. It was on this day that the advance of the 1st Marine Division was halted. After participating in the breakout from the Chosin Reservoir and upon his rotation back to the United States in April, Lieutenant Johnson was assigned to the Staging and Replacement Command at Camp Pendleton. There, he was given duties as a cold-weather training instructor and later as the Aggressor Platoon leader.

Years later Johnson could not recall if he and Colonel Hubbard had just happened upon Pickel Meadow or whether the local forest rangers from the district office in Bridgeport directed them there. However, inasmuch as either a temporary, or long-term, land use permit would eventually have to be approved by that agency of the government, Johnson believed it likely that Colonel Hubbard would

---

* The author was unable to determine whether this was an early reference name for what became the Pickel Meadow site, or if was a separate candidate site that was then under consideration.

* The incorrect use of "Pickle," vice "Pickel," occurs frequently in early correspondence and message traffic between HQMC and the commands at Camp Pendleton.

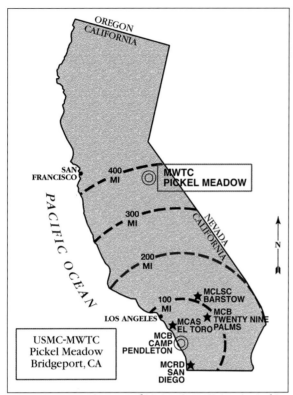

USMC Mountain Warfare Training Center Pickel Meadow Master Plan.

have, at the very least, consulted with the local rangers before walking the ground of any prospective site. Regardless of whether this reconnaissance party happened upon or was shown the landscape surrounding Pickel Meadow, Johnson does remember that they were quite impressed by the surrounding terrain.

Physically, this region of the eastern Sierra had not changed much since Frank Pickel built his log cabin above the West Walker River in the early 1860s. What had once been a rough mule and wagon trail over Sonora Pass was now a two-lane paved highway, California 108. Additionally, three miles to the west near Leavitt Meadows, there was now a small commercial fishing lodge and pack station. But the state of California did not maintain Highway 108 as an all-weather highway. Therefore, the road was customarily closed to vehicular traffic after the first snowfall in late October or early November and did not reopen until May. This, in essence, turned Pickel Meadow into a virtual cul-de-sac for six months of the year, providing all the isolation from civilian distractions that the Marines had been seeking.

As to the rest of the commanding general's guidance, the valley floor, which was at the 6,800-foot level, seemed to offer ample space for a logistics base to support both the permanent personnel and the Marines under instruction. From here, the mountains rose to over 11,000 feet, with the mountainsides dotted with large stands of pine, fir, and aspen trees. Interspersed among the forests were lush alpine meadows and tracts of open scrub sage, making it ideal for the maneuver of small infantry units. Most importantly, it appeared that the snow and extreme cold weather conditions at the higher elevations had not varied since John C. Fremont first recorded them in February of 1844. Colonel Johnson clearly remembered verifying this when he and Colonel Hubbard stopped for a sandwich at the Leavitt Meadows Lodge. The proprietor was a man who introduced himself as "Shorty." In addition to running the pack station and fishing lodge, he also sold groceries to the campers and cut hair on the side. After lunch, Colonel Hubbard asked what the winters were like in the area.

"Oh, they are awful," responded Shorty. "The drifts around here get to be 20 feet deep and the temperatures at night fall between minus 5-20 degrees. Even the snowshoe rabbits can't survive the winters up here."*

"And what do you do in the winter?" pursued the Colonel.

"Look at those sticks holding up the shutters," replied the proprietor, pointing to his store windows. "Well, when the first snowflake falls, I knock those sticks down and start buttoning this place up right away. Then I hightail it south out of here until the next spring."

Smiles broke out on the faces of the two Marine officers as they listened to Shorty's descriptions of the severe winter conditions. Hearing him rattle on about the prevailing freezing temperatures, both officers likely nodded and thought to themselves "Eureka! We have found it."[47]

After weighing all the advantages and disadvantages between the several prospective sites that the reconnaissance teams had reported, the only issue that may have given the Commanding Generals some pause before selecting Pickel Meadow as the most suitable area was the distance. Traveling by way of U.S. Highway 395, the new site was separated from Camp Pendleton by over 450 miles. Furthermore, ground transportation ferrying troops to and from the site would have to cross three passes over 7,500 feet in elevation, the last being the 8,000-foot Conway Summit, just to the south of the town

_____
* Just to the northwest in neighboring Calaveras County, the town of Tamarack averages more 37 feet of snow a year and holds the U.S., record for having the greatest depth of snow on the ground at any one time (not counting snowdrifts): 451 inches, nearly 37 ½ feet.

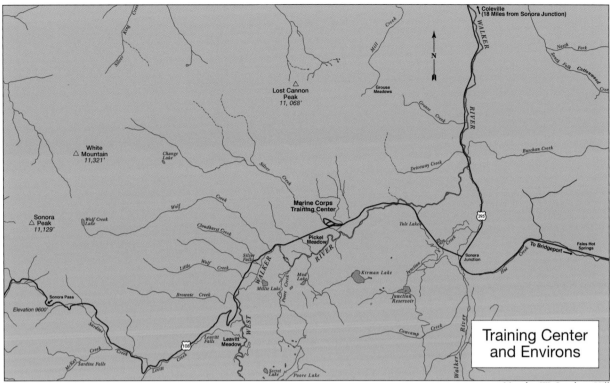

Training Center and Environs

Map by W. Stephen Hill

of Bridgeport. This could be problematic from December through March for those drafts who had to complete their training, yet return in time to meet firm sailing dates for Korea. Despite these risks and the logistical challenges, the area at Pickel Meadow seemed to have so many other advantages in its favor that ultimately it did become the recommended winter training site of both Generals Smith and Twining. After announcing this decision, an immediate request was sent to the 12th Naval District Headquarters asking that command begin negotiations with the U.S. Forest Service for a temporary land use permit.

Except for a few small parcels held in private hands, the vast majority of Pickel Meadow and the surrounding terrain were all within the boundaries of the Toiyabe National Forest. What President Theodore Roosevelt had first set aside in 1907 as a small National Reserve, by 1950 had grown to over three million acres, making the Toiyabe the largest National Forest outside of Alaska.[48] The administrative headquarters for this vast tract of land was located in Reno, Nevada, with a District headquarters 17 miles to the south in Bridgeport, California. While the Real Estate Division, Public Works Office, 12th Naval District worked with the local supervisor and district offices of the U.S. Forest Service to craft a temporary use permit, in Washington D.C. a higher level team from Headquarters U.S. Marine Corps and the Department of Navy opened negoti-

ations with the Department of Agriculture with a request for a more permanent lease agreement. Fortunately, both the Department of Agriculture and the U.S. Forest Service were very helpful and cooperative. Before the last day of August, the Marines had been granted the temporary use of over 60,000 acres of the Toiyabe National Forest with the promise that a more permanent joint policy agreement between the Secretary of the Navy and the Secretary of Agriculture would be concluded within the next six months. Therefore, at least one of the long-term solutions to a vexing problem was now well on the way to being resolved.

As the negotiators worked out the final details for the use permits and the amount of terrain that would be involved, it became obvious to the citizens of Mono County that something significant was about to happen in their community. On August 17th, the *Bridgeport Chronicle-Union* told its readers:

Bridgeport was abuzz last week with Marine Corps members who reportedly were in the area to make preliminary plans for a winter camp near Wheeler Ranger Station. Convoys of motorized equipment and personnel went through Inyo-Mono early last week, and were camped near Bridgeport. Further details of the proposed camp will be made in a later edition, if forthcoming from Marine Corps headquarters.[49]

Photograph of town of Bridgeport, California, early 20th century.

Activation of the Cold Weather Battalion

On 25 August 1951, the Commanding General, Training and Replacement Command, with Staging Regiment serving as its parent organization, activated the Cold Weather Training Battalion at Camp Pendleton.[50*] Shortly thereafter, the same officer who made the initial Pickel Meadow site survey, Lieutenant Colonel Donald B. Hubbard, was appointed as the battalion's first commanding officer. The 32-year-old Georgian had not served in Korea. But he did come with three years of wartime experience in the South Pacific during World War II. Serving initially as a company commander and then executive officer of a parachute battalion, at age 25, he was wounded in action as a major while commanding the 3d Battalion, 9th Marines, during the recapture of Guam. He later recovered in time to participate in the Iwo Jima campaign. His post-war years included a tour of duty at the University of California to study the Chinese language at Quantico, Virginia, where he was assigned first as a student and then as an instructor at the Amphibious Warfare School. During his 10 years of active service, the colonel had gained a reputation for being a tough taskmaster with a firm belief in the value of realistic field training.[51]

As Lieutenant Colonel Hubbard saw it, his mission was now threefold. First, he had to construct a temporary base camp at Pickel Meadow to provide housing, mess, and work spaces for the "permanent personnel" who would be assigned to his battalion. Second, he needed to organize and prepare his unit for the task of either training or supporting the training of the eight replacement drafts that were scheduled to undergo cold-weather indoctrination during the forthcoming winter months. The third task would be to supervise the conduct of each of those drafts through seven days of practical application and tactical field exercises. Time was of the

A winter view of the main street, Highway 395, of Bridgeport, California, in the 1940s. The Bridgeport Hotel is currently the Bridgeport Inn.

---

* On 11 September, the word "Training" was dropped and the organization was redesignated as: Cold Weather Battalion.

Courtesy of author

Lieutenant Colonel Donald B. Hubbard, Commanding Officer, Cold Weather Battalion, 1951-1952.

essence if he were to accomplish this mission before 18 September and the arrival of the 14th Replacement Draft.*

On 30 August, an advance working party of 40 Marines arrived at Pickel Meadow to start erecting the battalion's temporary base camp. Corporal John J. Schneider, a small arms weapons repairman who was scheduled to depart for Korea in December with the 16th Replacement Draft, was assigned temporary additional duty to this first contingent of Marines. "The valley was absolutely bare," Schneider related a half a century later. "We went right to work setting up the first two strong-backed pyramidal tents."

The first was located on the south side of Highway 108, later to be called the "Guard Shack." The second pyramidal tent erected was situated on higher ground among a grove of aspen trees on the east bank of Silver Creek. This tent was to be the living and work quarters for the commanding officer. During the remainder of his temporary additional duty, Corporal Schneider was assigned duties in the field mess hall, sleeping at night under the stars. By the time he left to return to Camp Pendleton, the valley floor on the north side of Highway 108 was filled with an imposing array of strong-backed pyramidal and general purpose tents to house the hundreds of instructors, aggressors, and

* The 14th Draft did not actually arrive until 22 September.

service and support personnel who were beginning to arrive for duty with the Cold Weather Battalion.[52] Construction on two large wooden frame buildings was also underway. One was used for the maintenance and repair of equipment while the other stored the battalion's organizational supplies. As the camp was nearing completion in late September through mid-October, it was not uncommon to see flights of Marine Corsair fighter-bombers from the El Toro air station, flying overhead at tree top level as the pilots made practice strafing runs on the recently established tent camp.

At a 4 September commanders conference hosted at Camp Pendleton by the Commanding General, Fleet Marine Force, Pacific, (FMFPac) it was the consensus view of the attending flag officers that the Cold Weather Indoctrination Program being afforded for the replacement drafts would also be beneficial to units of FMFPac Troops and the recently reconstituted 3d Marine Brigade, now commanded by Brigadier General Lewis B. "Chesty" Puller. Accordingly, staffs of the various commands involved began working out the details to implement the plan. Ultimately, it was decided that the Cold Weather Battalion would be augmented with six officers and 134 enlisted Marines who would be assigned temporary additional duty from FMFPac Troops from November through April of the following year. Most of these personnel would be integrated into the various sections of the Cold Weather Battalion, except for a separate Aggressor Platoon

Strong-back pyramidal tents constructed at valley floor of Pickel Meadow, October 1951.

Courtesy of Harold F. Haberman

Courtesy of Harold F. Haberman

The tent camp under construction, October 1951. Concerning the two wooden buildings on left, one was used for storage of the battalion's organizational supplies and the other for maintenance and repair of heavy equipment.

and a small training section. The latter would work under the direction of the FMFPac Troops Cold-Weather Training Officer, Lieutenant Colonel George G. Ryffel. Overall responsibility for training both the replacement drafts and the FMFPac Troops, however, would remain under Lieutenant Colonel Hubbard, the commanding officer of the Cold Weather Battalion.[53]

On 22 September 1951, the first training increment of the 14th Replacement Draft arrived by bus and by nightfall had set up a bivouac site among the sage brush, one half mile to the west of the Cold Weather Battalion's base camp. While the Aspen trees were turning yellow and there was a hint of

fall in the air, as yet, no new snow had fallen in the Sierras, even at the higher elevations. Nor had Lieutenant Colonel Hubbard received the full complement of 53 officers and 730 enlisted men that had been promised to him to flesh out his battalion. Nevertheless, the essential ingredients had come together and the stage was set.[54] The U.S Marine Corps' first Cold Weather Battalion was now open for business at Pickel Meadow.

Corsair fighter aircraft from Marine Corps Air Station El Toro conduct simulated strafing runs over the Pickel Meadow base camp under construction, October, 1951. Pictured is one of two wooden buildings built at the time.

Courtesy of Harold F. Haberman

Chapter 4

Cold Weather Battalion's First Year

This is the Law of the Yukon, that only
The Strong shall thrive;
That surely the Weak shall perish, and
Only the Fit survive.
        -Robert Service

"We've got to get 'em tougher to survive"

Throughout the Korean War, the responsibility for organizing and processing each replacement draft for embarkation to the Far East was assigned to the commanding officer of the Staging Regiment of the Training and Replacement Command. The Training and Replacement Command was located at the northern end of Camp Pendleton at Camp San Onofre. At that time it was commonly referred to as Tent Camp #2. Each month a numbered draft would be scheduled well in advance to depart on a certain day by sea transport from either the San Diego or the Long Beach naval bases. The drafts varied in size, but at the height of the conflict they normally numbered between 1,800–2,500 Marines. It should also be remembered that these drafts were made up of individual replacements, not organized units. Therefore, each was a mix of every occupational specialty and rank, running from private to major. During pre-deployment training the replacements were loosely organized into numbered battalions, each comprised of four or more provisional rifle companies of about 250 men each. Four platoons comprised a company, with each platoon made up of four rifle squads. Because assignments to a replacement unit were done randomly, it was a rare instance when more than two or three men might even be acquainted before being thrown together in the same platoon. The four platoon commanders assigned to these provisional "lash-ups" were usually newly commissioned second lieutenants, fresh from The Basic School at Quantico.

Before starting the cold-weather indoctrination phase of their training, every Marine in a company would draw a complete set of cold-weather clothing. As each man signed for his gear, the supply clerks would remind him of the cost of each item and that the total kit came to $126.13. Marines were expected to account for their gear or expect a pay checkage. The clothing issue was customarily followed by four hours of classroom instruction on such subjects as the principles of the cold-weather uniform layering system, cold injuries, individual mobility in deep snow and the rudiments of providing shelter and heat.[55] Throughout this instruction the acronym "COLD" was used to stress the main points for keeping oneself combat effective in a frigid climate: "C" for keeping clothes clean; "O" for avoid overheating; "L" for wearing layers, and "D" for keeping dry, which even the instructors had to concede was a challenge in the sometimes sleety conditions.

At about 0230 the following morning, the troops would form up at a designated assembly area, staggering in the dark under their 85-pound loads of cold-weather uniforms and equipment. Each man would also be carrying a sack lunch consisting of two bologna sandwiches and an apple, which he had drawn from the mess hall that morning. After a roll call, the companies would climb onto the waiting Pacific Greyhound or Continental Trailways busses and start out on their 10-hour journey for Bridgeport. The route took them north along U.S. Highway 395, with one stop for "head call" at an abandoned airstrip near the town of Lone Pine. Sometime after mid-day, the training units would arrive at Pickel Meadow and debark on the west end of the valley. Once there a team of instructors from Lieutenant Colonel Hubbard's Cold Weather Battalion would meet them. After being given a brief chance to get themselves sorted out on the ground, the troops would then start the first of their seven days of practical field maneuvers by trudging up the slopes to their first night's bivouac site at Tactical Area #1. Meanwhile, those provisional com-

Marines from the Korean War 15th Draft debarking from busses upon arrival at Pickel Meadow, November 1951.

Courtesy of author

Courtesy of author

The 15th Draft marching to higher elevations to begin cold-weather training at Pickel Meadow, November 1951.

panies that had completed their week of field training would be loaded onto the same busses on the east end of the valley. The luxury of being in a heated bus was a welcome change after being exposed for seven days to snow, wind and bone chilling cold. Usually, becoming warm again would have an immediate somniferous affect on the exhausted Marines. As a result, most of them would already be in a sound sleep before reaching the town of Bridgeport on their way back to Camp Pendleton.

It did not take long for the word to get around Tent Camp #2 that the training conducted at Pickel Meadow was distinctly different from any of the other standard processing activity at the Staging and Replacement Command. "Listen to what the instructors tell you and take it seriously," returning Marines would caution their buddies who had yet to go through the program. "It's tough up there!" For many combat commanders who were veterans of the Korean Conflict, the new Cold Weather Indoctrination Program was spot on. Certainly this rigorous training and the demands it placed squarely on the shoulders of the individual Marine were consistent with the philosophy of Lewis B. "Chesty" Puller, one of the most highly decorated Marine ever, and a recent veteran of the Chosin Campaign. When Puller returned to the United States from Korea he told reporters that "We've got to get our people tougher to survive. Throw all these girls out of camp. Get rid of the ice cream and candy. Get some pride in 'em–that's what we need now most of all, pride."[56]

Snow came early to the Sierra Nevada in the fall of 1951. By mid-October, the higher peaks were al-

ready blanketed under deep drifts. Even down at the Cold Weather Battalion's base camp at the 6,800-foot level, the accumulation was enough to make plowing and snow removal part of the daily routine. By this time, it was now also routine for the citizens of Bridgeport to look out on Highway 395 and observe a convoy of vehicles loaded with hundreds of Marines as they passed through the town enroute either to or from Pickel Meadow. An article appearing on the front page of the *Bridgeport Chronicle–Union* dated 28 October 1951 informed its readers of what was taking place at the nearby Marine training camp:

After careful inspection of all available training areas in California, the Pickle Meadow [sic] site was selected by veteran Marine Corps Officers as the location offering altitude, sub-zero weather and deep snow equal to the mountainous sections of Korea.

During a rugged training period the Marines toughen their bodies and develop confidence in themselves and their cold-weather equipment constantly watched by a highly trained instructor staff, many of whom are former ski experts, mountain climbers or veterans of Korean fighting. The trainees live in the field under simulated combat conditions.

Other instructors make up an enemy guerilla force, which adds realism to combat problems. These white clad raiders strike at the trainees supply lines, attempt to steal his weapons and raid his headquarters. In this manner, mistakes which might mean death or defeat in combat are vividly pointed out and eliminated.

Highly essential for surviving in the sub-zero cold, the Marine learns to keep his body warm and his fingers and feet free from frostbite. As some of our recruit Marines have never even seen snow and are sometimes apprehensive at the prospects of living in it, said the commanding officer, Lieutenant Colonel Donald B. Hubbard, this training shows the individual that we have means to overcome the rigors of winter warfare and how to use what nature offers to keep warm. He gains confidence in himself, his equipment and his fellow Marines.[57]

In his official after-action report, Lieutenant Colonel Hubbard expanded on this same theme by describing the metamorphosis that each training company went through during its seven-day cycle of cold-weather indoctrination:

> For the most part, the trainees were completely inexperienced in cold-weather and extreme wintertime conditions, or had never participated in a military operation under such conditions, although some may have been natives of harsh climatic regions. Upon arrival at Pickel Meadows, [sic] the trainees were ominously silent, reluctant to leave the busses,

Colonel Lewis B. Puller in 1950 while commanding officer, 1st Marine Regiment in Korea.
Marine Corps History Division

and hesitant to enter the bleak expanse of white wilderness. After several orientation lectures, demonstrations, and periods of application on care and use of equipment, clothing, shelter, food and water, and after direct contact with those weather characteristics, the silence gave way to a more jovial, but not particularly carefree approach. Upon completion of the field exercise and upon learning that movement through snow and cold at high altitudes was not only a possibility, but a practicality; the trainee attitude became one of confidence and at times cockiness. Invaluable lessons in leadership were learned by officers and noncommissioned officers in the discovery of the amount and intensity of command supervision necessary to move troops through snow, cold, wind, and blizzard conditions, yet maintain a sense of combat readiness.[58]

Keeping the training companies from becoming too lax or carefree was the task of Lieutenant Richard "Dick" W. Johnson and his 70-man Aggressor Platoon. Operating from their own self-contained base camps that were hidden away at the higher elevations, Lieutenant Johnson's white camouflaged squads would lie in wait along routes of march between the various night tactical bivouac positions and then swoop down on the stragglers of a company in column at the most inopportune moment. But the situations the aggressors most relished for launching their assaults were between midnight and the first daylight hours, or during a blizzard when visibility was severely reduced. Should unit commanders fail to post adequate security, or if their Marines were slow in getting out of their sleeping bags and into their fighting positions when the alarm was raised, they usually paid the price as the aggressors, firing blank ammunition, came charging through the company perimeter on skis or snowshoes knocking down shelters and carrying off captured weapons as they withdrew.

Despite living and operating in arctic conditions for long stretches, morale among the Aggressor Platoon stayed consistently high. Recalling those days a half-century later, Johnson attributed the high morale of the platoon to several factors. "First and foremost we had a great cook," recalled Johnson.

> He loved the isolation of the field and had a knack turning our rather drab rations into a delicious meal. His 'deer burgers' were a particular favorite. Most of the troops were young privates and privates first class, right out of

Courtesy of Col Richard M. Johnson

Cold Weather trainees setting up two-man shelter half tents while undergoing instruction at Pickel Meadow, early 1950s.

boot camp. Fortunately, I had some fine non-commissioned officers to lead them, some of whom had already been to Korea. Then, whenever we might have a break in the schedule, I would make arrangements to get the troops to Reno for a night or two of liberty. When they returned, we would sober them up and off we'd go again.

Johnson recalled that the Navy corpsman was the only one who had any previous experience on skis. "But we got to the point where we could get around on them pretty well."[59]

The Winter of 1951-1952

If the lack of snow and the absence of extreme cold vexed the Marine cold-weather trainers during 1950-1951, the opposite was the case in the winter of 1951-1952. From December through late March, currents of frigid air that streamed down from the Pacific Northwest collided continuously with warm winds coming from the south. This created tempest winds which erupted into a series of blizzards that blew directly over the Sierra Nevada range. Each storm was followed by periods of extreme low temperatures. According to Lieutenant Colonel Hubbard's official after-activity report, on 1 January the mercury dropped to –39 degrees Fahrenheit at his lower base camp. By the time the April thaw finally arrived, the local population had already declared it the worst winter to strike the region since 1891.

The Southern Pacific Railroad's streamliner *City of San Francisco* became snow bound and marooned as it tried to cross over Donner Pass in the middle of a particularly devastating storm. Emergency food supplies for the passengers had to be airdropped by helicopters during the 10 days it took for snow-plowing engines to relieve the stranded passenger train. Air Force National Guard C-119 "Flying Box Car" cargo planes were likewise kept busy through much of that winter and into early spring, air-dropping bales of hay to the many herds of stranded livestock that had become isolated and were in danger of starving.

Marines who went through that first winter at Pickel Meadow remember the harsh circumstances. The resident Cold Weather Battalion as well as the inexperienced 23,213 trainees who were there for only one week of indoctrination training suffered greatly in the fierce winter conditions.

One trainee was Lieutenant James Brady, future author and columnist. Writing 40 years later, Brady could vividly remember being at "the cold-weather training camp up near Tahoe where we had two feet of snow in October and the thin air burned our lungs."[60]

Before that harsh winter commenced, Staff Sergeant Harold F. Haberman, a Cold Weather Battalion Marine, drew his set of cold weather-clothing from the Training and Replacement Command on

A fire team moving out on patrol as "aggressors" from their base camp, sometime in 1951-1952.

Courtesy of Col Richard M. Johnson

Courtesy of Col Richard M. Johnson

The aggressors in hide position observing a provisional training company, sometime in 1951-1952.

5 September, and was soon on his way in his 1937 Chevrolet to join the Cold Weather Training Battalion. Upon reporting, he was assigned to work in the Battalion S-4 Section. Throughout his tour of duty with the Cold Weather Battalion, September 1951-April 1952, Staff Sergeant Haberman recorded what was going on around him by taking black and white photographs with his personal camera. Looking at an October snapshot, one can see how the snow blanketed the ground at the lower base camp. By November it has risen to waist deep. Photo-

graphs taken in December and January showed even deeper drifts, burying vehicles and equipment. By late January, the snowfall had become so heavy that the state of California snowplow crews were unable to keep Highway 395 open and the base became completely isolated for almost a week. As food and supply stores begin to run low, Staff Sergeant Haberman's camera caught the C-119 cargo planes that were parachuting critically needed supplies to the 1,500 Marines, who for a time, were completely cut off and snowbound.[61]

While this was going on, the numbers of stranded Marines at Pickel Meadow had troubling repercussions with regard to sailing schedules for the outgoing drafts. On 29 January 1952, Major General O. P. Smith wrote a letter from his headquarters at Camp Pendleton to the newly installed 20th Commandant of the Marine Corps, General Lemuel C. Shepherd, Jr. General Smith provided a personal assessment of the situation and the action that was being taken to overcome the "few complications" that the winter storms were causing:

Dear Lem:
      You have already been advised by dispatch of the completion of cold-weather training for the 17th Replacement Draft. California's worst winter in several years presented a few complications. U.S. Highway 395 from Bishop to Pickel Meadows [sic] (cold-weather camp) has been closed for most of January. Normally this route is kept open all winter. When snow first caused closing of the road we had over 2,300 trainees (draft and FMF) in the camp. Then the highway people were able to open the road

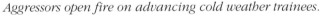
Aggressors open fire on advancing cold weather trainees.

Courtesy of Col Richard M. Johnson

Courtesy of Mr. Harold F. Haberman

Deep snow covers the Pickel Meadow base camp, January 1952. Members of the Cold Weather Battalion lived in tents throughout the winter.

long enough for us to get out 1,500 trainees. Then snow blocked the road again. While 800 trainees remained in camp snowbound, we sent two other increments (approximately 800 in each increment) to Bishop where they were bivouacked in a National Forest area and were given an abbreviated cold-weather training course. Finally, the state highway people opened up the road from Pickel Meadow to Nevada and we sent buses around to bring the remaining trainees from Pickel Meadow to Fallon, Nevada, from where El Toro planes airlifted them to Pendleton and El Toro. By 26 January all trainees (those from Bishop and those from Pickel Meadow) had returned to Pendleton. The permanent detachment remains at Pickel Meadow. During all this period it was necessary to evacuate only three men from Pickel Meadow (one appendectomy and two with respiratory trouble.) These went out through the Nevada side. There were ample rations and stove oil.

Cold Weather Battalion mess hall goes up in flames, January 1952.

Courtesy of Mr. Harold F. Haberman

Courtesy of Mr. Harold F. Haberman

A C-119 Flying Boxcar aircraft supplies Pickel Meadow base camp with critically needed fuel, oil, and rations in January 1952. Air resupply was necessary because winter conditions had halted rail traffic in the region.

Roads permitting we will send personnel of the 18th Draft into Pickel Meadow. If roads go out we will train at Bishop. While the Sierras are in the grip of winter we are reconnoitering for an alternate site for a cold-weather camp if training is continued next year. Possibly we can find a site where we can get snow and cold weather, but where the chances of the road being blocked are minimized.[62]

If General Smith held out some glimmer of hope that the worst was over and that winter would gradually start to loosen its grip on the Sierras, he was soon to be disappointed. Throughout February and March, severe storms continued to lash the Sierra Nevada. In March, Lieutenant Colonel Hubbard reported one blizzard that "deposited approximately five feet of new snow in a 24-hour period."[63] Again, snow-removal equipment and crews fell hopelessly behind, necessitating a repeat of Highway 395 being temporarily closed. However, by this time alternate routes through western Nevada had been

The burning mess hall was doused by pushing snow onto the fire with a snowplow, January 1952.

Courtesy of Mr. Harold F. Haberman

established, which allowed most of the troop-laden bus convoys to get in and out of Pickel Meadow.

But the severe weather was not the only complication to test the staffs at Camp Pendleton that were trying to keep the flow of troops and supplies to the Cold Weather Battalion on schedule. In January, in the midst of one of the worst storms of the year, the Bridgeport mess hall burned to the ground. The structure itself was simply a large tent over a skeleton metal frame. Thus it could be quickly rebuilt. However, the galley equipment was a complete loss and it took time to replace it all. According to Staff Sergeant Haberman, the source of the fire was never established.[65] Here again, his trusty camera

Bernard E. Trainor

One of the officers assigned to that mid-January training increment and who was precluded from reaching Pickel Meadow was a Korean bound second lieutenant by the name of Bernard E. Trainor. In a series of articles entitled: On Going to War, the first of which appeared in the April, 1996 issue of the *Marine Corps Gazette*, Trainor, by then a retired lieutenant general, provided a humorous personal account of the abbreviated cold-weather training he received outside of the town of Bishop. The reader will note that Lieutenant General Trainor's version differs somewhat from what General Smith had reported to the Commandant.

"The winter of 1951-1952 was particularly bad in the high Sierras; lots of snow. The Chicago Limited[*] on its way to San Francisco became snowbound for days in the Donner Pass and had to be resupplied by helicopter. It made the pages of *Life* magazine. All this by the way of introduction to the fact we never made it to Pickel Meadow. The busses were halted by the state police at Bishop, California, and the drivers told the highway was closed further north due to snow. Their advice was to turn around and go home. This put the little fat major in charge of the convoy in a state of near panic. He argued to the troopers that his wards were on their way to Korea and the Commandant had mandated that they go through cold-weather training first. As anyone who has ever tried to argue with a state policeman knows, the major's efforts got him nowhere. The police outranked the Commandant in California and they absolutely mandated that 'you shall not pass.' We were delighted with their firmness. We had no burning desire to go to Pickle Meadow. After all, our days along the Chopawamsic qualified us for nasty weather. Besides, an unscheduled return to Pendleton probably meant liberty call.

Poor Major 'No-Name' of course saw things differently. He just couldn't return to garrison with troops unqualified for winter warfare because of winter conditions. Think of the shame. Besides, it would throw the whole Marine Corps and its well greased replacement system out of sync. I will say this for him, he may have been a staff pouge with a dirty belt and unshined brass, but he was a dedicated Marine with a sense of mission and a knack for the famous field expedient. If Mohammed could not go to the mountain, he would bring the mountain to Mohammed. He blew a whistle and ordered everyone out of the busses. For the next three days and nights we tromped through the snow in the hills above Bishop, pretending we were in Korea, while the major set up his command post in a local motel. At the end of our trekking we piled into the buses and headed back to Pendleton. Upon arrival, noncommissioned officers were seated at portable tables stacked with our officer qualification record books. As we debussed and identified ourselves by name, an entry was stamped into our officer qualification records, 'Certified: Winter Warfare Qualified.' "[64]

---

[*] Gen Trainor mistakenly identified the name of the train; it was *The City of San Francisco*.

managed to record the blazing scene of bulldozers pushing piles of snow to extinguish the flames and contain the fire.

A second complication that caused more serious consequences occurred in March. This involved the Pacific Greyhound Lines and Continental Trailways being forced to cease charter operations because of a labor strike against both bus lines. After the strike began, new charters were given over to the Trona Stage and Tanner Greyline to make the long trip between Camp Pendleton and Pickel Meadow. Unfortunately, the aging vehicles of each line were near the end of their service lives. Consequently, a number of the training increments were stranded along Highway 395 waiting for replacement busses to come and transport these Marines on to their destination.[66] Unable to cope with this unsatisfactory service without risking further disruptions to the draft sailing dates, the leadership at Camp Pendleton reluctantly decided to cancel the cold-weather training at Pickel Meadow that had been scheduled for the 20th and 21st Drafts.

On 17 March, the Cold Weather Battalion concluded training and out posted the last increment of the 19th Replacement Draft. This was the last of the overseas drafts to receive the complete package of cold-weather indoctrination training that winter. However, by using its organic military transportation, Fleet Marine Force Units were able to hold to their original schedules. Therefore, cold-weather training for Brigadier General Puller's 3d Brigade and for Force Troops Pacific did not end until 6 April. By the middle of the month, the Cold Weather Battalion with its FMF augmenters began to drawdown to return to Camp Pendleton to rejoin their parent organizations. On 19 May 1952, the Cold Weather Battalion began shifting its headquarters back to Camp Pendleton, leaving only a small detachment to guard the camp and to police the various bivouac sites, once the snow had left the ground. On 28 May 1952, the unit was redesignated as Headquarters Company, Cold Weather Battalion, Marine Barracks, Camp Pendleton, California.

Thus, the first year of the Cold Weather Training Battalion at Pickel Meadow came to a close. It had been a busy nine months. Despite its hasty formation and the primitive conditions associated with living under canvas through one of the worst winters ever to hit northern California, the organization had accomplished its mission and had shown that it could deal with adversity. Moreover, only a handful of minor frostbite cases were reported during the entire training season. It was unfortunate that the bus strike

had prevented the 20th and 21st Replacement Drafts from taking advantage of this training experience. As Lieutenant Colonel Hubbard pointed out in his after-activity report:

> Despite the deep snow and the extra burden it placed on vehicles and unsuitable snow-removal equipment, it was never a serious threat or impediment to training. The weather, as well as the terrain, proved ideal for the indoctrination of cold, moisture, chill winds, blizzards and rapid temperature changes. Snow depths varying from two feet to 10 feet and drifting up to 30 feet produced ideal variety for troop movements, affording solid crust, breakable crust and shoulder-high powder snow.[67]

The Cold Weather Battalion had realized its purpose. No less than 23,213 Marines and sailors received indoctrination training that winter. Elliot W. Chassey, a member of the 15th Replacement Draft that sailed for Korea in December 1951, later recalled that "The training was the hardest, most demanding we ever went through, but it did a lot to save lives."[68]

If General O. P. Smith directed his staff to search for an alternate site for the next year's Cold Weather Indoctrination Program, as he had so indicated to the Commandant, there is no record of it. Perhaps two factors might have dissuaded him from doing so. First, despite the disruptions and problems encountered from snow blocked highways and a bus strike, all the reports he received pertaining to the ideal winter conditions and the expansive areas open for troop maneuver were absolutely glowing in their praise for the existing camp. Second, "Joint Policy between the Department of the Navy and the Department of Agriculture Relating to the Use of National Forest Lands for Defense Purposes" was agreed upon and had been formally approved by Secretary of the Navy Dan A. Kimball and Secretary of Agriculture Charles F. Brannan on 19 February. (See appendix D) Under the terms of this agreement, the Department of Agriculture granted to the Navy Department at no cost, exclusive use of 40 acres for the base camp and joint use of over 60,000 acres of Toiyabe National Forest lands so long as it was determined that the lands are "essential for the defense effort."[69] Opening new negotiations for land use elsewhere may not have resulted in such a favorable outcome for the Marine Corps. Therefore, General Smith apparently reasoned that it was better to let things stand as they were and to press on with the plans for improving the existing site.

Chapter 5

Making Improvements, 1952-1956

No Marine training was ever tougher or more practical for the purpose.
-Colonel Robert D. Heinl Jr.

Introduction

Throughout the winter and spring of 1951-1952, Lieutenant Colonel Donald B. Hubbard, commanding officer, Cold Weather Battalion and his counterpart, Lieutenant Colonel George G. Ryffel, officer-in-charge of the Pickel Meadow Detachment of Force Troops, Fleet Marine Force Pacific, submitted numerous recommendations to their respective superiors at Camp Pendleton. Most of this correspondence was aimed at improving the future of cold-weather training and operations at the new site. The two officers seemed to concur on most matters. Their final reports were submitted within 10 days of one another and as one reads through them, it becomes readily apparent that the two reports had been closely coordinated. The majority of the recommendations originated by the two commanders suggests that their most pressing priorities fell under one of the four following areas: facilities, organization for training, cold-weather clothing and equipment, and command relationships.

Facilities

A Cold Weather Battalion Staff Study, signed by Lieutenant Colonel Hubbard on 13 March 1952, begins with several assumptions. Among them are "that cold-weather training will be continued on an annual basis in the Pickel Meadow area near Bridgeport, California" and "that cold-weather training will recommence in September of each year and conclude each annual training period in May of the following year." This staff study then went on to make the case for constructing a permanent camp one-fourth mile east of the present tent camp with barracks, heads and office "buildings to consist of insulated Quonset type construction with concrete decks, while maintenance and utilities building to be of frame type construction to fit utilities required." The stated preference for Quonset construction was because "of fire security in high winds and the shorter time and ease of construction by Marine engineer units." A table of organization that proposed a permanent Cold Weather Battalion of approximately 53 officers and 730 Marine and navy enlisted men, accompanied the staff study.[70]

In his final report to the commanding general, Force Troops, Fleet Marine Force Pacific, Lieutenant Colonel Ryffel echoed the same need for the immediate construction of a permanent camp. "The living conditions and facilities offered to permanent personnel are not adequate nor up to minimum standards for permanent duty . . . . It is considered a necessity that all quarters, offices, and facilities

The Cold Weather Battalion base camp at Pickel Meadow in the summer of 1952 before the construction of a more permanent facility that year. Highway 108 runs horizontally through the middle of the picture and the West Walker River is in the background.

Courtesy of MWTC

move out of tentage and into Quonset-type construction." But he also made it quite clear that this condition pertained to the permanent personnel only. Facilities for those under instruction, he stressed in a succeeding page, "should remain at a minimum level in order to provide a hardship of conditions and to develop self-reliance and improvisation."[71]

Organization for Training

Neither Lieutenant Colonel Hubbard nor Lieutenant Colonel Ryffel spared much criticism of the preliminary Cold Weather Indoctrination Program conducted by the Staging Regiment at Camp Pendleton. In their view, the program was lackluster. It was too short, lacked substance, and what was being imparted to the troops was often "inconsistent with the principles being taught by the instructors of the Cold Weather Battalion." Moreover, regimental supply had made no effort to size the cold-weather clothing to the man as it was being issued. Therefore, wholesale exchanges in boots, gloves and outer garments between the men of each training increment had to be made after they had arrived at Pickel Meadow.

Lieutenant Colonel Hubbard proposed that each replacement draft training company be given an opportunity to make a half-day conditioning march in cold-weather uniforms to ensure proper fit. This was to be followed by an overnight bivouac at Camp Pendleton, prior to departing for Pickel Meadow.[72] Similarly, Lieutenant Colonel Ryffel recommended that "the introductory lectures at Camp Pendleton be given under the control of FMFPac Troops (vice Staging Regiment) to insure a complete and accurate coverage." In addition, Ryffel recommended, "prior to the movement to Pickel Meadow, provisional infantry units be given a field training phase at Camp Pendleton of approximately two days in which a bivouac is established and elementary small unit tactics is practiced."[73] The recommendations of both officers were subsequently adopted.

Cold-Weather Clothing and Equipment

Notwithstanding the local problem associated with ill-fitting cold-weather uniforms, significant improvements were made to the cold-weather clothing and equipment kit for the individual Marine during 1951-1952. What became known as the M1951 cold-weather clothing system came into general service in mid-1952. It replaced the bulky, overly restrictive parka, thereby reducing the total weight of the kit somewhat. Otherwise, it was based on the same "layering" principle as before, and included a loose-fitting white undershirt and drawers, half-wool long underwear, wool shirt and trousers, a standard Marine wool sweater and a field jacket with liner that was water repellent. A parka and over trousers could be added for exceptionally frigid weather.

But unquestionably, the greatest single advancement in the cold-weather uniform was made in the footwear. Up until November 1951, the M1944 Shoe-Pacs continued as the standard boot of issue. Over time, the sub-standard Shoe-Pacs, which accounted for many of the frostbite injuries suffered during the Chosin Reservoir campaign, was replaced with what was briefly known as the "Bristolite" boot, produced by the Hood Rubber Company. According to Lieutenant Colonel Hubbard, these early models also "proved too inflexible and caused chafing."[74] However, by February 1952, Major Vernon D. Boyd, the Headquarters U.S. Marine Corps project officer and a representative from the Hood Rubber Company were back at Pickel Meadow to test and evaluate a new model of the insulated rubber boots. This model boot proved highly successful and was immediately adopted for use and designated as the M1952 "1952 boot, insulated rubber."[75] Dubbed the "Mickey Mouse" boot by the troops, this thermal boot used the vapor barrier principle of airspace trapped between inner and outer layers of wool pile insulation, both of which were completely sealed off by rubber from any contact with moisture. Furthermore, as the insulated rubber boot replaced the Shoe-Pacs among the infantry units of the 1st Marine Division in Korea, it was noted that the absence of a steel shank in the new boot also reduced foot injuries from exploding land mines.

With respect to equipment improvements, both Hubbard and Ryffel agreed with everything that had been said before about the inadequacy of the 1941 Marine Corps Pack System in cold-weather operations. Throughout the year, trainees and instructors alike at Pickel Meadow conducted comparison tests between the U.S. Army's mountain rucksacks versus the waterproof bag, lashed to a wooden pack frame, in order to determine which was best suited to carry the cold-weather load. Both officers faithfully reported their troops' conviction that the rucksack was the superior load-bearing system for movement in the mountains and in deep snow.[76] Nevertheless, the pack frame with waterproof bag soon became the accepted standard for use in the Marine Corps and it would be another 30 years before the rucksack eventually replaced this system. Finally, Hubbard pointed out, while the new cold-weather uniform was an improvement, there was still insufficient insulation between the sleeping bag and the snow. The poncho, he said, simply did not serve well and forestry restrictions prevented using branches and shrubbery for this purpose. "Therefore," he recommended, "that some consideration be given to the possibility of providing cold-weather trainees and personnel with air mattresses."[77] By the following year, air mattresses had indeed become part of the cold-weather equipment list, despite some grumbling from "old timers" that this was clear proof that the Corps was becoming soft.

Command Relationships

Back in August and September of 1951, the Cold Weather Battalion had been hastily drawn up and thrown together. Then, time was of the essence. The battalion had to be formed quickly in order to meet the scheduled arrival of the 14th Replacement Draft. Some Marines filled billets under permanent orders, while others were assigned from parent organizations on a temporary additional duty (TAD) basis for an unspecified period. Still others were carried as augmenters, such as the majority of Lieutenant Colonel Ryffel's detachment from Force Troops, Fleet Marine Force, Pacific. The result was an administrative nightmare. Individual members of the battalion flowed in and then were recalled at the whim of the parent organization back at Camp Pendleton. In some cases, both officer and enlisted personnel who were assigned turned out to be completely unsuited for the duty and their orders were terminated for the good of the command. According to Colonel Hubbard, these temporary additional duty personnel, as well as those from Fleet Marine Force (FMF) units, also "suffered from lack of interest by their parent unit which retained their service record books; thus creating an arrangement that left much to be desired in pay, testing, fitness reporting and markings."[78]

With respect to the complexities of coordinating daily requirements with activities outside his established chain-of-command, Lieutenant Colonel Hubbard had even more to say:

> The Cold Weather Battalion worked with the following activities during the past training period: Air FMFPac, FMFPac Troops, Dept of Pacific, Depot of Supplies San Francisco and Barstow Annex, 12th Naval District, Marine Barracks, Hawthorne, Nevada, Marine Barracks, Camp Pendleton, Training and Replacement Command and Staging Regiment. Because of the large number that this battalion necessarily dealt with, and because of the number of echelons in the chain-of-command, it was often difficult to retain a clear-cut con-

cept of command policy and often difficult to obtain decisions without delay. In view of the distance from Camp Pendleton and the large number of Marine Corps and Naval activities that this Battalion by its very nature will necessarily deal with, *every consideration should be given to establishing as much autonomy as is practical.*[*] [79]

In his report, Lieutenant Colonel Ryffel addressed the same issue in almost identical terms:

> A five months view of the command relationship of the Cold Weather Battalion as it concerned logistical support, administrative matters, and operational control leads me to believe that a much more effective and efficient relationship could be put into effect. The Cold Weather Battalion, in effect, dealt directly with three separate staffs in its chain of command, besides coordinating with FMFPac Troops and its subordinate units, and the Depot of Supplies at San Francisco and Barstow. As a result, decision and responsibility was sometimes a nebulous thing, and other times an all hands act. In view of the distance from Camp Pendleton and the necessity for on-the-spot decisions with respect to training and weather, and in view of the personnel and facilities that suffer from being a part of so far distant a command as Camp Pendleton, *it is believed that the Cold Weather Battalion should have as much command autonomy as possible, even to the extent of being a separate command patterned after a Marine Barracks.*[*] [80]

What Lieutenant Colonel Hubbard was likely seeking with this quest for "greater autonomy," was to remove his battalion from the administrative and operational control of Camp Pendleton altogether. In essence, his 13 March 1952 Staff Study suggests exactly that in the fourth and final assumption: "That the Cold Weather Battalion will be under the Department of the Pacific for administrative and logistical control, and under the Commandant of the Marine Corps for operational control."[81] While it is doubtful that Major General Oliver P. Smith was willing to recommend such a drastic change, he was likely sympathetic to the notion of streamlining. This he did by eliminating the two layers that had previously existed between himself and the commanding officer of the Cold Weather Battalion. For in his final report of 26 May 1952, Lieutenant Colonel Hubbard closes by noting: "The transfer of

---

* Emphasis by the author.

Courtesy of MWTC

New Quonset huts constructed at Pickel Meadow base camp, July 1952.

this battalion on 19 May 1952 to Marine Barracks, Camp Pendleton—was definitely a step in the right direction."[*][82]

Building a Camp, 1952

While not all of Lieutenant Colonel Hubbard's many recommendations for improving the status of the Cold Weather Battalion bore fruit, some did receive prompt response. From the standpoint of troop morale, the most significant was the construction of semi-permanent facilities for living and workspaces at Pickel Meadow. Because of the lack of a permanent lease agreement and the need for speed, the commanding general, Camp Pendleton approved Lieutenant Colonel Hubbard's recommendation that construction be of a "temporary nature" consisting largely of Quonset and Butler type structures. This task was assigned to the 7th Engineer Battalion, Force Troops, Pacific. With a completion deadline set for mid-October, the 7th Engineers lost no time in laying out the rudiments of a new camp. By late May, as soon as the last of the winter snow had left the floor of the valley, construction crews were already at work bulldozing the hillside to the east of the tent camp and beginning to pour the concrete slabs that would serve as foundations or hardstands for most of the buildings.

Throughout the summer of 1952, construction continued at a fast pace. Before the winter season set in 54 Quonset huts and 12 Butler buildings were erected, plumbed and wired for electricity. In addition, several

frame structures were constructed, one of which was to serve as the stables for pack animals. Individual Quonsets were largely used for officer, staff noncommissioned officer and sergeant and below billeting spaces and heads. Multiple Quonsets of two or more huts were extensively modified to serve various purposes. For example, the battalion headquarters and the medical facility both consisted of six huts; the staff noncommissioned officer's club two huts; the recreation building three huts; and the commanding officer's quarters two huts. Butler buildings were erected to house the mess hall and commissary, motor transport and heavy equipment shops, supply warehouses, fire house and one that was to serve as the post exchange, theater and "slop chute" or club for corporals and below. Four 75 kilowatt diesel generators supplied electrical power.[83] Water was piped directly out of Silver Creek through two 10,000-gallon storage tanks. This system only worked marginally well and in 1956, $294,000 would ultimately be appropriated by Congress to build a dam across Silver Creek to supply fresh water for the camp and for the installation of a sewage system.[84]

Lieutenant Colonel Hubbard did not remain as the commanding officer, Cold Weather Battalion, long enough to witness his new camp's completion. In the summer of 1952 he received orders directing him to report for classified assignment with the Central Intelligence Agency and on 22 September 1952, command of the Cold Weather Battalion passed to Lieutenant Colonel Donald M. Schmuck. Schmuck, widely known as "Buck," had a reputation for being a tough, resourceful officer who brought with him much combat experience, gained the from the country's two previous wars. Commissioned in 1938 after graduating from the University of Colorado, this highly decorated officer had served in a number of command billets throughout the Pacific, including battery commander in the 2d Defense Battalion; rifle company commander in the 3d Marines; and as an infantry battalion commander in the 4th Marine Division. In Korea, he had commanded the 1st Battalion of Colonel Puller's 1st Marine Regiment throughout the intensive combat periods of Inchon, Seoul and at the Chosin Reservoir campaign. Prior to Lieutenant Colonel Schmuck's assignment to the Cold Weather Battalion, he had been serving in Hawaii as the assistant G-3 at Headquarters, Fleet Marine Forces, Pacific.[*][85]

---

* The lineage certificate for the Marine Corps Mountain Warfare Training Center gives the redesignation date for transferring the Cold Weather Battalion directly under Camp Pendleton as 28 May 1952.

---

* During a personal phone intvw, the author asked BGen Schmuck whether he had requested to be assigned as the commanding officer, Cold Weather Battalion inasmuch as he had been reared in Colorado and had also commanded a battalion during the withdraw from the Chosin Reservoir. "Hell no," he replied, "I was very happy to be in Hawaii. It was Puller and Shepherd who had conspired to send me there."

Courtesy of MWTC

Marines of 7th Engineer Battalion, Force Troops Pacific, construct Quonset huts at Pickel Meadow base camp, October, 1952.

The day that Lieutenant Colonel Schmuck took command, the Cold Weather Battalion numbered approximately 350 officers and enlisted men. By now most of the battalion was comprised of veterans from Korea. Doubtless then, with temperatures falling, they must have been a happy group when orders finally came down to abandon their pyramidal tents in favor of the more luxurious billeting afforded by the newly constructed Quonset huts.

A few months earlier, on 28 June 1952, President Harry S. Truman signed what became Public Law 416, 82d Congress. Under its provisions, Congress authorized the Marine Corps to "be so organized as to include not less than three combat divisions and three air wings, and such other land combat, aviation, and other services as may be organic therein."*

In anticipation of this legislation, on 7 January 1952, the 3d Marine Brigade at Camp Pendleton had been reconstituted as the 3d Marine Division. By fall, the division was up to full strength. Meanwhile on the Korean Peninsula, the 1st Marine Division was entering its third year of continuous combat operations. Its earlier participation in Operations "Killer" and "Ripper" in the eastern sector of the Korean Peninsula had helped to blunt massive Chinese counteroffensives in the spring of 1951 and 1952. Subsequent to these operations, the 1st Marine Division was shifted 180 miles to the west where it occupied a battered ridgeline known as "The Hook," which overlooked crossing sites on the

Imjin River. After fighting a series of vicious struggles to hold this vital ground throughout October, the division began to settle in for another dreary winter campaign. By now however, the number of noncombat casualties reported by division surgeons due to frostbite or to other types of cold injuries had been virtually eliminated. Clearly, the combination of the improved vapor barrier boot, the fielding of the 1951 cold-weather clothing kit, and the insistence by the Commandant that all ground combat replacements undergo the Cold Weather Indoctrination Program prior to shipping out for Korea, was paying off.

As the winter approached, the Cold Weather Battalion resumed its seasonal cycle of providing practical cold-weather field indoctrination training to over 1,000 Korea bound Marines each week. By this time, most of the logistical and administrative problems that had previously frustrated the trainers had now been ironed out. Thus, the second training year at Pickel Meadow started well and ran smoothly throughout most of the winter and spring. Moreover, the bus strike that had caused major disruptions to movement schedules in the previous year had also been resolved, thereby allowing the more reliable Greyhound and Continental lines to resume their charter services. And, although a foot of new snow did manage to fall in Summit Meadow just in time to greet the first training increment of the year, the winter of 1952-1953 would be remembered as mild, compared to what the Sierra Nevada had experienced the year before.

The instructors' banter of this being but a "mild"

---

* U.S Code, Title 10, Chap 503, Sec 5013.

winter compared to the last provided little solace to the new crop of replacements that were encountering their first taste of living in extreme cold. Sergeant Major Maurice J. Jacques, was an infantry squad leader in the 26th Replacement Draft and was among those who underwent his first cold-weather indoctrination at Pickel Meadow that October. Later, he wrote:

Most of our instructors were veterans of Korea and knew what would be expected of us there, so they made our training as realistic and demanding as possible. They wanted us to learn not only how to survive in the cold but how to be successful in cold-weather combat. Even Mother Nature lent her helping hand toward realism—the cold clear weather we had found when we first arrived had changed by late on our second day, and it began to snow heavily. Marines were posted to brush the snow off our shelter halves to keep them from collapsing, but by the time the snowstorm had passed, nearly a foot of wet snow blanketed the ground.

The three day war of company-level tactics was not designed to see who could win and who could lose, but what it also revealed, an even more important issue—who could be

Lieutenant Colonel Donald M. "Buck" Schmuck, commanding officer of Cold Weather Battalion, cuts the cake during the Marine Corps birthday celebration inside the battalion mess hall, November 1953.
Courtesy of MWTC

trusted not to fall asleep on post, who exhibited common sense and leadership, and, of course, who among us was selfish and could not be trusted. These were all part of the lessons learned while we were training under conditions made much more difficult by the cold weather. We learned how demanding it was to survive in the cold while moving steadily through snow and carrying heavy packs. As a team, we learned to overcome such difficulties, and those lessons would help us through the most trying times because they were the hard lessons that we would take into combat. I cannot ever recall being as cold as I had been while I was at Pickel Meadow [sic]. [86]

February brought an end to the training of replacement personnel headed to the Far East for Fiscal Year 1952-1953. In March, the Cold Weather Battalion hosted winter field exercises for two battalion landing teams from the 3d Marine Division at Camp Pendleton. In addition, some 800 selected key officer and enlisted personnel from Fleet Marine Force, Atlantic and Fleet Marine Force, Pacific were sent through a special five day Cold-Weather Indoctrination Program, bringing the total number of Marines trained at Pickel Meadow during the Fiscal Year to approximately 15,000. [87]

With the winter training season over, Lieutenant Colonel Schmuck turned his attention toward improving the living conditions and recreational opportunities for his Marines who were required to live year round in this remote, austere camp. Years later he could still recall that he wasn't getting much assistance from the staff at Camp Pendleton. His efforts to obtain Marine Corps busses for liberty runs to Carson City and Reno, for example, or to have saddle horses brought up for riding in the summer months were either ignored or rebuffed. "Then," he said,

one morning in the spring of 1953, who should drive up to my headquarters building completely unexpected and unannounced, but General Lemuel Shepherd, the Commandant of the Marine Corps, accompanied by his Chief of Staff, Colonel Victor H. Krulak. They spent several hours with me while I showed them around the camp before they departed for Camp Pendleton. I don't know what words the Commandant might have had with the commanding general at Camp Pendleton; but thereafter, I started getting regular telephone calls from the staff wanting to know what I needed and how could their office be of service to the Cold Weather Battalion. [88]

The main gate, Cold Weather Battalion, in the 1950s. This was the original entrance to the base.

Cease-Fire in Korea

Finally, after months of drawn out negotiations between the U.N. Command and the People's Republic of North Korea, often punctuated by periods of intense combat, at 2200, 27 July 1953, all firing along the main line of resistance ceased. In the months that followed, the truce remained an uneasy one, even as both sides went through the process of exchanging prisoners of war. For the 1st Marine Division, this would mean remaining in Korea for 18 more months. Meanwhile, in August, the Joint Chiefs of Staff had ordered the deployment of the 3d Marine Division to Japan as a strategic reserve, in the event fighting should again break out on the Korean Peninsula.

On 27 March 1954, Lieutenant Colonel Schmuck was transferred to Headquarters, Marine Corps, where he was assigned as the Head of Operations and Training Branch, G-3 Section. Relieving him as the new commanding officer of the Cold Weather Battalion was Colonel Clayton O. Totman. Colonel Totman was no stranger to living and operating in cold climates. Reared in Massachusetts, he had attained a bachelor of science degree in forestry at the University of Maine before being commissioned a second lieutenant in the Marine Corps in 1935. Shortly before and after the outbreak of World War II, he had also seen service at the naval air stations at both Sitka and Kodiak, Alaska, before being assigned to the 2d Marine Division in time for the

Martin Russ

A month later, a young Marine by the name of Martin Russ also underwent cold-weather indoctrination training at the High Sierra camp. Within five years he published his first book, describing his experience:

"This area is breath-taking, literally and figuratively, for the air is rarefied. The mountain streams yield the sweetest water I've ever tasted and the coldest, for there are large fields of snow about.

Within several days we have climbed a semicircle of mountains with Pickel Meadow [sic] below us. We have been attacked at least twice a day by a group of 'aggressors' who are Marines permanently stationed here. Most of them are Korean veterans, and some of them speak a few words of Chinese, which they yell during their charges. The other night one of them yelled, 'Tluman is a bassard!' Their tactics are along Red Army lines, their charges preceded by whistles, yells, gongs and bugles. We all use blank cartridges, of course, and are very brave. The worst thing that could happen would be to get captured by the aggressors; they are rough on prisoners. Two nights ago, while on guard duty, I caught an infiltrator crawling toward our camp. I chased him for a full minute, thinking what I would do to him when I caught him, but he got away."[89]

A Marine from Aggressor Platoon climbs aboard tracked vehicle for "liberty run," in the 1950s.

Mariana and Okinawa campaigns. In Korea during 1952-1953, he commanded the West Coast Island Defense Unit, under U.N. Naval Forces Command.[90]

Although hostilities in Korea had ceased, there was no immediate reduction to the tempo of training taking place at Marine Corps Base, Camp Pendleton, or its Cold Weather Battalion in the High Sierras. Indeed, with two Marine divisions now deployed to the Far East, the flow of replacements needed for Asia and the two Marine barracks in Alaska nearly doubled. According to Marine Corps records, in Fiscal Year 1953-1954, nearly 32,000 replacements were processed through Camp Pendleton that year, with 16,534 receiving instruction at the Cold Weather Battalion.[91] Nevertheless, by the time the 1st Marine Division was finally rotated back to Camp Pendleton in January 1955, it was becoming increasingly clear that the era of the Korean War was about to end, and the new Marine Corps theme of maintaining a "balanced force-in-readiness" was at hand. Summing up the former period, one Marine historian, Colonel Robert D. Heinl, concluded that:

> Marine Corps Schools, Camp Pendleton, and El Toro, carried the burden of training for the war—the Schools for training out junior officers, and Pendleton and El Toro for

preparing and processing the steady flow of replacements for the Far East. By the end of the war, 60 percent of the Corps had traveled that path and fought in Korea. Conspicuous in Pendleton's cycle was the ordeal of cold-weather training, which all ranks below colonel had to undergo at Pickel Meadow [sic] in the snow-girt High Sierras; no Marine training was ever tougher or more practical for the purpose.[92]

On 17 July 1955, Lieutenant Colonel Sidney F. Jenkins replaced Colonel Clayton O. Totman and became the fourth, and last officer to command what was called the Cold Weather Battalion at Bridgeport, California. Training individual replacements for cold-weather operations remained the primary mission of the battalion. Still, it was evident that the Marine Corps was beginning to think in terms of using the excellent training afforded at Pickel Meadow for purposes other than just cold-weather operations. In his annual report to the Secretary of the Navy for Fiscal Year 1956 the Commandant noted that 15,000 Marines had completed cold–weather training during the year. "Replacements intended for Alaska and the Far East, and some tactical, formed the major portion of the student load." Furthermore, he went on to state that "The site of this training is potentially useful for year-round training in mountain warfare and survival. This matter is being studied." In another section of this same report, the Commandant provided a second clue as to what may be afoot with respect to the future of Pickel Meadow when he advised the Secretary that "Temporary trailers are being procured for the Cold Weather Training Battalion at Bridgeport, California to meet family housing needs."[93]

In 1956, the provisional rifle companies that were dispatched to Pickel Meadow for cold-weather indoctrination training were not exclusively made up of overseas replacements. Mixed in with them, were also the winter graduates from Camp Pendleton's Infantry Training School at Camp San Onofre. Members of those provisional companies that underwent training in mid February of that year will never forget being treated to the unusual sight of Marine Corsairs once again flying over the valley at tree-top level, followed by command detonated explosions on some distant ridgeline. Nor will they forget observing a Marine unit trudging single file down a road dressed in 1950 cold-weather garb, including Shoe-Pacs, while large wind machines caused billowing snow to be blown into their oncoming grizzled faces. Hollywood, the trainees

A still photograph taken at Pickel Meadow in February 1956 during filming of Hold Back the Night. *An HRS helicopter is in the background.*

were told, had come to Pickel Meadow to film a motion picture called *Hold Back the Night.**

The film was an adaptation of Pat Frank's novel about a rifle company, portrayed as Company E, 2d Battalion, 7th Marines, which was tasked to serve as flank security to the 1st Division during the withdrawal from the Chosin Reservoir to Hungnam. John Payne played the starring role as the Reserve company commander recalled to active duty during the Korean War, with former Marine Chuck Connors in the supporting role of the company gunnery sergeant. The picture was produced by Allied Artists and was originally scheduled to be filmed in February of 1955, but because of technical problems, was postponed until the following year. The Marine Corps cooperated fully in the production of the film. Lieutenant Colonel Harold S. Roise, who had commanded the 2d Battalion, 5th Marines, at the Chosin Reservoir, was assigned by the Corps to be the technical advisor. In addition to making the Pickel Meadow training area available to the film makers for 30 days, 200 troops were also furnished by the 3d 4.5 Rocket Battery of Force Troops FMF Pacific, and trainees from MCB, Camp Pendleton. The 3d Marine Aircraft Wing provided Sikorsky HO3 Dragonfly helicopters along with Chance-Vought F4U Corsair aircraft.[94]

In a later critique of this picture, Dr. Lawrence Suid, a military historian and author of several books relating to film productions about the military, ironically noted that "although filmed in snow and low winter temperatures, *Hold Back the Night*

---

* The author was then a PFC and a member of one of the provisional rifle companies that witnessed some of the filming of this picture.

simply lacked the feel of the bitter weather the Marines had experienced in Korea and that *Retreat, Hell* had managed to recreate on the "painted hills" of Camp Pendleton. Moreover, it failed to provide any real sense of the actual desperation that the retreating Marines had felt, perhaps because the war in Korea had been over for three years by the time *Hold Back the Night* appeared in 1956."[95]

Another addition to the Pickel Meadow training site, and perhaps a subtle indication of the Corps' interest in its year-round use was the establishment of "Camp Cloudburst." One mile to the west of the main camp, just off Highway 108, was a three-acre flat that overlooked the West Walker River. Having been trained as a forester, Lieutenant Colonel Totman must have reasoned, why not develop this into an encampment that would offer personnel of all services and their families the opportunity for an inexpensive camping experience in the High Sierras? The commanding general, Camp Pendleton lost no time in endorsing Totman's plan. Thus in the summer of 1955, this novel recreational facility was opened with 10 hard-backed pyramidal tents, each furnished with oil stoves and iron bunks. Operating under the Special Services Section from 1 May to 1 October, the facility soon became so popular that over the next two years the number of individual tents was doubled to 20 over the next two years.[96]

Although morale and welfare funds had been made available for creating and operating an enlisted club, noncommissioned officers' club and staff noncommissioned officer's club, no similar facility had been planned for the commissioned officers assigned to this remote post. Therefore, the

Movie stars of Hold Back the Night *were John Payne depicting a rifle company commander and Chuck Conners, a former Marine, as the company gunnery sergeant.*

officers decided, it was high time to take matters into their own hands and build a club themselves. During 1954-1955, with the help of the Seabees, but largely through their own labor during off-duty hours, they erected a frame, one story "L" shaped clubhouse in an aspen grove on the east bank of Silver Creek just below the commanding officer's quarters. The outside was stained and the interior finished with wood walls of knotty pine. A local mason was contracted to build a large rock fireplace in the center of the main hall. Adjacent to the main hall was a bar and grill for beverages and light meals. This opened on to a large outdoor porch offering a beautiful view of the surrounding moun-tains and valley below. Directly below the porch, Rainbow and Brook trout were kept stocked in a pond that was constantly fed with fresh water from a diversionary stream taken from Silver Creek. The set-up allowed this club to offer a fare of grilled trout caught only minutes before by the members themselves.[97]

By the summer of 1956, it had become evident that the name Cold Weather Battalion was no longer appropriate if the mission of the organization was to be broadened. Therefore, on 15 September 1956, the organization at Pickel Meadow became officially known as the Cold Weather Training Center (CWTC), Bridgeport, California.[98]

Chapter 6

Expanding the Mission, 1957–1958

*A Force-in-Readiness Means a Force Ready to Face
all Types of Terrain and Climate.*
-Description of a Traditional Marine Corps Mission

Introduction

The notion of using Pickel Meadow for summer training as well as for winter operations was not a new concept that suddenly came up in 1956. As early as 17 May 1952, Lieutenant Colonel George G. Ryffel, the officer-in-charge of the detachment of Fleet Marine Force, Pacific, troops that had augmented the Cold Weather Battalion advised in his after-action report that "the use of the Pickel Meadow area for training in mountain warfare during the summer months for battalion landing teams is believed to be practical and desirable. The advantages of the available terrain and the existing camp facilities seem to offer a made-to-order situation for such a training program."[99] Over the next few years, succeeding commanders of the Cold Weather Training Battalion would make similar pleas for expanding the mission beyond just preparing replacements for cold-weather operations. None of these recommendations received serious consideration until the mid-1950s, when the newly formulated national security strategy for containing the

An aerial view of the Cold-Weather Training Center in early 1957. The lower base camp has the pyramidal tents for housing training units; there are eight HRS helicopters in landing field in lower right to the left of highway indicating more than ground training was conducted. To the left of the helicopters are three Quonset huts that served as classroom and billeting spaces for the Mountain Leadership Course. The base stables were located directly behind Quonset huts.

Courtesy of MWTC

Sino-Soviet Bloc came into being. The deployment of the Corps' Fleet Marine Forces following the Korean Armistice reflected the new strategy. Most of the 3d Marine Division, teamed with the 1st Marine Aircraft Wing was to be permanently stationed in Okinawa and Japan providing the United States with a strong expeditionary force ready to quickly reinforce U.N. Forces in Korea in the event hostilities should break out again. The 1st Marine Brigade, comprised of a reinforced infantry regiment from the 3d Division and a Marine air group from the 1st Marine Aircraft Wing, constituted a reserve in the Central Pacific. The 1st Marine Division was now back home at Camp Pendleton, teamed with the 3d Marine Aircraft Wing at El Toro. On the East Coast, the 2d Marine Division and the 2d Marine Aircraft Wing had resumed the earlier mission of providing ready combat forces afloat for deployment to the Atlantic, Caribbean and Mediterranean regions. The emergent naval doctrine of providing a balance fleet of air, surface and landing forces to project U.S. power and influence at flash points throughout the littorals of the globe was coming of age. For the embarked Marines and for those who were deployed forward, this implied being ready and able to fight in any clime or place during any season of the year.

The enormous training implications of this naval doctrine carried new imperatives for the Marine Corps. The prevalence of severe climate and difficult terrain in many of the potential areas of operation where Marine amphibious forces might be employed was obvious to strategic planners. No one understood this better than Colonel Donald M. "Buck" Schmuck, the former commander of the Bridgeport training facility. From 1954 until 1957, following his tour in the Sierra Nevadas, Colonel Schmuck served in the G-3 Division at Headquarters, Marine Corps as the Head of the Operations and Training Branch.[100] Thus in the spring of 1956, he was in a key position and likely played a major role in persuading the newly installed Commandant, General Randolph McC. Pate. To initiate a study of the Pickel Meadow site in order to seriously examine its potential use for year-round training in mountain warfare and survival.

Using the impetus of the study, which was approved by the Commandant, the Head of the Operations and Training Section at Headquarters Marine Corps thus lost no time in taking a second step. Schmuck directed Lieutenant Colonel Sidney F. Jenkins, the Commanding Officer at Cold-Weather Training Center (CWTC), to establish two new pilot training courses as a matter of priority.[101] The first was to be a Mountain Leadership Course designed for the small unit infantry leader in the rank of sergeant through company grade officer. A separate syllabus to conform to both the winter as well as summer months would be established. The second was a formal course in escape, evasion and survival aimed primarily at Marine aviators and air crewmen up to the rank of lieutenant colonel, but might include ground reconnaissance personnel and others who might find themselves behind enemy lines. The G-3 also made it clear that he expected both courses to be ready to accept students starting in early 1957; yet, he went on to declare that "CWTC should not expect any additional funding, nor an increase to its current table of organization in meeting this commitment." In other words, keep these courses austere and basic. In order to pay for the personnel and training costs of the new all year program, General Pate had also approved the recommendation of his G-3 to discontinue the Cold Weather Indoctrination Program for replacement drafts to the 3d Marine Division at the end of the winter season in March of 1957. This decision would not only free up thousands of instructor duty hours, but also result in an annual savings of $373,000 in training dollars. The G-3 planners correctly estimated this would more than underwrite a more diverse year round program.[102]

Of the two pilot courses, escape, evasion, and survival perhaps warranted the greatest priority. On 17 August 1955, President Dwight D. Eisenhower had signed the Executive Order establishing for the first time a Code of Conduct to guide U.S. servicemen who may become war prisoners. The code, devised as a means of fighting Communist "brainwashing" tactics, had been drafted by the Secretary of Defense's 10-man Advisory Commission which had studied the treatment of U.S. prisoners of war held by their Chinese and North Korean captors during the war in Korea. The Executive Order noted that every serviceman was "expected to measure up to the [code's] standards." It pledged: "that every man liable to capture shall be provided with specific training and instructions designed to better equip him to counter and withstand all enemy efforts against him and shall be fully instructed as to the behavior and obligations expected of him."[103]

Changes to Command Relationships

Up until the summer of 1956, the Cold Weather Training Battalion had been regarded as little more than an extension of Camp Pendleton. However, as the Marine Corps began to recognize a long-term need for its mountain outpost, then in the process of being renamed the Marine Corps Cold Weather Training Center, Headquarters Marine Corps started

A winter scene of commanding officer's quarters at the Cold Weather Training Center in 1957.

to take a more direct role in solving the camp's problems as well as shaping its future. While Camp Pendleton would continue to serve as the next higher administrative headquarters, henceforth, in matters of training, the center would come under the direct supervision of the G-3, Headquarters Marine Corps. For logistical support, instead of submitting requests for supplies and equipment through Camp Pendleton, the Marine Corps Supply Center, Barstow would now become the direct source for the bulk of the center's supplies and for providing fourth and fifth echelon maintenance of its equipment. And, in an effort to reduce the almost 100 percent annual turnover of personnel, which the organization had suffered for the past several years, beginning on 15 August 1956, the Personnel Department at Headquarters assumed responsibility and control for making all personnel replacement assignments to the training center. Eventually, this action stopped the hemorrhaging of proficient instructors and those assigned to key support and maintenance billets, thereby giving the training center greater stability for staffing its personnel. Furthermore, as early as 6 March 1957, Headquarters, Marine Corps had published a new table of organization for the CWTC. This table of organization

called for a headquarters and two companies: a headquarters company and a service company—the latter largely comprised of occupational specialties in motor transport, maintenance, supply, food service, and heavy equipment. To meet its new missions, the Center was authorized a total strength of 31 officers and 405 enlisted men. A medical officer and dental officer, plus 12 corpsmen and one dental technician were authorized separately from the allowance prescribed from the Naval Dispensary and Dental Clinic, Camp Pendleton.[104]

Between the two new courses of instruction he had been tasked to develop, Lieutenant Colonel Jenkins likely had a personal interest in the syllabus of the Escape, Evasion, and Survival Course. Raised in northern California, Jenkins had received his commission as a second lieutenant in the Marine Corps on 1 July 1939. One year later found him serving as a rifle platoon commander with the 2d Battalion, 4th Marines, in Shanghai, China. Subsequently, he was still with this regiment as a first lieutenant during its gallant defense of Corregidor in the Philippines Islands when war broke out in the Pacific. After that island fortress capitulated to the Japanese Army on 6 May 1942, Lieutenant Jenkins was interned at the Philippine Military Prison

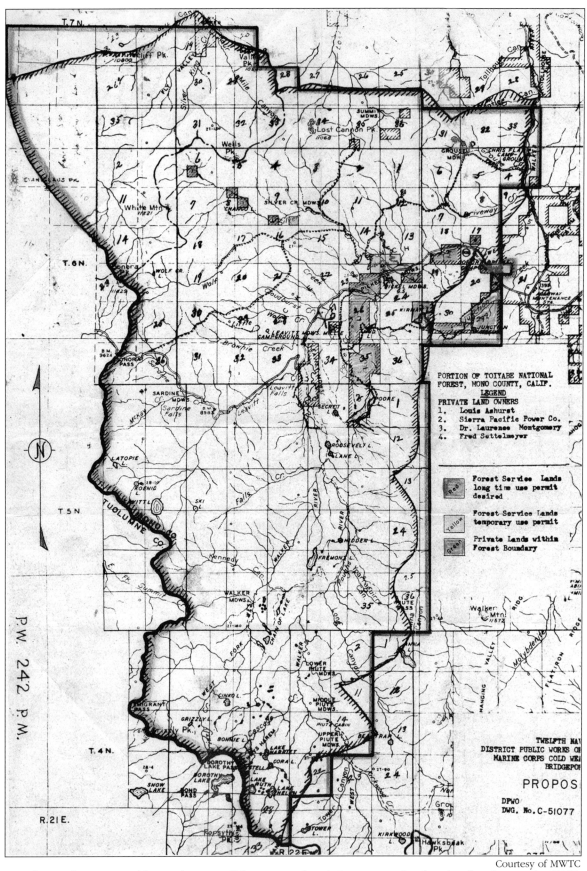

A 12th Naval District public works map of the proposed training center site showing land usage in 1957.

Camp #1. Consequently, he himself endured over three years as a prisoner of war before being liberated at Jinsin, Korea on 7 September 1945.[105]

Although Lieutenant Colonel Jenkins can be credited with laying the groundwork for the new year-round program at CWTC, his transfer to a new duty station on 30 March 1957 meant that refinements to the program would have to be left to his successor, Lieutenant Colonel Alexander W. Gentleman. The new commanding officer accepted this challenge with aggressiveness and flair while demanding meticulous, detailed planning from his staff. Commissioned in the Marine Corps in 1940, Lieutenant Colonel Gentleman had seen combat as a young officer at Tarawa, Saipan, Tinian, and Guam during World War II. He had also seen service in the Korean campaign, commanding the 1st Battalion, 5th Marines, in 1951-1952. Thus, he too could claim personal experience and a keen appreciation for warfare conducted in severe climates and difficult terrain.

Since the signing of the original agreement between the Secretary of Agriculture and the Secretary of the Navy in February 1952, the 64,000 acres that was initially allotted for Marine Corps use by the U.S. Forest Service had by 1957, almost doubled in size. Relations between the local forest ranger at Bridgeport and the Forest Supervisor's Office in Reno, Nevada and each of the succeeding commanders at the Pickel Meadow training site had remained consistently close and cordial. Through special use permits negotiated by the Real Estate Division, Public Works Office, 12th Naval District during the previous five years, over 102,000 acres of the Toiyabe National Forest were now open to CWTC at no cost. These permits included the right to construct certain roads, "which are in the interest of both the Marine Corps, for training, and the Forest Service, for land management and fire protection." (See appendix D) The exclusive use permit that covered the land in the immediate vicinity of the camp area had also been enlarged from 40 to 200 acres. Although the use of explosives was prohibited, as was the firing of any weapon larger than the service rifle, practical restrictions on use of this vast tract of land were few, amounting to the same restrictions found on most Marine Corps bases. California Fish and Game authorities interpreted State game laws as: "not applicable to survival training."[106] In addition, 20 miles to the south of Pickel Meadow lay the Saw Tooth Ridge/Twin Lakes region. Here, the ridges' serrated granite peaks rose almost vertically to elevations over 12,000 feet above sea level. Abutting the eastern escarpment were local glaciers with moats and crevasses that made it comparable to any alpine terrain in the world. Consequently, when Lieutenant Colonel Jenkins was directed to establish the Mountain Leadership Course, he requested that students and instructor and guides of this course be granted temporary access into this area for the purpose of teaching snow and ice climbing exercises and crevasse rescue techniques. The U.S. Forest Service quickly granted this request.

It was a CMC Letter of Instruction to the commanding officer, CWTC that ultimately codified and established the new training program to be conducted at CWTC as follows:

(a) Cold Weather training indoctrination in season.
(b) M76 Amphibious Cargo Carrier crew training in season.
(c) Evasion, Escape, and Survival training throughout the year.
(d) Mountain leadership training throughout the year.
(e) Reserve Unit training as directed,
(f) To provide specialized instruction and technical advice and assistance to FMF or Reserve Units as may be required while such units are in training at CWTC.

Collateral missions included:
(a) Develop, for approval, tactics and techniques incident to the conduct of operations in extreme cold and snow, in mountains, and in the techniques of escape and survival.
(b) Testing equipment and material required in these operations.[107]

Organization for Meeting the New Training Mission

Following the last cold-weather indoctrination course conducted for replacements in 1957, the S-3 Operations and Training Section at CWTC was reorganized into four sections:

(a) *Headquarters Section* consisting of the S-3, his assistance and administrative personnel to provide supervision, coordination and administrative support for its subordinate groups.
(b) *Evasion, Escape, and Survival Section* responsible for preparing, reviewing and conducting formal classroom and practical field instruction to 13 classes of 45 students annually, each of a two-week duration, in the technique of Evasion, Escape and Survival.
(c) *Mountain Leadership Section* responsible for preparing, reviewing and conducting formal classroom and practical field instruction of 16 classes of 25 students annually, each of a three week duration, in the techniques of leading troops at high al-

titudes over steep mountainous and snow-covered terrain.

(d) *Unit Training Section* responsible for preparing, reviewing and annually conducting basic instruction relating to mountain and cold-weather operations to eight FMF battalions, five Organized Reserve units, and five cold-weather indoctrination classes of 110 students of company-grade officers and noncommissioned officers from the FMF and Reserves, for a duration of six days.

(e) *Otter Training Section* formed a fifth training section, but did not fall under the S-3. The Motor Transport Section provided instructors for this course. However, the S-3 was responsible for the content of the syllabus, reviewing lessons plans, and the generally quality of the course. Five classes of 36 students, for a six-day duration were scheduled annually for FMF and Reserve enlisted Marines on the operation and maintenance of the Amphibious Cargo Carrier M76 "Otter." At the time, the M76 was the only over-snow vehicle available to the Marine Corps and 16 of these vehicles were assigned to CWTC.*

Evasion, Escape, and Survival Course

The U.S. Air Force had been conducting formal training in evasion, escape and survival at its Stead Air Force Base, located some 15 miles north of Reno since the early 1950s. Thus the original cadre of Marine escape, evasion, and survival instructors, consisting of two officers and 11 staff noncommissioned officers and noncommissioned officers, were sent to Stead Air Force Base to undergo training in its instructor's course. From this experience and through an intensive and thorough study of all available publications on escape and evasion, much valuable information was gained for developing a similar program of instruction for the Marine Corps. This included a two-day prisoner of war compound exercise, which realistically simulated the harsh treatment, the interrogation techniques and political indoctrination the Chinese and North Korean military had used against American prisoners during the Korean War. Unlike the Stead Air Force Base model, however, which conducted its compound exercise at the end of the course, the Marines reversed the procedure by subjecting students to the compound exercise at the very beginning. This "shock treatment" at the outset enabled students to reflect on their own mistakes when the time came for the classroom instruction to impart to the students how they

could and should have organized themselves to resist and withstand their captors' efforts more effectively. The second half of the course was largely devoted to survival, evasion and field craft improvisation techniques, culminating in a four-day practical field exercise in survival and evasion.

The first pilot course commenced in late 1956. During the first year of its existence, the Escape, Evasion and Survival Camp was located four miles east of the main camp near the Sonora junction with Highway 395. It consisted of a prisoner compound and four Quonset huts: two for billeting, one for a classroom, and one as a storage and office space. However, the disadvantages of this site soon became apparent. Therefore, to reduce the logistics needed to support the operation, the first task that was assigned to the detachment of the Navy Construction Battalion that reported to CWTC the following spring involved relocating the prisoner of war compound to the flats on the west side of the main camp off Highway 108, and reconstructing the two billeting, classroom, and office and storage huts adjacent to the Mountain Leadership Course near the base stables. The complete outfitting of the Escape, Evasion, and Survival Training Course was accomplished at a cost of $8,882. This included the purchasing of live rabbits and poultry that were issued to student teams for the field survival phase. Initially, the dark brown Soviet-style uniforms that were used during the prisoner compound exercise came from the "hand-me-down" uniforms that Captain Robert F. Eggers, the officer-in-charge of the Escape, Evasion, and Survival Course, had managed to scrounge from the Air Force through his counterpart at Stead. Students for the Escape, Evasion, and Survival Course arrived from FMF commands throughout the Marine Corps and the Organized Reserve, except for those stationed in the Far East. Customarily, the classes would be assembled on one coast or the other and flown by military air transport to the Naval Air Station at Fallon, Nevada. There, they would be met by a CWTC bus that two hours later would deliver them to Pickel Meadow. Alternatively, a few might arrive via the Reno airport on individual travel orders.[108]

Mountain Leadership Course

Similar to the escape evasion, and survival instructors who had gone to Stead Air Force Base for assistance, the original cadre of Mountain Leadership instructor-guides also went outside the Marine Corps in search of help and expertise. In this instance, they turned to the U.S. Army Mountain and Cold Weather Training Command at Camp Hale, Colorado. First Lieutenant Edward C. Goodman, who had been appointed senior instructor, along

---

* The term over-snow vehicle is a misnomer. This heavy tracked vehicle would flounder in deep snow. It was primarily used to keep the roads to the extended training sites open by packing the snow after each new snowfall.

"The Capture:" Initial phase of the Prisoner of War Compound Exercise as conducted by the Evasion, Escape, and Survival Training Course, Marine Corps Cold Weather Training Center, Bridgeport, California. Students are herded from this point where they had been ambushed a few moments before to the compound.

"The People's Pool:" At the compound, recalcitrant leaders are segregated and given coercive treatment in an effort to achieve cooperation of the group. The entire group is forced to witness this treatment which results in a feeling of dread and anxiety in the minds of many.

with Lieutenants Billy B. Buck, Joseph P. S. Brown, Robert A. Utter and Ralph V. Walker, Jr., who were assigned to the training course as assistants, spent almost two weeks at Camp Hale going over its program of instruction, receiving instruction in mountaineering techniques and examining equipment lists, lesson plans, training films and the Camp's large reference library of military and civilian mountaineering publications. Later, a three-man Army training team from Camp Hale spent two weeks at CWTC honing the climbing skills of the five officers and 14 enlisted instructors of the Mountain Leadership Course and the two officers and 24 enlisted instructors who had been assigned to the Unit Training Section. This team was made up of a highly qualified Army officer and two civilians, Hans Wagner and Knut Smith, who were recognized authorities on training military mountaineers.

The general objective of the Summer Mountain Leadership Training Course was to "train the trainer." That is to say, to provide at least two to three highly skilled military mountaineers in every Marine rifle and reconnaissance company within the FMF. The concept being that graduates would

Courtesy of MWTC

A view from the watchtower showing the interior of the compound, the tin huts and condition of the "prisoners." This compound is modeled after those used by North Korean and Chinese Communists in the Korean War. A rigorous 30 hours in this compound shows the student what life as a prisoner of war would probably be like.

be qualified to: (1) instruct their units in the "basics" of military mountaineering techniques such as rock climbing, rappelling and the construction of rope installations upon returning to their home stations, and (2) in combat, lead an assault climb against a cliff face that the opposing force might believe is impassable and therefore leave it lightly, or even undefended; and, by anchoring a number of fixed ropes from the top, thereby enable the entire assault force to scale the heights and perhaps outflank the enemy defenses.* The training objectives for graduates of the Winter Mountain Leadership Training Course was similar in scope, but with a few differences. In this instance, a graduate's primary task may be to assist his commander in restoring the mobility of the unit back to one or two miles per hour, when moving through deep snow in mountainous terrain. This might be accomplished through instruction on the use of snowshoes or

cross-country skis. Also, he could become an advisor to the commander in such field craft as route selection, construction of improvised shelters during survival situations, organization for trail breaking, crossing snow bridges and avalanche control. Ideally, any Marine designated as a unit mountain leader would be a graduate of both the summer and winter courses. But only in a few rare instances was this goal ever achieved.[109]

Separate syllabi for both the winter and summer courses were quickly drafted, keeping the above training objectives in mind and acknowledging the 20-training day limitation. Training schedules were written, instructors were assigned to subjects and a host of administrative details were firmed up. Fortunately, the field manuals of the U.S. Army pertaining to mountain operations, military operations in snow-covered terrain, and arctic operations were current and soundly based on the first-hand knowledge and practical lessons learned by the U.S. Army's famed 10th Mountain Division. Moreover, appendices to these manuals provided detailed

---

* During the closing days of World War II, the 10th U.S. Mountain Division successfully carried out such an assault at night against German defenders of the Gothic Line in northern Italy.

Communists kept prisoners in solitary confinement for months and even years to aid in breaking the prisoner down by interrogation. Students subjected to such confinements in training reported that experiencing a taste of it made them more confident of their ability to resist interrogation in an actual situation.

guidance for structuring training programs. Therefore, all that was needed to turn any reasonably dexterous, physically fit infantryman into a skillful military mountaineer was to put them into action.

Easing the chore of course development was the wide selection of nearby choice training locations. For the winter course, looking for areas in which to instruct students in snowshoes, downhill and cross-country skiing, skijoring etc., was never difficult. Grouse Meadow, Silver Creek or Wolf Creek, where small bivouac sites, consisting of one or two Jamesway temporary shelters had been established, could serve this purpose during most of the winter season. In light snow years, the instructors need only take their students to the higher elevations on the Finley Mine Road, or even to the 11,000-foot summit of White Mountain. For the summer course, four miles to the west of the main camp across Highway 108 from Leavitt Meadows was a massive outcrop of solid granodiorite rock. At the topmost tier of the outcrop, a glaciated cliff face rose almost 300 feet high and was approximately 1,200 feet

across. This area was considered ideal. It afforded every type of terrain needed to instruct mountaineering techniques from simple balance climbing and rappelling, up to and including severely difficult two and three party climbing on Mountaineering Classification 5 routes that required the use of direct aids. Behind the cliff face was the Brownie Creek area, where vertical 80-foot cliffs of slate rock offered unique challenges for constructing rope installations, such as vertical hauling lines. Furthermore, sites for teaching rope bridges, stream crossing techniques and building suspension traverse lines across the fast moving West Walker River were also plentiful in this area. And, as for practical application in the techniques of ascending and descending glaciers and crevasse rescue, instructors could teach all these subjects on the steep, high altitude slopes of Horse Creek, under the shadow of the Saw Tooth Ridge in the Twin Lakes area, 14 miles to the southwest of Bridgeport.[110]

The mountain leadership school itself was located in the lower base camp in the vicinity of the base stables. It consisted of four Quonset huts: two for billeting students, one for a classroom and one for the storage of ropes and special equipment issued to the students. The equipage needed to open the course called for 30 individual sets of such special items as nylon climbing ropes, thousands of feet of various dimensions of manila rope, rucksacks, crampons, ice axes, different types and sizes of snap links, pitons, piton hammers, military skis with different bindings and hitches to permit downhill as well as cross-country movement, ski boots,

The interrogator is attempting to create an attitude of gratitude in the subject by offering cigarettes and food, and thereby achieve his cooperation. No trick is too dirty or mean if the interrogator achieves his objective; getting the subject to talk.

Courtesy of 1stSgt Carl H. Raue

A Mountain Leaders Course practice knot tying in 1957. Before graduating, students were required to tie 28 different knots blindfolded. Technical Sergeant Carl H. Raue Jr., third from left, is instructing students.

akio, sleds and five-man mountain shelters. The initial outlay for starting the course in 1957 came to $17,431.[111]

In August 1956, 25 junior officers and staff noncommissioned officers from the 1st Marine Division attended the pilot summer mountain leadership course conducted at CWTC. [112] By the following year, when the course became fully established, the majority of quotas to the Mountain Leadership School alternately went to either the 1st Marine Division or the 2d Marine Division. The students from Camp Lejeune and Camp Pendleton would customarily arrive by military air via Naval Air Station Fallon and thence by bus or truck to CWTC. A sprinkling of reservists, who were granted quotas, usually arrived under individual travel orders.

Unit Training

Unit Training was the largest of the three training sections that was supervised by the S-3. In 1957, it consisted of two elements with one officer and

about a dozen instructor and guides assigned to each. To ensure uniformity and consistency of instruction throughout the center, in order to become an instructor-guide of the Unit Training Section, one had to first graduate from both the summer and winter Mountain Leadership Training Courses.

One element of the section was responsible for the liaison and the instruction provided to the eight FMF battalions from the 1st Marine Division, which were at that time deploying from Camp Pendleton to CWTC for two-week periods of training and field exercises under both summer and winter conditions. Depending on the season of the year, this element normally provided the initial five days of basic instruction on such subjects as shelter and heat, cold-weather medicine, backpacking, over-snow movement, stream crossing survival, animal packing, rock climbing and rappelling. Thereafter, the instructor-guides would remain with the battalion as advisors during the organization's field exercise phase. The second element provided similar

Courtesy of 1stSgt Carl H. Raue Jr.

Students in the Mountain Leader Course practices the body rappel technique in the Leavitt training area in the late 1950s. This technique was the safest means of descending a cliff face.

blocks of basic training to the five Reserve companies that were scheduled during the summer months and for the five Cold Weather Indoctrination Classes scheduled for the winter months. The latter course consisted of six days of living in the field and was largely comprised of company-grade officers and staff noncommissioned officers from all Marine Corps commands inside the United States. In addition to the two elements above, a 50-man Aggressor Platoon to oppose students and add realism during field exercises, plus serve as prison guards for the escape, evasion and survival compound exercises, was also assigned to the Unit Training Section.[113]

Camps for the unit training courses were in several locations. The main cantonment was established on the flats to the north of the small grass landing strip. Here some 70 strong-backed pyramidal tents had been erected for student and unit billeting, together with several strong-backed general purpose tents that served as mess tents, heads, and as the shelter for a portable shower unit. In addition, smaller camps were established at the Silver Creek Meadow and Upper Wolf Creek bivouac sites. During duty hours the base theater could serve as an indoor classroom for the larger classes, but for the most part, the instructor-guides from unit training conducted their classes and demonstrations at informal outdoor training areas, regardless of weather conditions.

Perhaps a few instructors at this time might have regarded the specialized escape, evasion, and survival, and the Mountain Leadership Courses as being more glamorous than the programs provided

Three student mountain leaders learn techniques for crossing a glacier aided by ice axes and crampons at the Sawtooth Ridge Area in the late 1950s.

Courtesy of 1stSgt H. Raue Jr.

Unit training instructors give classes in snowshoeing in the Silver Creek area to members of a Marine infantry battalion in the late 1950s. Vehicles in the background are M76 Otters.

by the Unit Training Section. In reality, nothing could have been further from the truth. Each succeeding commanding officer and his respective S-3 at CWTC had come to appreciate that whenever the justification for continuing CWTC was questioned, it was always the total number of input and output of trainees that counted with Headquarters U.S. Marine Corps. At the end of FY 1957, Lieutenant Colonel Gentleman could still rightly make the claim that over 11,000 Marines had undergone instruction at CWTC, even while his organization made the transition to year-round training. But it was largely the substantive courses under the cognizance of the Unit Training Section that allowed those numbers to be achieved.

In the fall of 1957, General Randolph McC. Pate, Commandant of the Marine Corps, accompanied by Major General Reginald H. Ridgley Jr., Commanding General, Camp Pendleton, made a formal visit to CWTC to get a first-hand look at the effectiveness of the new training programs being offered at CWTC. All indications suggest that from what he

saw during the demonstrations and heard during the command brief, General Pate was favorably impressed by the efforts of the staff and the progress being made at the training center.

Among the numerous agenda items Lieutenant Colonel Gentleman briefed to the Commandant was the 3d Marine Aircraft Wing's plan to deploy a helicopter squadron for a week in each quarter of Fiscal Year 1958 "in order to obtain experience in high altitude operations and to determine aircraft lift capabilities and limitations at this altitude." On a less positive note, he also presented CMC with a complete update on the issue of a proposed dam on the West Walker River. In 1955, the Commandant was briefed that the Bureau of Reclamation of the Department of Interior had completed a reconnaissance report that indicated favorable cost/benefit ratios might be achieved if a dam were constructed across the West Walker River. Two possible project sites had been recommended. The primary was located on the Hoye Canyon area near Wellington, Nevada. The alternate was a dam at the narrows of

Courtesy of MWTC

An honor guard comprised of the Cold Weather Training Center Aggressor Platoon and Headquarters personnel fall-in while in front of headquarters before rendering honors to Commandant of the Marine Corps General Randolph McC. Pate in the autumn of 1957.

the eastern entrance of Pickel Meadow, one mile to the east of the CWTC main gate. According to local officials of the Bureau of Reclamation, a feasibility study of the project was in progress that should be completed by 1959. Depending on the results and the succeeding authorization and appropriation of funds by the Congress, it was possible that construction at one of the two proposed sites could commence as early as 1964. But, Gentleman went on to stress, given the local hostility to the project, it was unlikely that any construction could begin before 1966. Nevertheless, should the project go forward at Pickel Meadow, the present main camp would be under water, thereby necessitating a relocation of the main camp upslope to the vicinity of Tactical Area #2. Gentleman's report estimated the cost of rebuilding a permanent camp at this location at 18 million dollars.[114]

When the Commandant returned to Washington D.C., with a favorable report on the solid progress he had witnessed in the Sierra Nevada Mountains, not everyone on his staff at headquarters shared his enthusiasm. Indeed there were those, particularly in the Personnel Department, who seriously ques-

General Randolph McC. Pate, Commandant of the Marine Corps; Major General Reginald H. Ridgely, Jr., Commanding General, Marine Corps Base, Camp Pendleton, and Lieutenant Colonel Alexander W. Gentleman, Commanding Officer, Cold-Weather Training Center, during the Commandant's visit.

Courtesy of MWTC

Courtesy of MWTC

General Randolph McC. Pate, casts for trout at the officers club pool during visit to the training center. Lieutenant Colonel Alexander W. Gentleman appears left of General Pate.

tioned whether the current manpower levies and monetary expenditures were worth the limited results. As a consequence of the critical commentaries that continued to be voiced, at the end of 1957 a decision was made at Headquarters U.S. Marine Corps to assign an evaluation team to pay a visit to the Sierras in order to determine whether the training center held realistic potential to provide any truly significant value to the future of the Corps' war fighting capabilities.

Chapter 7
Winners Never Quit, 1958–1961

As long as I was commanding officer there, the major effort would be to keep the Center alive for generations of Marines yet to come.[115]
-Lieutenant Colonel Gerald P. Averill

Introduction

The evaluation team that went out to Cold Weather Training Center (CWTC) at the end of 1957 to assess its future value to the Marine Corps returned to Washington and briefed the Commandant on its findings and recommendations. It was a jarring report. The concluding recommendation of the team strongly urged that the center be reduced to a caretaker status and that all organized training there be immediately suspended. When the Commandant asked General Ridgely, the Commanding General, Camp Pendleton for his views on the matter, this veteran, who had himself been a prisoner of war of the Japanese Army during World War II, let it be known that he was unalterably opposed to the contents and the final recommendation of the report. Echoing a statement that he had made earlier General Ridgely stated that "had Marines received such training, the outcome of operations in Nicaragua, in World War II, and in Korea would have been quite different; that this is the type of training that Marines need to meet the variety of conditions they are likely to face."[116] To further counter the negative findings, General Ridgely directed Lieutenant Colonel Gentleman to send him the most recent post-course student evaluation reports in order that the Commandant could read for himself the glowing comments that young officers and staff noncommissioned officers were making regarding the effectiveness of the training they had received at CWTC. In the end, General Pate did decide in favor of keeping the training center open at the same tempo and level of operations. But it was with the provision that there be a 45 percent cut in the training center's personnel staffing. Gone would be such luxuries as the security guard force, the Aggressor Platoon, and the inordinately large complement of officers and staff noncommissioned officers who were assigned to instructor duties. Henceforth, the revised table of organization would reduce the authorized strength of the training center to 18 Marine officers and 235 enlisted. The size of the Navy component of medical, dental and chaplain personnel would remain unchanged.[117]

These personnel cuts had already been imple-mented when Lieutenant Colonel Gentleman was ordered to report to Paris, France as a student in the North Atlantic Treaty Organization (NATO) Defense College. He departed on 6 July 1958, leaving his executive officer, Major Richard F. Dyer, temporarily in command.

In the late afternoon of 1 August, the new prospective commanding officer of CWTC, Lieutenant Colonel Gerald P. Averill, arrived along with his wife, three school-aged children, and their Saint Bernard dog "Samson," and moved into their new quarters.* Major Curtis James, the CWTC operations and training officer, had previously served with Averill in the late 1940s. Therefore, he had already forewarned the troops on what they could expect. However, it was not until the morning formation of 3 August that all hands got a good look at this wiry, 5 feet and 6 inches lieutenant colonel who had been sent out to lead them. The adjutant, Captain Charles H. Clipper, read the appointing and assumption of command orders. The traditional passing of the training center's standard followed, while every man in ranks eyed their new commander closely, searching for clues as to what "the old man" might have in store for them. It was not in Averill's nature to keep his troops guessing very long.

"Zum Gipfel"

Lieutenant Colonel Averill spent his first month in command acclimatizing to the high altitude, observing the various courses of instruction and taking increasingly strenuous physical conditioning workouts while he waited for a leg injury, suffered in a parachute jump at Fort Benning, to heal completely. On 17 September, he enrolled himself as a student in the Summer Mountain Leadership Class 3-59. He later explained:

> For several reasons I had wanted to train in that class–first, I had no formal training in mountaineering and wanted it; second, during

---

* The quarters, the only set on the post, were essentially two Quonset huts butted together to form a "T." The head of the "T" contained the kitchen, dining and living room, which boasted a very large rock fireplace and picture window that looked out on the surrounding mountains and valley below. At the leg of the "T" were the bathroom and bedrooms. Heating was provided by a propane heater and from a fire in the fireplace. In 1964 a second set of quarters was erected below the commanding officer's quarters and designated for the surgeon assigned to the training center.

Gerald P. Averill

Lieutenant Colonel Gerald P. Averill was born and raised in Maine, where he attended high school and spent one year at the University of Maine. With war clouds on the horizon, he enlisted in the Marine Corps on 11 August 1941 and underwent recruit training at Parris Island, South Carolina. After completing parachute training at Naval Air Station Lakehurst, New Jersey as a corporal, he was sent to Quantico, Virginia to attend a Special Reserve Officers Class and on 16 December 1942 was commissioned a second lieutenant. From there he joined the 2d Parachute Battalion on New Caledonia. He saw his first combat as a rifle platoon commander in the raid on Choiseul. After the Parachute Regiment was disbanded in 1944, he became the executive officer of Company H, 3d Battalion, 26th Marines, 5th Marine Division. During the assault on Iwo Jima, Lieutenant Averill was seriously wounded by machine gun fire and was evacuated to the Army hospital on Guam. He was awarded the Silver Star and Purple Heart medals for his actions on Iwo Jima and after recuperating from his wounds, rejoined the 26th Marines and participated in the occupation of Japan. Subsequent tours of duty included one as a naval air observer in the 2d Marine Division, company commander in the 6th Marine Regiment and another as a student at the Amphibious Warfare School, Junior Course. In February 1951, Captain Averill was assigned as the Operations Officer (S-3), 2d Battalion, 5th Marines; promoted to major he became the S-3 of the 5th Marines, where his service won him the Legion of Merit with Combat "V." In the mid 1950s, he served as a tactics instructor at the Amphibious Warfare School and as the S-3 and executive officer of the 3d Battalion, 6th Marines. Prior to coming to the CWTC, Lieutenant Colonel Averill had spent two years at Fort Benning, Georgia as the liaison officer with the Infantry Board (ConArc Board #3) from the Marine Corps Landing Force Development Center at Quantico.[118]

According to Averill's own account, it was Captain Paul X. Kelley who had made several jumps with him at Fort Benning and who was then an assistant to the director of personnel, who first proposed his name as a candidate to take command of CWTC. "In later years," wrote Averill, "I would thank Paul X. Kelley more than once for his recommendation to the director of personnel. I loved Bridgeport."[119]

my time in the Corps I never had asked a Marine to do anything that I could not do; and third, I had perceived that we would need to cross train as quickly as possible a number of permanent personnel-cooks, mess men, maintenance men, drivers and mechanics, in mountain and winter warfare specialties. There was no slack in the line to take up, manpower wise. It was bowstring taut already.[120]

Once having completed the summer rock-climbing course, which in his own words he did "passably well," the new commanding officer next instituted changes to the daily routine of the training center, and to the formal courses of instruction that became the pattern for the next two years during both winter and summer. Averill later remembered:

With the loss of the Aggressor Platoon, troops from the mess force, the maintenance section, motor transport, and the headquarters sections constituted the enemy forces for the compound exercise and field problems. At times there would be no one in the main camp except a communications watch, the officer of the day, the gate sentries, a generator crew and a skeleton mess force. Everyone else was in the boondocks. My family saw little of me during the summer and fall for I, too, was a part of the training force, participating in mountain leadership demonstrations as a guide/rappeller for cliff evacuation and long rappeller—200–feet–during the climbing demonstrations. I also acted as an enemy soldier of the defense force on White Mountain, humping an A-4 light machine gun to the 11,000-foot crest of the mountain and remaining there to run opposition against the students as they attempted to seize a portion of the heights.[121]

In order to prepare himself and his troops to be physically able to undertake these additional duties, Lieutenant Colonel Averill next launched his command into an intensive physical fitness program. Each morning between 0600 and 0700 regardless of the weather, all hands not on an essential watch, or engaged in student instruction in the field, mustered in front of the headquarters building in sweat clothes and combat boots for calisthenics, or "cali-

The staff of the Cold Weather Training Center in 1959. Standing in front of headquarters building in the center front is commanding officer Lieutenant Colonel Gerald P. Averill and his officers. Marines on the left are the enlisted staff of the Mountain Leadership Course, while the Marines on right are the enlisted staff of Unit Training Course.

hoopies" as the troops referred to them. Once warmed up, Averill and his sergeant major led the troops for a run along Highway 108. Initially, the runs were four miles round trip; as the months went by, the runs were extended to the junction at Highway 395 for a total distance of 10 miles. These runs made at just below seven thousand feet of altitude caused a number of Marines, especially the new arrivals who were not acclimatized or used to such a strenuous regime, to vomit their last meal along the way.* Added to the morning workouts, were monthly nights conditioning marches with full packs and weapons for all permanent personnel. The length of these marches varied between 12 to 15 miles and was always led by the commanding officer and his sergeant major, first James M.

"Jim" Westerman and later William J. "Bill" Conley. Moreover, because everyone might be assigned to stand a watch during the 48-72 hours escape evasion and survival prisoner of war compound exercise, Lieutenant Colonel Averill established the policy that all newly arrived to permanently as-

Marine Corps Birthday celebration at the center in November 1959. Commanding officer Lieutenant Colonel Averill stands third from right. Second from right is the sergeant major, Sergeant Major William Conley.

---

* Old timers who were stationed at CWTC at the time can still recall waiting for their stomachs to settle after the morning run and then after 1000, slipping down to the mess hall where sympathetic cooks would prepare a late breakfast for them. This late meal became know as "Calihoopie Chow."

Courtesy of Capt John F. Baltes

Lieutenant Colonel Averill led by example as Cold Weather Training Center commanding officer. Here he prepares to demonstrate a seat-hip rappel at Leavitt Training Area in the summer of 1959.

signed Marines, regardless of rank, were required to go through the first week of instruction at the next scheduled escape evasion and survival class. This included the prisoner of war compound exercise and classroom instruction on prisoner of war conduct and resistance techniques to interrogation and indoctrination. The aim was to ensure that anyone playing the future role of a camp guard, for example, would understand the objectives of the exercise and thereby reduce the potential for abusive treatment of the students.[122] This policy stayed in effect until the prisoner of war compound exercise was significantly modified in 1964 at the direction of Headquarters U.S. Marine Corps.

Shortly after Lieutenant Colonel Averill had taken command, a sign, in Marine Corps colors of red and gold, appeared in front of the training center headquarters building. It read: "Winners never quit— Quitters never win," succinctly suggesting the expected standard of all who reported to Pickel Meadow for either duty or training. Convinced that all the various courses presented there were absolutely invaluable, the commander of the training center wanted to encourage anyone who may have been of faint heart or mind not to let this golden opportunity for self-examination slip by. He later wrote: "To be there pitted against the stresses of nature and the physical and psychological contrivances of man, could not fail to produce a better warrior, a better balanced Marine—an experience immensely profitable to the man and to the

Corps."[123] By this time, the troops and students alike had given the new commander the sobriquet: "Old Iron Balls." If this nickname fazed him, he never showed it. Indeed, if anything it probably encouraged him to make each of the training packages even more realistic and strenuous. Within a year of his arrival, CWTC had taken on a reputation for offering the most practical, yet physically challenging courses available in the Marine Corps. In each course of instruction, leadership by example became the watchword, placing constant pressure on the individual Marine to reach well beyond his comfort level and self-imposed physical limitations. For example, graduates of the Army Ranger Course would often remark in their course evaluations that they had found the Mountain Leadership Course far more challenging and arduous than what they had experienced at Fort Benning.[124]

One feature of the Escape, Evasion, and Survival Course that Averill disliked was the location of the POW Compound that had been constructed a short distance from the course classroom area. He would later recall, "There were always curious people

Captain Charles Clipper, longtime adjutant of Cold Weather Training Center, stands in front of headquarters. The motto on the sign was introduced by Lieutenant Colonel Averill.

Courtesy of Leatherneck

poking about, prying into things that did not concern them—a bad situation for the instructors, even worse for the students."[125] Funding for construction of a new compound had been appropriated, but had not been released by Camp Pendleton. After concerns about abuse were made by the G-3 of the 1st Marine Division after witnessing students undergoing the prisoner of war compound exercise, Lieutenant Colonel Averill was able to convince General Ridgely to have those funds released early. Consequently, in the spring of 1959, the 7th Engineer Battalion was allowed to move the prisoner of war compound and its outbuildings to a new location. The site that had been selected was close to one of the former Aggressor Platoon's field campsites in an aspen grove several miles to the east of Tactical Area #2. Also, by damming up the stream that ran alongside the enclosure, the engineers were able to create an added feature. This was a small pond that thousands of students hereafter would come to know as "The People's Pool."

In making improvements to the Mountain Leadership and Unit Training Course curriculums, Lieutenant Colonel Averill insisted that not only the individual techniques of skiing, or mountain climbing be taught, but that equal attention be given to their tactical military applications when fighting as small unit teams. "Why don't we climb with weapons and equipment?" Averill would ask the course instructor and guides. "Wouldn't we do so in combat?"[126] As a result, such classes as night climbing assaults against defended positions were added to the mountain leadership syllabus, and the course culminating with a pre-dawn assault on the rocky crest of White Mountain.

The consequences of these and many other practical improvements that Averill and his staff of instructors were to bring to the training center were significant. At the close of the first year of operating at the reduced strength, the center had not only raised the bar on the quality of its training, but had exceeded the number of trainees established by Headquarters U.S. Marine Corps.* For his part, the Commandant had kept his promise and funded the center for another year, leaving in place the same stipulations on manpower.

During Lieutenant Colonel Averill's second year at the training center the pace he set for the command never slackened. Once the summer routine was underway it became customary for the Mountain Leadership and Escape, Evasion, and Survival

Marine Corps History Division

A VMO-6 aircraft flying over Pickel Meadow. While acting as an aerial observer in such an aircraft flying near Sardine Lake, Captain Ernest C. Cheatham Jr.'s military career nearly came to an end when the aircraft stalled and crashed in the vicinity of Finley Mine Road.

Courses to graduate a class on a Saturday and receive the next incoming class on the following Monday. The Unit Training Section was kept equally busy furnishing instruction to the regular and Reserve battalions, which were clamoring to get away from their home stations and take advantage of the unique terrain. It was also during his second year that Averill decided to test the mettle of about 45 of his Marines by leading them on a weeklong hike. The route he laid out was from the main gate, north along Highway 395 to Carson City, Nevada and back—a distance of some 150 miles. Starting off early on a Monday morning with helmets, marching packs and weapons, Sergeant Major Conley remembered that each succeeding day became hotter. By the time the column reached Carson City on the third day and started its return south, badly blistered feet had caused the evacuation of over half of the number who had set out. By the fourth day, the number of hikers had been reduced to the commanding officer, Sergeant-Major Conley and a half a dozen other Marines before even the hard driving Averill decided it was time to halt the hike and call for a truck to take the remnants of his column back to the training center.[127]

As it had done in previous years, in October of 1959, the 1st Reconnaissance Battalion deployed from Camp Pendleton to CWTC for the entire month. Supporting the reconnaissance battalion was an aviation detachment from the 3d MAW, consisting of a number of Sikorsky UH-34 Seahorse helicopters and two Cessna OF-2 observation aircraft

---

* Base training figures for that year reported: EE&S 585; MLC 400; CWI 550; FMF Battalions under Unit Training 6,400; for a grand total of slightly under 8,000 for the year.

from Marine Observation Squadron 6. The aircraft not only provided troop lifts, but also was used as platforms for high altitude parachute jumps. On 13 October, Company B was in the process of preparing for a mounted road reconnaissance exercise toward Sonora Pass, using secondary and tertiary roads. Before launching the exercise, the Company B commander, Captain Ernest C. Cheatham Jr., was scheduled to make an aerial route reconnaissance flight in one of the aircraft with himself as the observer. After completing the flight pre-briefing, one of the pilots handed Captain Cheatham his hard hat and said: "Here, you had better replace your soft cap with this." Shortly thereafter, the flight took off from the small grass strip, and then circled over Pickel Meadow to gain altitude before heading west toward Sonora Pass. Unfortunately, while flying near Sardine Lake, the pilot found himself too low inside a box canyon. Attempting to maneuver out of the canyon the engine stalled and the plane immediately started into a downward dive. Within seconds it had crashed into some trees and was upside down on the north side of Highway 108 in the vicinity of the Finley Mine Road. When Captain Cheatham became conscious, he managed to extricate himself from the observer seat and lower himself to the ground. In removing the helmet that had been loaned to him, he noticed that it was almost

Lieutenant General Ernest C. Cheatham, Jr. as Deputy Chief of Staff, Manpower.

Marine Corps Photo

split in half. Unaware that both his legs were broken, Captain Cheatham then proceeded to unstrap the unconscious pilot and to drag him out of the cockpit and away from the wreckage. By this time as he was regaining consciousness, the pilot suddenly remembered that he had failed to cut the switch to the fuel tank. This meant that the plane might explode into flames at any moment. Captain Cheatham thus dragged himself back to the wreckage a second time to turn off the fuel switch. Then, moving the pilot and himself some distance away to a clearing, Captain Cheatham spread out his parachute and laid down to await the rescue team that he was sure would soon be on its way. First to arrive on the scene was the company gunnery sergeant, accompanied by Captain Warren Wiedhahn, Jr. The two had come by jeep from the base camp via the Finley Mine Road, thereby beating the main rescue party that had proceeded up Highway 108. Captain Wiedhahn had only recently joined the battalion and was yet unassigned. As he and the pilot were being bundled into the ambulance and made ready for the trip to the Reno hospital, all that the dazed Captain Cheatham could remember in his half conscious state was Warren Wiedhahn cheerfully telling him: "don't worry Ernie, I'll take your company for you." And this he did.[128]

1960 Winter Olympic Games

The following January found the training center tasked with a new and unusual challenge—provide support for the 1960 Winter Olympic Games. Years earlier, the small ski resort known as Squaw Valley, which lay midway between the town of Truckee, California and Lake Tahoe, had entered the international competition for hosting the 1960 winter games. Its selection by the Olympic Committee, however, caught everyone off guard and caused the state of California to launch a massive public works program to build an Olympic Village at the site along with a new highway infrastructure over the Sierra Nevada Mountains to handle the expected surge in traffic. Traditionally, snow slopes used in Olympic ski competition are constantly packed and groomed by skiers, not machines. Thus the U.S. Olympic Committee had submitted a request to the Commandant of the Marine Corps asking that the Corps furnish a detachment of Marine skiers to support the 1960 Winter Games. The Commandant approved the request and directed the commanding officer, CWTC to serve as his executive agent and on-site representative.

The guidance received from Headquarters U.S. Marine Corps made it clear to Lieutenant Colonel Averill that the Olympic games would take priority over all other activities at the training center. Accordingly, several of the formal training courses were virtually suspended during January and February while a composite unit of approximately 45 Marines representing the very best skiers from the training center, augmented by troops from the 1st Marine Division was formed under officers and noncommissioned officers from the Mountain Leadership and Unit Training Sections. After being clothed and equipped and long hours of reviewing the techniques of sidestepping, herringbone, and sideslipping, the unit deployed to Squaw Valley. There, the Marines moved into an expeditionary camp of strong-backed pyramidal and general purpose tents that had been established near the Olympic Village. Working under the supervision of the ski-patrol, the unit could be seen daily packing and repacking the ski runs until the Games ended in February.* [129]

A Change in the Watch

In the spring of 1960, it was common knowledge at CWTC that Lieutenant Colonel Averill was making it known to his superiors and to the director of personnel at Headquarters U.S Marine Corps that he was very interested in extending his tour at the training center for a third year. However, for whatever reasons, Major General Alan Shapley, the Commanding General, Camp Pendleton, did not concur in this request. The table of organization authorized a colonel to command the training center. Therefore, perhaps he believed this was a good time to assign one. General Shapley's nomination to the director of personnel was his base G-3, Glen E. Martin, who had recently been promoted to the rank of colonel. As a captain, Averill had served as Lieutenant Colonel Martin's S-3 in 1951 when the latter commanded the 2d Battalion, 5th Marines, in Korea. Once he learned that this officer, for whom he had great respect, had been nominated as his replacement, Averill gave up his lobbying efforts to extend his tour and made plans to depart in June. Despite his disappointment in not being allowed to remain for an additional year, in just 22 months Lieutenant Colonel Averill had managed to turn the reputation of the training center from something of questionable value, into one of the premier training facilities of the Marine Corps. As he was to write in his autobiography, "The land itself, with all of its desolate spaciousness, its pristine loveliness, its terrible loneliness, became a part of me, the yearning to remain with it was a twisting, burning pain in my gut. Being kind of king of the mountain made other as-

* The U.S. Marine Band was also on hand to participate in the opening ceremonies of these winter games.

Photo by William Brier, courtesy of author

Marines from the Cold Weather Training Center and Camp Pendleton make the daily run down the ski slopes to pack the snow for the Winter Olympic Games. The best skiers were used for this under the supervision of the local ski-patrol..

signments commonplace and drab. I had glimpsed Shangri-la."[130]

Raised in Iowa, Colonel Martin received a bachelor of arts in economics from Colorado College in Colorado Springs in 1941. That same year he enlisted in the Marine Corps and received his commission in August 1941. As a platoon commander and later company commander during World War II, he participated in a number of the major amphibious landing operations in the Pacific Theater, earning the Navy Cross in the Marshall Islands. Other awards included two Silver Stars and two Bronze Stars. At the end of World War II he left active duty, but remained in the Organized Reserve. At the outbreak of the Korean conflict he was recalled to active duty and sailed with the 1st Replacement Draft. Having arrived at Kimpo Airfield during the fight to recapture Seoul, Major Martin assumed command of Weapons Company, 2d Battalion, 5th Marines. He continued to serve in that capacity throughout the Chosin Reservoir campaign, during which he earned his third Silver Star and third Bronze Star medals. Promoted to lieutenant colonel in January 1951, he assumed command of the 2d Battalion just in time to lead it in Operations Killer and Ripper during General Ridgeway's counteroffensive to regain the 38th Parallel. For his final three months in Korea, he served as the assistant operations officers (G-3A) of the 1st Marine Division. After accepting a regular commission, his subsequent tours included duty at Marine Corps Schools, Quantico, the Military Assistance Advisory Group, Formosa, as G-2 and G-5 at Air FMF-Pac, El Toro and as the commanding officer, 1st

Courtesy of 1stSgt Carl H. Raue Jr.

Marines from center participated in recovery of the bodies of two civilian mountain climbers killed in a fall in the Montgomery Peaks Ridge area, Mono County, May 1959. Lieutenant Colonel Averill personally supervised the effort and the seven instructor-guides were temporarily deputized by the Mono County Sheriff for this purpose.

Battalion, 7th Marines, at Camp Pendleton.[131]

Lieutenant Colonel Averill and his family had already departed by the time Colonel Martin assumed command on 1 July. Shortly thereafter, he and his wife Virginia and their two boys and two girls, ages 13, 11, 9, and 7 respectively, moved into the Quonset quarters that would be their home for the next two years. In 1957, as a Lieutenant Colonel serving in the Plans Division at Air FMFPac, Colonel Martin had wrangled a quota to attend the U.S. Army six-week Cold Weather Indoctrination Course at Fort Greely, Alaska. It was there, he said, "that I had become reasonably proficient in cross-country skiing." However, the new commander could claim no experience in military mountaineering. Consequently, like his predecessor, Colonel Martin enrolled himself as a student in the next scheduled Mountain Leadership Course. [132]

Marines who served at Pickel Meadow during the tenures of Lieutenant Colonel Averill and Colonel Martin fondly remember both officers as superb leaders; nevertheless, many acknowledge that their personalities and leadership styles were quite different. Where the former was dynamic, aggressive, and naturally prone to being combative, the latter came across as soft-spoken, reflective, and

unpretentious. Yet by their own unique ways and actions, both commanders inspired in their subordinates a high sense of duty and confidence that the training being conducted at Pickel Meadow was very meaningful to the individual Marine and therefore important to the overall health and well-being of the Corps. One must recall that these were challenging years. Both the U.S. Army's and Marine Corps' conventional forces and budgets had been declining ever since the Eisenhower Administration had adopted nuclear deterrence as its primary national defense strategy. Economy measures had already caused the Marine Corps to cadre several of its infantry battalions and when Colonel Martin arrived at CWTC he was greeted with the news that his table of organization had been further reduced by 45 enlisted positions. This brought the total strength down to 180 and meant that all hands would be required to wear several "hats" and participate in the training programs in addition to fulfilling their primary duties.[133]

Another issue that Colonel Martin had to confront soon after he arrived involved compliance with the California Game and Fish laws. Contrary to the earlier policy of allowing the escape, evasion, and survival students to trap small game and to fish out of season, the attorney general of the state of California ruled this practice to be illegal. A letter signed by the attorney general to this effect was received at the command a month before Colonel Martin assumed his duties there. General Shapley cautioned his new commander at CWTC "not to turn a blind eye to the attorney general's ruling in the hope of not getting caught." After conferring with the local agent of the Fish and Game Commission, Colonel Martin made several trips to Sacramento to plead a case for making a change to the law incident to formal survival training. California State Senator Jones, who was then chairman of the Forestry Sub-committee was sympathetic to Colonel Martin's arguments and agreed to hold a hearing on the issue.

As a result of Colonel Martin's testimony at this hearing, the law was changed, thereby permitting the escape, evasion and survival students to have survival fishing rights year round. "Money was so tight then," recalled the colonel. He added that whenever he had to travel to Sacramento he and his driver would depart at 0300 that he would pay for the driver's lunch from his own pocket and that they'd start back for the base after 1600. "I would have liked to have stayed overnight, but we had no per diem funds to speak of in those days."[134]

This change to the California Fish and Game Law not only benefited the Marine survival course, but also the survival program at Stead Air Force Base, which had been suffering under the same proscription. Impressed by what the Marines had achieved, the commanding officer of Stead Air Force Base and several key staff members paid a visit to CWTC to express their thanks to Colonel Martin and to look over the Marine Escape, Evasion, and Survival Course. One of the outcomes of the good relations that followed between the two commands was Stead's gift of additional sets of Soviet-style uniforms for use in the Marine POW Compound exercise. "Some uniforms were used," recalled Colonel Martin, "but most of them were brand new."

Up until the time Colonel Martin assumed command, it had been the practice of the Mountain Leadership Winter Course to issue students a ski boot that had been designed for use by the U.S. Army's 10th Mountain Division. This was a stiff, square-toed, low-cut boot of brown leather. But

BGen Lewis W. "Lou" Walt, assistant division commander of the 1st Marine Division, at left; and Col Glen E. Martin, commanding officer of the Cold Weather Training Center, at right, during a prisoner of war compound exercise in 1961. Both officers are wearing the dark brown Soviet-style uniforms that were used by the school staff.
Courtesy of MWTC

Courtesy of *Leatherneck*

Improvised field-expedient pack made by a student in the Escape, Evasion, and Survival Course during the evasion phase of the course, early 1960s.

since the standard footwear for all Marines in any future conflict in snow-covered terrain would be the insulated "Mickey Mouse" boot, the new commanding officer directed that students learn their over-snow techniques using this boot. With minor modifications to the hitches of the Northland skis and the addition of Arlberg straps wrapped tightly above the ankles of the boots, sufficient control in downhill ski techniques could be achieved. Thus the new order soon became standard practice.

Other than this modest change, Colonel Martin made no alterations to the curricula of the formal courses or their training practices. Instead, he turned his attention toward improving the cost effectiveness of the base and its habitability standards for both permanent personnel and students. In the summer of 1960, the 7th Engineers constructed a wood frame head and shower facility with heated flooring in the schools area for students undergoing instruction in the Escape, Evasion, and Survival and Mountain Leadership Courses. The students and instructors regarded this facility as a major improvement over the outdoor heads and expeditionary tent shower unit that had been used during the previous four years.

In 1961, at the end of Colonel Martin's first year of duty at the training center, Lieutenant Colonel Nathaniel H. Carver reported for duty as his executive officer. Carver was a 1302 engineer officer.

Courtesy of MWTC

An M76 Otter struggles, belly-up, in deep snow at the center in the early 1960s.

Thus to him fell the task of implementing one of Colonel Martin's most ambitious undertakings: the conversion of the training center to commercial power. Since its earliest days, electrical power for the base was furnished by four 75-kilowatt, and later four 100-kilowatt generators, with two of these on line operating at 10-day intervals with the other two. In addition to a heavy consumption of fuel, the power plant required four men rotating the watch around the clock. Earlier attempts to convert the base to commercial power several years before had been unsuccessful. Nevertheless, Colonel Martin was eager to try again. After encouraging nearby ranchers and property owners to join in on this venture and after several trips to Los Angeles, Colonel Carver eventually succeeded in negotiating a contract with Southern California Edison to extend its power services to the training center. The project was started in 1962 and conversion to commercial power was completed the following year.[135]

Another legacy left by Colonel Martin was the introduction of the Thiokol Snowcats (commonly called Trackmasters) to the training center. Since the 1940s the only vehicle in use by the Marine Corps in snow-covered terrain was the Pontiac M-76 Otter Amphibious Cargo Carrier. Because of its weight, however, this tracked vehicle was fit for crossing through marshes, or marginal terrain, than it was for traversing deep snow. Unplowed roads with snow over 18 inches would usually cause the vehicle to founder and lose its traction. Therefore, in order to keep the roads open to the training areas

at the higher elevations, it became standing operating procedure to run the Otters day and night during snowstorms just to keep the new snow packed down. Needless to say, this inefficient use was costly in terms of both driver hours and fuel. Moreover, Colonel Martin later recalled, "by the end of every winter we found that we were blowing out two or three transmissions every year. At the time, the Barstow Supply Center was charging us $18,000 just to replace one transmission. I tried to get them to reduce that price since we were the only user of the vehicle, but they would not go along with it. About that time, I found that we could purchase a new Thiokol Trackmaster for $10,000."[136] Colonel Martin directed that two of the Thiokol Trackmasters be purchased for trial and evaluation. These vehicles arrived in December 1962. Capable of traversing steep slopes over snow-covered terrain while carrying up to 11 troops inside (with skis and packs lashed to the top) these two test vehicles quickly proved their worth. Both the Winter Mountain Leadership and Unit Training Courses were now able to extend the range of student bivouac sites to the highest slopes where the best snow conditions could be found. Further, their road speeds of up to 25 miles per hour also made this wide-tracked vehicle ideally suited for skijoring up to two squad-sized infantry units. As a result, the Otters were phased out and the Trackmaster fleet was increased to 10 vehicles over the next several years.[137]

Ski troops skijoring behind Thiokol Trackmaster in 1963. This oversnow vehicle extended the capabilities of the Mountain Leadership and Unit Training sections to reach higher elevations. It could reach of 15-25 miles per hour in deep snow.

Courtesy of MWTC

Chapter 8

Mountain Men, 1962–1965

We aren't no thin red 'eroes, Nor we aren't no black-
guards too,
But single men in barricks, Most remarkable like you,
An' if sometimes our conduck, Isn't all your
fancy paints,
Why, single men in barricks, Don't grow into
plaster saints.
–Rudyard Kipling

Marines Who Proved a Match for the Mountains

By the early 1960s, thanks to a series of several exceptionally qualified and energetic commanding officers and in response to the needs of the Marine Corps to be a force in readiness in "every clime and place," CWTC had earned a reputation for offering some of the most challenging and sought after training programs in the Corps. To many of those who had served there, the training center had clearly demonstrated its value. True, the Personnel Department at Headquarters U.S. Marine Corps did continue to challenge the cost effectiveness of some training programs and did continue to send out evaluation teams from time-to-time to determine whether this or that course could not be shortened or done away with altogether. However, after witnessing the training being conducted and reading the student post graduation comments, invariably these teams would come back with reports essentially declaring that the Marine Corps should continue this vital training. One such favorable report even resulted in the CWTC table of organization receiving a slight increase in its enlisted strength.[*]

However, it was not just the commanders who convinced visitors of the viability of the training center. Equally impressive was the dedication, professionalism, and enthusiasm of the Marines and the Navy personnel that made up the command. Regardless of their assignment, whether instructional, service, or support, most seemed convinced that what they were doing was vitally important to the Corps. Throughout these years, Headquarters U.S. Marine Corps listed CWTC as a "hardship post." This was especially true for those with wives and young children. For the husband, service at the training center might well be viewed as an "opera-

tors" dream; but for his spouse, isolated and living in an eight by 20-foot trailer it could become a nightmare if the marriage was not a solid one. Even the bachelor officers and staff noncommissioned officers affectionately referred to the Post as "Fort Bleak" and the masthead of the post newspaper carried the name *Last Outpost*. Yet its permanent complement above the rank of corporal was consistently made up largely of volunteers who had submitted written requests to be assigned there. Moreover, many were serving extended tours of duty, or had returned for a second tour. While it is impossible to list all of those who may have left their mark on the training center during this era, this monograph seeks to document the contributions of influential Marines who later became consequential figures.

Among the officers, perhaps the one who could claim the longest continuous service at Pickel Meadow was Captain Charles H. Clipper. He reported for duty at CWTC as the S-1 and adjutant under Lieutenant Colonel Gentleman in 1958. Capt Clipper continued to hold that billet until 1964. He made his home in Reno, Nevada and thus for six years he would embark on the base liberty bus at 0500 in Reno and disembark after 1900 every working day of the week. Captain Clipper also became a very popular figure among many prominent citizens and hotel and casino owners in the Reno area, always ensuring that a large contingent of Marines would be on hand to support the local Red Cross blood drives and other events. During Charlie Clipper's tenure, it was customary for the Mapes, Riverside, or some other large casino or hotel to host the CWTC Marine Birthday Ball at no cost, other than for individual drinks.[*]

Captain Stanley "Ski" Wawrzyniak was serving as the provost marshal at the Subic Bay Naval Base, Philippine Islands, in 1959 when he requested and received orders to CWTC. Initially, he became the S-3 under Lieutenant Colonel Averill. Colonel Martin later made him the officer-in-charge of the Unit Training Section and subsequently, senior instructor -guide of the Mountain Leadership Course. At his own request his additional duty was the base mess officer. Even before reporting to CWTC, this five feet and six inches barrel-chested captain had al-

---

[*] In 1963 the authorized strength at CWTC was raised to 17 Marine officers, 207 enlisted Marines, three Navy Officers (a chaplain was now added,) 13 Navy enlisted, and five civilians (figures extracted from the S-3 portion of a 1963 MWTC command brief in possession of the author).

[*] Capt Clipper later retired as a realtor in Reno. Unfortunately, he died in 2002 before the author could interview him in person.

Courtesy of MWTC

Living quarters of Cold Weather Training Center permanent personnel, who often affectionately referred to the post as "Fort Bleak."

ready earned a Corps-wide reputation for being one of the most fearless, toughest and inspiring combat leaders to have come out of the Korean War. During his two-year extended tour on the Korean Peninsula, he went from staff sergeant to master sergeant, and while serving with the 2d Battalion, 5th Marines, was awarded two Navy Crosses, (the first while under Colonel Martin, the second coming from his actions during the following year was down-graded from a recommendation for the Congressional Medal of Honor) a Silver Star, and three Purple Hearts. In Vietnam he went on to earn two Bronze Stars and his fourth Purple Heart.

Humorous Captain Wawrzyniak stories continued to reverberate through Pickel Meadow long after this colorful and unique leader had departed for duty at Quantico in 1961. One story that was related for years to come told of the incident when he was going through the Mountain Leadership Course as a student in the summer of 1960. The class was undergoing ice climbing and crevasse rescue techniques on a glacier beneath the Saw Tooth Ridge. As Wawrzyniak took his ordered practice fall, his student-climbing partner who was suppose to arrest his fall came out of his belay position. As a result, he slid headlong into the blue ice of the open crevasse. Fortunately, he landed on a sunken connecting snow bridge, thereby preventing what surely would have been a fatal fall. Even so, after

he was retrieved, Wawrzyniak was found to have suffered a broken sternum and was in deep pain. The corpsman who was with the class wanted to administer morphine and have the captain littered back to Twin Lakes. But characteristically, he refused both.[138] Those readers who have trekked out of Horse Creek Canyon can appreciate what a jarring experience that can be, even when one is at

Training center staff stretched out on the fireplace at the Cold Weather Training Center Staff Noncommissioned Officers Club, around 1964.

Courtesy of *Leatherneck*

the top of his form. But at his insistence, Wawrzyniak managed to slowly struggle down those steep talus slopes under his own power, aided only by the shoulders of the strapping instructor and guide, Corporal Roger Shelton. Upon reaching the parking lot at Twin Lakes, only then did this iron man finally let go and collapse.

Lieutenant Wiley M. Clapp Jr., served with the Escape, Evasion, and Survival Course from July 1959 to November 1961 and was the officer-in-charge of the section during the summer and fall of 1960. During his tenure, Lieutenant Clapp managed to add more and more realism to the course of instruction that he and others had inherited from their predecessor, Captain Robert F. "Bob" Eggers. As a result, the Escape, Evasion, and Survival Course offered one of the most practical and useful learning experiences then offered by any formal Marine Corps school of the time. Writing as one of those who went through the course during Lieutenant Clapp's tenure, can anyone ever forget his masterful presentation on The Code of Conduct Later, Wiley would credit a Gunnery Sergeant John C. Sheridan, an early instructor in the Escape, Evasion, and Survival Section, for first developing the powerful mes-

sage it carried.[139] Nevertheless, in the history of the school, no one ever quite perfected this lecture to the same degree, or delivered it with more passion and belief than did Wiley Clapp.

First Lieutenant Vincent R. Lee requested assignment to CWTC after completing an unaccompanied overseas tour as an infantry officer in the 3d Marine Division. His request was granted and in the late spring of 1962 he reported for duty and was assigned to the Mountain Leadership Section as an instructor-guide under Captain John B. Morris. Reared in Westchester County, New York, Lieutenant Lee had developed an early enthusiasm for rock climbing in the Hudson River valley, an avocation that he continued to pursue while an undergraduate at Princeton University. During his two years at CWTC, Lieutenant Lee became known for his willingness to share the new techniques he had learned as a civilian mountaineer with his fellow instructors. Over time he skillfully modernized the syllabus of the Mountain Leadership Course by introducing the latest climbing techniques and lightweight equipment that he believed would have equal application in military mountaineering. As a result of his singular efforts, the standing operating procedures for the

Stanley Wawrzyniak

From 1959 through 1961, Captain "Ski" served as operations officer, senior instructor of the unit training section, and as the additional duty mess officer during his several years at the Mountain Warfare Training Center. But most significantly, he ran the Mountain Leadership Course as senior instructor and guide. There are many "Ski" stories that Pickel Meadow old-timers love to share at reunions, but the "Ski's" official record needs no embellishments.

From Gary, West Virginia, Stanley Wawrzyniak enlisted in the U.S. Navy during World War II at Buffalo, New York, serving as a boilermaker third class. He joined the U.S. Marine Corps in 1946. When the Korean War began, he was a staff sergeant with 2d Battalion, 5th Marines and landed at Inchon with the 1st Marine Division. During two separate tours in Korea, he was wounded three times, which included a six-week stint on the USS *Consolation* (AH 15). He was decorated with the Silver Star and two Navy Crosses and promoted to the rank of master sergeant when the conflict ended. Encouraged by the Commandant of the Marine Corps, General Randolph McCall Pate, Wawrzyniak was commissioned a second lieu-

tenant in 1953. After serving throughout the United States and the Far East, Major Wawrzyniak served in Vietnam in 1966-1967 with 3d Battalion, 3d Marines, earning two Bronze Star Medals and another Purple Heart. He retired as a lieutenant colonel and died in 1995. After Ski's death, stories circulated of his countless adventures, which involved everything from stealing a jeep to breaking his back in a glacial crevasse.

Major Tony Milavic circulated many of these in a narrative of exploits including those at Bridgeport. Occasionally, some Marines sought to step away from the challenges of the demanding Mountain Leaders Course that then Captain Wawrzyniak supervised. One sergeant tried to quit while in agony as a group climbed the 11,321-foot White Mountain. Ski would not let him quit, and tied a rope around him to literally pull him within a few feet of the summit. After untying the rope, the wayward sergeant fell back down the slope. Wawrzyniak turned to Milavic and gave him the rope, saying "Go bring that ungrateful b****** back up here!" According to Milavic, "Ski did not try to move mountains; he moved Marines and conquered mountains."[140]

Staff Sergeant Anthony F. Milavic, an instructor of the Escape, Evasion, and Survival Course, poses in Soviet-style uniform used in the Prisoner of War Compound Exercise in the summer of 1961.

Mountain Leadership Course were completely revamped and modeled along the lines he suggested, culminating in a challenging five-day alpine counterguerrilla exercise in the rugged Saw Tooth Ridge area.

Similar to the officer community, there were several legendary characters among the enlisted ranks that are also deserving of special mention. One should not forget the contributions of Staff Sergeant Carl E. "Pappy" Scheer in the area of service and support. This dedicated Marine spent nine years at the training center as the noncommissioned officer-in-charge of the heavy equipment section. Another notable character was Gunnery Sergeant John Marjanov, who reported for his first tour of duty at the training center in 1964 and was also assigned as heavy equipment chief until his transfer to Vietnam in 1966. As a staff sergeant in Korea, John Marjanov was for a time attached to a contingent of British and Canadian Forces. For his actions and services, he was awarded the British Empire Medal (BEM) at a formal ceremony at the British Embassy in Washington D.C. in July 1955.[141] Consequently, his fellow staff noncommissioned officers at the training center never referred to him to as anything but "Sir John."

Remarkable figures among the Mountain Leadership Section included Staff Sergeant Theodore E. "Boone" Neal, Gunnery Sergeant William R. "Bill" Lightfoot, and Gunnery Sergeant Lonnie "Moose"

Henderson. Staff Sergeant Neal was reared in Colorado and spent his youth on ranches breaking horses before enlisting in the Marine Corps. His first tour of duty at CWTC started in 1957. As a corporal, he ran the base stables and taught animal packing for the Mountain Leadership and Unit Training Courses. Following a tour in the 1st Marine Division, Staff Sergeant Neal returned for a second tour at CWTC in 1962 and was assigned to the Mountain Leadership section. "No one could 'read' or had a better sense for the mountains than Boone Neal," said Gunnery Sergeant Ronald "Ron" Burtsell, unit chief of the Mountain Leadership section. Bill Lightfoot joined the Mountain Operations Group as a staff sergeant in 1958 under Lieutenant James V. "Jim" Knapp. During his last two years at the training center until his transfer to the 1st Marine Division in late 1963, he served as the chief of the Mountain Leadership Section. One could count on Bill Lightfoot to be levelheaded and consistent, and to run things "by the book." The six feet five inches "Moose" Henderson was raised on a tobacco farm

A Marine prepares to use a three rope bridge to safely cross the Walker River at the stream crossing site near Leavitt Lodge. He is supervised by two legendary training instructors in the white helmets; Sgt Hank Vozka on the left and Capt Stan Wawrzyniak on the right.

Gerald H. Turley

"Gerry" Turley's account of the only escape from the enemy prisoner compound:

"Inside the compound there were several steel sheds in which we gathered to get out of the chilly weather. The shed I was in was near the south (downhill) side wire. I observed the guards routine for several hours, and then felt that if an escape went early and quickly, it would probably be more successful than later during our confinement.

So we slowly began moving the shed closer to the fence, and after about two hours it was within four feet of the eight-foot fence. The lowest side of the shed (about five feet high) faced the inside of the compound. The high side, which was almost seven feet high, faced the barbed wire fence.

We noticed the guard in the one tower was having problems with his EE-8 telephone, and he was bending over pulling up a new phone on a rope. I had earlier told a big strong Marine of my idea to run and leap on someone's back to get onto the shed's roof, and from there, to just keep moving toward the wire. While the guard was distracted, the big Marine quickly assumed a leaning position against the shed. I stepped back about 20 feet, and ran as fast as I could, and putting one foot on his back I leveraged myself up onto the roof. Never stopping, I then made a wild leap from the shed up over the fence. It all happened so fast that not one of the cadre was even aware that I had escaped.

Once over the fence, I landed in some brush, headed down the hill for about 100 yards, and then turned to the west for another 200 yards, and then began to climb back around and above the POW camp. I concealed myself and then just sat there and watched the cadre scramble when they discovered someone was missing.

I remained out about four hours and then voluntarily returned to the compound. The cadre people were not pleased, but they treated me fairly. All in all it was a good day, and the training experience proved valuable many times over."[142]

In reality, the instructors considered this the perfect escape from the compound exercise of the escape and evasion school; it was organized, all students participated and the escapee got away before a guard could react. In their collective memory, this was the first for the course.[143]

in southern Virginia. Before joining the Marine Corps, he went to Africa where he worked as a tracker and white hunter for a safari company. In 1963, he was an instructor at the 1st Marine Division's Counterinsurgency School at Camp Pendleton. The newly appointed senior instructor-guide of the Mountain Leadership section was a student in the course and was so impressed by Henderson's instructor abilities and knowledge of the subject matter that he induced him to ask for an immediate transfer to CWTC. Henderson joined the Mountain Leadership Section three months later and went on to become one of its ablest instructor-guides.

Perhaps the enlisted instructor in the Escape Evasion, and Survival Course who consistently left the most lasting impression on his students during this era was Staff Sergeant Anthony F. Milavic. Before reporting to CWTC in 1960, he served a two-year tour of duty with the 1st Marine Air Wing at Iwakuni, Japan. There he studied Japanese and became a belted instructor in a particular form of martial arts known as Wadoo Ryu Karate. These courses, combined with his serious study of the interrogation and political indoctrination techniques used by the Chinese Communist Forces in Korea, aided him in becoming an instructor of the highest quality. During the prisoner of war compound exercise, Staff Sergeant Milavic often played the role of the empathetic and "understanding" indoctrination officer. Normally, the students undergoing the exercise would be absolutely tight-lipped under interrogation. Then, around 0200 while in an entirely different setting, invariably the smooth-talking Anthony Milavic dressed in civilian attire would all too easily seduce members of the class into talking on a host of seemingly harmless subjects, thereby causing them to unwittingly break the precepts of the Code of Conduct. This became a valuable learning lesson during the classroom instruction that followed. Two other highly esteemed instructor-guides who left their mark with the Escape, Evasion, and Survival Section were Staff Sergeant Eugene L. "Gene" Ewing and the section chief, Gunnery Sergeant Raymond A. Montoya. Both served at the training center between 1962 and 1964.

Typical among the many able and dedicated instructor-guides who served in the Unit Training Section was Corporal Henry Vozka. The lean, five feet and 10 inches bachelor corporal had completed three years in the 1st and 3d Marine Divisions before reporting for duty at the training center in April

1959. Raised in Michigan and therefore no stranger to cold-weather, the likable Vozka quickly adapted to life at CWTC. After completing all of the courses of instruction and receiving a promotion to acting sergeant, Vozka acquired a Keeshond puppy, which he named Hondo. The two became inseparable. Until his transfer in October 1962, on off-duty weekends Vozka and Hondo would often be seen bivouacked together along Silver or Wolf Creeks while his hut mates were off to Reno on the base liberty bus. One former instructor and guide who served at CWTC during the same time wrote the following account which characterizes Sergeant Vozka's outlook toward his duties:

> In 1960, I was stationed at the Marine Corps Cold Weather training center, Bridgeport, California when those in the infantry field were authorized "proficiency pay." For the center, it amounted to a three-month increase in pay of $30.00 a month on a rotating basis for one or two of the instructor and guides in each of the three sections: Escape, Evasion and Survival, Mountain Leadership and Unit Training. The first to receive this pay in the Unit Training Section was Sergeant Henry Vozka. At the time, a sergeant's base pay was about $150.00 a month and $30.00 amounted to a significant increase in pay.

During that summer of 1960, Sergeant Vozka and his section were preparing for a class on river crossing for a unit from Camp Pendleton. In the process, Vozka tied one end of a two-rope bridge to a tree on the bank of the West Walker River. Unfortunately, there were two trees there and the one Vozka picked was not the favorite of Master Sergeant Chad J. Palmer, the noncommissioned officer-in-charge of the Unit Training Section. This resulted in the "Top" giving Vozka some "corrective guidance." Well, the other members of the section who were witnesses to the event took pleasure in razzing Vozka by asking: "How could someone on proficiency pay screw-up like that?" This chiding continued into the unit training billeting Hut 4018 that night. The next morning, Vozka confronted the center's disbursing officer and said: "Sir, I'm returning this 'pro-pay' and I want you to stop paying it to me." The disbursing office looked at the $30.00 in cash on his counter and replied: "Sergeant Vozka, I can't take it back. You have the money and its yours." "Lieutenant, I don't want it and I won't take it back," said Vozka as he promptly walked out of the disbursing office. On returning to the Unit Training Section, he announced, "I am no longer on 'pro-pay,' so get off my ass! Stunned speechless,

his fellow Marines did just that.[144]

There were certainly a number of extraordinary enlisted Marines who served at Mountain Warfare Training Center during this period of time whose personal mettle proved every bit as hard as the granite peaks that surrounded the meadow. But in terms of sheer colorfulness, few, if any, could quite measure up to the legendary Richard R. "Big Red" Ebert, Jr., he strapping six feet and four inches tall, 220 pounds, red-thatched Ebert entered the Marine Corps before World War II. He had fought in several Pacific campaigns, including Iwo Jima, and later in Korea as an artilleryman. "Perhaps this was the reason for his booming voice," Sergeant Major Daniel J. "Dan" Flynn wrote of him.[*] In 1964, "Red Ebert" arrived at CWTC and relieved Sergeant Major Harry A. Stoneburner as the training center sergeant major. One staff noncommissioned officer who at the time was serving at the training center remembers: "He was the original hard case. He snarled rather than spoke and his mere presence could generate an aura of fear in everyone in the room, from master sergeant to private." There was no room for anything but superb performance in Sergeant Major Ebert's book and even senior staff noncommissioned officers who admired the hell out of him would tend to give him a wide berth when they saw him making his daily inspection rounds of the training center. Although tough, he could also show a softer side by simply giving a good counseling session to any Marine for whatever errant behavior, and then reach right down to pull him back up and send him on his way–the right way. "Red" was a bachelor who lived in the staff noncommissioned officers quarters. However, only a few of his fellow staff noncommissioned officers were aware that whenever he was in garrison, he would retire to his room and place a nightly telephone call to his widowed mother. [145]

Shifts in the Wind

In the early 1960s the strategic focus in the western Pacific began to slip away from the Korean Peninsula toward Southeast Asia and the civil war that had been re-ignited between the two Vietnams. During March of 1961 the battle lines spread to the Plans de Jars causing a temporary crisis in Laos. In order to help stem the flow of the increasing number of Viet Cong who were infiltrating from North Vietnam, in October, President John F. Kennedy, Jr.

---

[*] In the 1955 motion picture *Battle Cry*, it is not an actor, but rather "Red" Ebert who is the bearded figure standing on the beach at Guadalcanal who in a gravelly voice, contemptuously welcomes Van Heflin's battalion as it wades ashore with the words: "Well, if it ain't da pogey-bait Sixth finally coming to the war."

authorized the Military Assistance Advisory Group in the Republic of Vietnam be increased from 600 military advisors to 15,000; shortly thereafter, this number would rise to 18,000. In 1962, the *Marine Corps Gazette* devoted each of its 12 issues to counter-guerilla warfare. Later "counterinsurgency" eventually became the term of choice. Later in the year, Headquarters Marine Corps issued guidance directing that 25 percent of all classroom and field training within the Fleet Marine Forces would be devoted to unconventional warfare or counterinsur-

gency Operations. During December of 1962, Major Kenneth J. "Ken" Skipper, the CWTC S-3 briefed Colonel Nathaniel H. Carver and the staff on several changes to training center's formal schools program for the next calendar year:

(1) The Escape, Evasion, and Survival Section would conduct its normal load of 20 courses of 12 training days each. The anticipated total load of students would number about 760, including those newly arrived CWTC personnel who would attend the first week of escape, evasion and survival in-

Coy D. Ziglar

"Zig" Ziglar retired as a gunnery sergeant in 1967, after a 20-year career which included a stint with the China Marines. While he served in many billets in many places, but his favorite duty station was the Mountain Warfare Training Center in Bridgeport, California:

"The years I spent at Pickel Meadow with Colonel Gerald P. Averill and Colonel Glen E. Martin were the highlights of my career," claimed Ziglar, who is also known as Zig.

Fifty years after checking into MWTC, Zig still recalled Colonel Averill's eight-mile runs.

"I lost almost 30 pounds during my first month up there!" said Ziglar. "When Colonel Martin came in, we went back to three-mile runs.

Zig was also known as the "Game Warden."

"Colonel Martin appointed me base Game Warden after I shot four sage hens by mistake," recalled Zig. "I thought they were quail! The colonel called me a poacher and said that as Game Warden I'd have to learn what animals and birds were on base, and which were protected."

Zig took his Game Warden duties seriously. He once gave the base chaplain a citation for shooting a doe. The chaplain coughed up a fine of $125, which went to Navy Relief.

"I remember another time when the commanding officer needed three Christmas trees to send down to Camp Pendleton, El Toro, and Barstow," said Zig. "We went up into the mountains and found three good ones and cut them down. Later we learned we'd only taken the tops of the trees, as the snow was 10 feet deep where we made the cuts!."

Ziglar fell in love with more than the mountains above Pickel Meadow. In 1963, he married a "Bridgeport girl" as the local village hosted its first-ever Marine/military wedding.

Zig and Darlene returned to Bridgeport after he retired and in 1968 they opened a main street business location, which over the years included a laundry-mat, sporting goods store, and boutique.

The former Marine also got into local politics. Zig was elected as a county supervisor in 1976, and he reestablished mutually beneficial ties to the recently re-opened base.

"We had a deputy sheriff get hurt out in the boondocks, and Colonel George A. Knudson responded right away to my request for help," said Zig. "He sent men right away and we got the guy out."

Circa 1978 there was an incident in Bridgeport village when a Marine on liberty made suggestive or threatening comments to a local girl. A complaint was filed and the situation began to receive publicity.

Soon thereafter, the Camp Pendleton Base Commander, the 1st Marine Division Commanding General, and several colonels arrived in town to demonstrate command interest.

Zig went to the meeting as county supervisor, and recalls the commanding general making a light-hearted comment about being nervous around politicians.

"Well, I'm a retired Gunny and I get nervous around generals," responded Zig. The room filled with laughter and the situation was satisfactorily addressed.

Zig could have postponed his retirement.

"Colonel Martin was talking to me back in '67 and said I was up for first sergeant, if I stayed in," recalled Zig. "I said the only way I wouldn't retire is if I could get orders back up to Pickel Meadow. There was no billet so I retired. But I loved Bridgeport."

As of 2009, Coy and Darlene Ziglar were still living in that house they built in 1968 in beautiful, downtown Bridgeport.

An improvised shelter constructed by students during the Evasion Survival Field Exercise. Shelters are constructed using native materials, ponchos, and parachutes. Camouflage is important since they are operating in enemy territory.

struction. However, in order to comply with the latest JCS Pub-1 term, escape, evasion, and survival would henceforth be referred to as survival, evasion, resistance, and escape (SERE).

(2) The Training Branch at Headquarters U.S. Marine Corps had directed that the name of the Mountain Leadership Course be changed to Mountain Operations Course. Furthermore, it had approved the recommendations of the training center that the course be extended from three weeks' duration to four, in order that both classroom instruction and a 96-hour counter-guerrilla exercise could be integrated into the course syllabus. A total of 10 classes would be conducted, three winters and seven summers for a total of about 310 students. This would include newly arrived CWTC instructor-guides, as well as four officers from the Korean Marine Corps and about eight officers and staff noncommissioned officers from the Chilean Marine Corps.*

(3) The Unit Training Section was expected to host

---

* About 1961, it became the practice to send Republic of Korea Marine Officers who had graduated from The Basic School during the winter to the Winter Mountain Leadership Course before returning home. The Chilean Marine Corps, which had the responsibility for garrisoning Chile's disputed borders with Argentina in the harsh climate of Tierra de Fuego had also requested quotas for its junior officers to attend the Winter Mountain Leadership Course upon graduation from The Basic School, and for its staff noncommissioned officers graduates from the Drill Instructor School at MCRD, San Diego. These requests were granted and administered through the bi-lateral Military Assistance Program agreements between Chile, Republic of Korea and the United States.

about 7,000 trainees during the year between its 10-day winter indoctrination courses, hosting five infantry battalions from the 1st Marine Division and provide two weeks of training to five rifle companies of the Organized Reserve during the summer.

During May 1963, Major Edwin A. Deptula reported from Marine Corps Recruit Depot, San Diego and replaced Major Skipper as the training center S-3. Major Deptula had earned a Silver Star and Purple Heart as a rifle platoon commander in the 5th Marine Regiment during the Chosin Reservoir campaign. Within a week after reporting to his new duty station, the major enrolled himself in the Mountain Operations Course that was just getting underway.[146]

In July of the same year, a reception was held at the base officer's club to welcome the new commanding officer, Colonel Frank R. Wilkinson, Jr., and his wife Catherine to the training center. Like his S-3, Colonel Wilkinson had transferred from Marine Corps Recruit Depot, San Diego where he served as a battalion commander in the Recruit Training Regiment and as the G-2/Depot Inspector. The 46-year old Wilkinson was born and raised in Illinois. He had graduated from the University of Michigan in 1941 and received his commission as a second lieutenant in the Marine Corps in April 1942. Lieutenant Wilkinson served his first five months of active duty as a White House Aide to President Roosevelt, followed by four months of training with the British Royal Commandos at Rosneath, Scotland. From early 1944 until Japan's surrender in September in 1945, he served in the Pacific theater as the commanding officer of the detachment aboard the USS *Bataan* (CVL 29), participating in combat operations off Okinawa and the Japanese home islands. During the Korean conflict Lieutenant Colonel Wilkinson earned the Bronze Star Medal with Combat "V" and the Army Commendation Medal for his meritorious service as commanding officer, 1st Amphibian Tractor Battalion, and later as a negotiator with the U.N. Military Armistice Commission at Panmunjom, Korea. Following his service as an instructor at Quantico, in 1958, he was appointed as Senior Marine Advisor to the Vietnamese Marine Corps and served in that capacity for two years, earning his second Army Commendation Medal before receiving orders to the Marine Corps Recruit Depot in San Diego.[147]

The energetic and outgoing new commander lost no time in further promoting good relations with the local community. Calling at the Forest Service Office in Bridgeport, he assured the district ranger that the provisions of the joint use agreement would

The Mountain Leadership Course included fixed rope installations. This picture shows a student crossing the West Walker River using a suspension traverse system in the early 1960s.

continue to be scrupulously observed and respected. He promised further that the Marines stationed at CWTC stood ready to augment the Toiyabe National Forest fire-fighting crews if the need should arise. Likewise, he told the county supervisors and the sheriff of Mono County that while he was in command, they could continue to count on the training center to immediately furnish experienced search and rescue teams for civilians who became lost, injured, or were killed during climbing accidents within Mono County.[*]

During that summer, Colonel Wilkinson personally welcomed two distinguished visitors to the training center. The first was the 22d Commandant of the Marine Corps, General David M. Shoup, who

---

[*] Over the years it had become common practice for local officials to call upon Marine Search and Rescue Teams upwards of 10 to 12 times each year. Most of the incidents happened during the summer months, but occasionally they might involve a winter search for a missing cross-country skier. If the task involved the recovery of a mountaineer who was known to have fallen from a great height, the officer-in-charge of the team would be "deputized" by the local sheriff before setting out, in order that the victim could be officially pronounced dead once the body had been located. Invariably, the instructor-guides who participated always learned new lessons and gained valuable experience from these rescue missions.

arrived in July. In the morning, General Shoup received a briefing by the Executive Officer, Lieutenant Colonel Carver, on the current status of the dam that had been proposed by the Department of Interior across the West Walker River back in 1956. Lieutenant Colonel Carver pointed out that the local ranchers and property owners still remained strongly aligned against the project. "Frankly," he opined, "it is highly unlikely that a dam will ever be constructed across the West Walker." After receiving additional briefings from the S-3 and the three officers-in-charge of the formal schools, the Commandant was taken to the Leavitt Meadows training site where he met the members of the Mountain Operations Course and witnessed a demonstration of the summer mountaineering techniques taught in the course.[148]

Soon after Labor Day, Under Secretary of the Navy Paul B. Fay Jr., became the second distinguished official to visit the training center that year. Reared in San Francisco and a pre-war graduate of Stanford University, Paul Fay received his commission in the U.S. Navy as a line officer in 1942. During the Solomon Islands campaign he and John F. Kennedy Jr., were fellow PT-boat skippers in the

Courtesy of author

Colonel Frank R. Wilkinson Jr., Commanding Officer, Cold Weather Training Center, jumps from a cliff face to demonstrate the suspension traverse at Demonstration Rock, Leavitt Training Area in the summer of 1963.

same squadron. "The friendship between the boyish-looking, lanky Kennedy and the energetic, fun-loving Fay was immediate, and, after the war, ripened into a warm and deep relationship."[149] The still youthful-appearing and spirited Under Secretary enthusiastically praised all that he saw and heard during his daylong tour of the center. After witnessing the afternoon rock climbing demonstration, however, the Secretary did express some disappointment at not being allowed to ride down the 200 foot "slide for life."

Within days of taking command, Colonel Wilkinson eagerly applied himself to learning all aspects of the various training programs being conducted at CWTC. He soon became an active participant in the monthly summer rock-climbing demonstrations, underwent training as a student in the Survival, Evasion, Resistance, and Escape Course, personally took part in the graduation exercises of all formal schools and also took a keen interest in the instruction given at FMF and Reserve unit training and

bivouac sites. As the new commander's appreciation for the broad range of summer military mountaineering skills and survival techniques grew, the more convinced he became that the old 1956 designated name Cold Weather Training Center was outdated. The colonel therefore proposed through the chain-of-command that the name be re-titled Mountain Warfare Training Center. This recommendation was quickly approved. On 1 November 1963, the Post was officially re-designated Marine Corps Mountain Warfare Training Center, Bridgeport, California.[150]

The winter of 1963-1964 turned out to be light in terms of accumulated snowfall. As a result, the Mountain Operations and Unit Training Sections were forced to maintain their respective training bivouac sites at locations above the 9,000-foot level. However, the mild winter conditions did give the 7th Engineer detachment that deployed from Camp Pendleton that year the benefit of getting an early start on the construction of Colonel Wilkinson's next building priority: an indoor gym. Recognizing that the base offered little in the way of recreational activities for the unmarried Marines and sailors during the long winter nights, he had plans drawn up for a Butler building that would house indoor courts for basketball and volleyball, a weight-lifting room, and a head and shower facility. The new gym was located uphill from the enlisted barracks area and was open for business before summer ended. He also directed that the engineers install a round stained glass window above the altar in the Quonset hut that served as the base chapel. The window was a gift and depicted the image of Saint Bernard, the patron saint of mountaineers.*

During mid summer of 1964, Colonel A. J. S. Crockett, OBE, the senior Royal Marine colonel assigned to the Defence Staff at the British Embassy in Washington D.C. made an official tour of the major U.S. Marine Corps installations located in the western United States. His itinerary included a two-day visit to MWTC. On the second day, while Colonel Wilkinson and his Royal Marine guest observed students of the Mountain Operations Course practicing two-party climbs under the watchful eyes of their instructor and guides, Colonel Crockett turned to his host and said something to the effect: "although equipment and techniques might vary slightly, it appears to me that your mountaineering program very closely parallels what we teach our Marines at the Assault Climbing Wing at Lympstone during the summer and in Scotland during the winter. Would you be interested in establishing an of-

---

* Today, this same window can still be seen in the beautiful base chapel that overlooks the meadow.

Courtesy of *Leatherneck*

A Quonset hut served as the base chapel; Colonel Wilkinson arranged that a stained-glass window be installed into the rear wall of the hut above the altar.

ficer exchange program between our two schools?" Being a graduate of the World War II Commando Course himself, Colonel Wilkinson unhesitatingly agreed and said: he thought it was "a splendid idea that would be beneficial to both our Corps." "Done then," replied the Royal Marine Colonel. "But I believe if I was the one to initiate our little scheme through the Commander, British Navy Staff at our embassy in Washington, our proposal may stand a chance of getting to our respective Commandant's for a decision faster, then if you were to do so." Colonel Wilkinson also agreed to this suggestion.[151] Within two months, the captain selected by Headquarters U.S. Marine Corps to be the first officer to represent the U.S Marine Corps under this new exchange program that was slated to start in January 1965, was enrolled as a student in the Mountain Operations summer course.*

It was also in 1964 when Major General Robert E. Cushman Jr., Director of Training at Headquarters U.S. Marine Corps issued a directive that caught all ranks at MWTC, including the commanding officer by complete surprise. Effective immediately, the directive said, students at Survival, Evasion, Resist-

ance, and Escape Courses would no longer undergo prisoner of war compound exercises in the present format, whereby students were treated as if they were actual prisoners of war. Instead, students

The stained-glass window in the base chapel depicts Saint Bernard, the patron saint of the mountaineer.
Courtesy of *Leatherneck*

---

* Unfortunately, this officer, although a qualified parachutist, suffered from acrophobia and therefore was administratively dropped from the course at its midpoint. Headquarters, Marine Corps subsequently selected Capt George Douse for this assignment.

Courtesy of author

Major General Robert E. Cushman, Jr., Commanding General, Marine Corps Base, Camp Pendleton with his staff, and Colonel Frank R. Wilkinson, Jr., Commanding Officer, Cold Weather Training Center, on General Cushman's left, observe rock-climbing at the Leavitt Training Area in September 1964. The Marine in summer dress is Marine Barracks, Hawthorne, Nevada, commanding officer Lieutenant Colonel Lewis R. Webb.

would be walked through the compound while instructors would explain and point out the type of treatment they might have to endure should they ever become a prisoner of war, but such treatment could only be described and not physically applied against them.[152] When this directive was published, instructors and former students alike believed the new policy was a mistake. Even new students to the course sometimes felt "cheated" for not having the chance to test their own stamina under stress. Notwithstanding their deep disappointment and belief that the effectiveness of the training had been severely diminished, there was nothing the instructor-guides of the Survival, Evasion, Resistance, and Escape and Mountain Operations Courses could do, but comply and make the best of it. Shortly after issuing this directive, Major General Cushman became the Commanding General, Camp Pendleton and made a personal visit to the training center before the summer programs had ended for the year.

On the day following the 10 November 1964 Ma-

rine Birthday Ball in Reno, a heavy storm lashed the Sierra Nevada Mountains bringing three-to four-foot drifts on the valley floor at Pickel Meadow. A promise of good snow conditions was in the air as instructor-guides packed away climbing gear and once again started practicing their downhill and cross-country ski techniques. In early December Major Deptula, the S-3, predicted that over 8,500 Marines would undergo training at MWTC in1965. But by now, Captain James P. "Jim" Sheehan, First Lieutenant Richard R. "Dick" Mannila, and their unit chief, Gunnery Sergeant Bernard G. Goddard, who collectively headed up the Unit Training Section, had become veteran instructor-guides. Captain William S. "Bill" Moriarty, who was relatively new to the training center, had already relieved Captain George A. Knudson as the officer-in charge of the Survival, Evasion, Resistance, and Escape Section and was anxious to get started. The senior instructor and guide of the Mountain Operations Section had just been transferred, but Captain Robert A. "Bob"

Johnson, a graduate of the course, was slated to arrive and would soon take over those duties. In the meantime, First Lieutenant Douglas W. "Doug" Gow and the unit chief, Gunnery Sergeant Ronald L. Burtsell, were more than capable of leading this highly experienced team of instructor and guides, whose adopted motto for the course was "*Zum Gipfel*" (To the Top).* Moreover, the added week of instruction in counterinsurgency subjects to the Mountain Operations syllabus had by this time been perfected and proven to be a good fit with the overall objectives of the course. A U.S. Air Force colonel from the Counterinsurgency Coordination Office of the Joint Chiefs of Staff arrived at Mountain Warfare Training Center in

Courtesy of author

Instructors staffed the training village of "Alpino" near the headwaters of Cattle Creek in the Hoover Wilderness Area. The village was used in counterinsurgency training as part of the Mountain Operations syllabus. Students were trained to cooperate and communicate with indigenous inhabitants. Here "villagers" include, left to right, Staff Sergeant Lonnie Henderson, Gunnery Sergeant Ronald Burtsell, and Staff Sergeant Theodore Neal.

October 1964 to get a first-hand look at the final field exercise conducted in the Twin Lakes region. The colonel's report concluded that the exercise was one of the most realistic and demanding scenarios that he had ever witnessed. By now, Navy SEALS (sea, air, land) team members had also been added to the list of students enrolling in the summer Mountain Operation's courses. And the Navy was requesting more quotas for its SEAL teams during the 1965 training year.

As the 1965 winter courses were getting underway, two new bachelor officers reported for duty at the training center. The first to arrive in mid January was the first Royal Marine to be formally appointed as an exchange to MWTC. His name was Captain James N.A. Goldsworthy. Jim Goldsworthy had been born to coffee planter parents in Kenya in 1936 where he spent his early years. After com-

pleting school in England, he was given a commission as a second lieutenant in the Royal Marines in 1955. While still undergoing training, he served in the Cliff Assault Troop, 42 Commando, during the Anglo-French combined assault to seize the Suez Canal. Upon completion of his training in 1958, he was assigned to the 45 Commando as a platoon leader where he served until 1960. He spent one year at the Recruit Depot, Royal Marines, and then was assigned as an instructor at the Cliff Assault Wing, Royal Marine Infantry Training Center. While there, he had undergone winter training at the Norwegian Army Winter School and also became a qualified parachutist. Captain Goldsworthy was serving on HMS *Gurkha* in the Persian Gulf when he received his orders to report to the U.S. Marine Corps Mountain Warfare Training Center.[153] Jim Goldsworthy later recalled that Captain Bill Moriarty drove him to the training center after meeting him at the Reno airport. That night, he attended a mess night at the officers' club, where General Cushman was welcomed as the guest of honor. "Thus my timing for getting to know all of the training center officers could not have been more fortuitous," he would later remark. The next officer to report for duty as an instructor was First Lieutenant Harry W. Jenkins Jr., a native Californian who was commissioned a second lieutenant in the U.S. Marine Corps in 1960 upon receiving a bachelor's degree from

---

* This team included Lts Hugh L. Scott III and Robert L. "Bob" Gray Jr., SSgts Lonnie "Moose" Henderson and Theodore E. "Boone" Neal, Sgts William T. "Billie" West, John Spofford, Marvin K. Moore, William E. Hoke, and Cpl T. Trinidad. Lt Gray was a native of Putney, Vermont and became a competitor on the U.S. Cross-Country Ski Team; Sgt Hoke was killed in action in Vietnam while serving with the U.S. Army; Cpl Trinidad was later awarded the Silver Star Medal for his gallantry in Vietnam. After completing his tour of duty at MWTC, Lt Gow joined the ranks of the FBI, where he distinguished himself by eventually becoming its Director of Operations (third highest office within the Bureau) during the 1990s.

Then Captain O.K. Steele, one of the authors, while a Mountain Leader Instructor at the MWTC during this period.

San Jose State College. After completing tours as a platoon commander in the 1st and 3d Marine Divisions, Lieutenant Jenkins was posted to the Marine Barracks, San Francisco Naval Shipyard, where he served as the barracks executive officer until joining the instructor staff at MWTC in late January 1965. Before the year was out, Captain Goldsworthy and Lieutenant Jenkins, who served side-by-side in the Unit Training Section, were to form a lasting friendship that would pay dividends during the conduct of Marine Corps winter field operations in northern Norway two decades later. [154]

As the winter season of 1965 passed smoothly,

the morale, professionalism and qualifications of its staff of instructors and support personnel seemed to have reached its zenith since the activation of the post nearly 14 years earlier. After going through years of growing pains, and fears of being misjudged as irrelevant and of little value, it now appeared to those serving at the training center that there was nothing that could come in the way of Colonel Averill's vow to keep the center alive for generations of Marine's yet to come. Nothing perhaps, except for the yet unforeseen adverse circumstances of a six-year major military commitment that the United States would soon undertake in Southeast Asia.

Royal Marine Captain James N. A. Goldsworthy, while an instructor in the Cliff Assault Wing, Royal Marine Infantry Training Center, prior to the exchange tour with the U.S. Marines.

Chapter 9
In the Doldrums, 1966–1979

The northern half of Mono County, California, is the locale for two interesting ghost towns, both about 20 miles drive from the county seat at Bridgeport. As ghost towns go they are quite dissimilar. The most famous is Bodie, to the southeast. It lies dormant in a state of preservation and is visited by tourists, but Bodie will never re-awake. The other, the Mountain Warfare Training Center at Pickel Meadows, also is sleeping and is being preserved. But nobody comes to visit.
-Nevada State Journal, 28 July 1968

Vietnam War Backdrop

By early 1965, General Westmoreland's Military Advisory Command, Vietnam (MACV) had already established a number of U.S. installations and air bases throughout South Vietnam. These airfields gave the United States the means to provide unlimited helicopter and close air support to South Vietnamese ground forces and their American advisors, as well as the added capability to launch limited air strikes against North Vietnam. In February, however, the Viet Cong succeeded in conducting a strong ground attack against the American Army helicopter base at Pleiku causing severe damage to a number of U.S. aircraft. As a result, General Westmoreland made a request to the Joint Chiefs of Staff (JCS) that U.S. ground forces be dispatched to Vietnam for the purpose of providing ground security for these installations. The JCS concurred with this request and President Lyndon B. Johnson gave his approval on 25 February. Subsequently on 8 March, the JCS directed the Commander-in-Chief Pacific Forces (CinCPac) to start landing the 9th Marine Expeditionary Brigade (9th MEB) at Da Nang, South Vietnam. By nightfall, the two reinforced infantry battalions of the 9th MEB (one battalion landing team was airlifted from Okinawa) had taken up defensive positions around the Da Nang air base. The Joint Chief of Staff instructions relayed through CinCPac to the 9th MEB commander, Brigadier General Frederick J. Karch, made it clear that the mission of the 3,500-man force would be limited to the security of the air base and that "Marines will not, repeat, will not engage in day-to-day actions against the Viet Cong."[155] In mid-April, the president approved the recommendation of the secretary of defense that two additional battalion landing teams be sent to the 9th MEB, one to Da Nang and the other to the airfield at Phu Bai, plus a U.S. Army infantry

division to other parts of Vietnam.

As the year progressed, General Westmoreland continued to propose additional U.S. ground deployments to Vietnam. As a consequence, between the end of March and the beginning of July—a period of only three months—the force levels climbed incrementally from 33,000 to a new presidential approved force level of 180,000. At the same time, President Johnson also decided to relax any restrictions on the use of these forces and to "move from the mission of base security to the mission of active combat in whatever way seems wise to General Westmoreland."[156] "Search and destroy" would soon become the strategy for American forces in Vietnam.

MWTC on the Slippery Slope

On 6 June 1965, Colonel Frank Wilkinson passed the MWTC organizational colors to his Executive Officer, Lieutenant Colonel Lester V. "Swede" Swenson and departed for Vietnam. Until this time, the increase in the force levels being dispatched to Vietnam had not caused a significant reduction to either the student loads or the FMF infantry battalions reporting to MWTC for training. But now, lead elements of the 1st Marine Division were also starting to deploy toward the expeditionary airfield under construction at Chu Lai; therefore, it would not be long before the entire division would join with the 3d Marine Division and the 1st Marine Aircraft Wing as a part of the III Marine Amphibious Force (III MAF) in the I Corps Tactical Area of Operations.

In mid August, the III MAF headquarters was alerted to an impending attack against the Chu Lai air base by the *1st Viet Cong Regiment*. Major General Lewis W. "Lou" Walt, the Commanding General of III MAF, decided to take the fight to the enemy before they could move to their assault positions. On 16 August, III MAF launched Operation Starlite, which consisted of a coordinated regimental-size attack from the sea and by air. This was one of the first major engagements for the Marines since the Korean War. For six days the two sides battled at close quarters until the enemy withdrew from the field. Operation Starlite proved to be merely a sample of the intensity and scope of the many combat operations that lay ahead.

On 7 June, Lieutenant Colonel Swenson's first day in command, MWTC suffered one of its worst and most unfortunate training accidents. During the afternoon, a rifle company from the 1st Battalion,

Courtesy *Leatherneck*

A Reserve Marine practices stream-crossing techniques near the Leavitt Meadows Campground. The "commando crawl" technique depicted here on a one-rope bridge was the technique being attempted by Staff Sergeant Kilfoyle when he and First Lieutenant Straehl lost their lives.

25th Marines, which was there for two weeks of Reserve annual training, was undergoing practical application in stream-crossing techniques. The site was on the West Walker River, just below the Leavitt Flat public campground. While crossing a one-rope bridge, using the "commando crawl" technique, Staff Sergeant John F. Kilfoyle lost his balance and fell into the fast moving water. The instructor-guide from the Special Training Unit, who was assigned downstream as the safety swimmer for the exercise and was roped up, immediately dove into the water to pull the floating staff sergeant to shore. About the same time, First Lieutenant Richard L. Straehl, one of the company officers who was standing on the bank, also jumped into the stream to assist. In the ensuing confusion, the safety swimmer became overpowered by the floundering of both men. As a result, both reservists missed catching the downstream safety rope. Before anyone could get a second line to them, they were swept away by the current and drowned in the churning white waters and whirlpools of the narrow gorge that lay several hundred yards downstream. Two years earlier in the late spring of 1963, three enlisted Marines who were in an off-duty status from the MWTC Motor Transport Section had drowned in the same stretch of water on a Sunday afternoon while attempting to shoot the rapids using 6x6 truck tire inner tubes

that they had lashed together. Weeks of searching for their remains in the gorge and along the banks of the river proved futile. It was not until several months later that their bodies surfaced and were discovered by fishermen in the meadow below.[157] Similarly, it was nine weeks later before a fisherman reported finding the remains of Staff Sergeant Kilfoyle. His body was recovered on 30 July 1965. The body of Lieutenant Straehl was not recovered until 27 August.[158]

On 16 July, while the investigation and search for the two drowned Marines was still going on, Lieutenant Colonel Swenson relinquished his temporary command of the training center to Colonel John B. Bristow. John Bristow was a veteran of over 23 years of active Marine Corps service and was the G-3 at Headquarters, FMFLant when he received orders to take command of MWTC. The 45-year old commander had been born in Shanghai, China and had entered the Marine Corps in March of 1942 after graduating from Colgate University. During World War II, he served as an artillery officer in the 10th Marines during the assaults on Tarawa, Saipan and Tinian. Following the war, he was assigned to attend an 18-month Chinese Language Course at the University of California. After graduating from the course in 1946, Captain Bristow was ordered to North China where he became the intelligence officer (S-2) for the 4th Marine Regiment and later served as the assistant Chief of Staff, G-2, for the Fleet Marine Force, Western Pacific. During the closing campaigns of the Korean War, Major Bristow served as the executive officer of the 2d Battalion, 1st Marines until June 1953, when he was assigned duties as the Marine liaison officer on the U.N. Peace Commission in Korea. Subsequent tours of duty before reporting to Headquarters, FMFLant, included two assignments to Formosa as an advisor to the Chinese Marine Corps, assistant director for recruiting with the 4th Marine Corps District, three years with the 2d Marine Division as Commanding Officer, 1st Battalion, 2d Marines; Executive Officer, 2d Marines; and finally commanding the regiment.[159]

Like his predecessors, Colonel Bristow took a keen interest in the welfare of his troops and in the unique training courses that the training center provided. During his first six months, the trailers that had served for the last eight years as enlisted family housing outside of Walker in Antelope Valley, were replaced with 40 three-bedroom mobile homes procured from the U.S. Air Force. A platoon from the Naval Construction Battalion, Port Hueneme, California made other improvements to the Antelope Valley Housing area including the addition of a 10,000-gallon liquid propane storage tank, which gave sufficient fuel storage capacity to last the winter season, and the installation of a master television antenna.

However, with the 1st Marine Division now fully deployed to Southeast Asia, Colonel Bristow must have foreseen that it would not be long before he was presiding over a command with diminishing prospects for the future. With the exception of the Survival, Evasion, Resistance, and Escape Course, which trained 153 officers and 236 enlisted during the last six months of 1965, student loads for the other course programs were clearly on a downward spiral. For the same period, five summer Mountain Operations Courses had graduated only 33 officers and 82 enlisted, who for the most part came from the east coast, or the Reserves.* Similarly, the Special Training Unit could claim it had provided training for only 48 officers and 836 enlisted, a fraction of its normal summer training load. Most of the seats were filled by units of the Marine Corps Reserve.[160]

On 10 November that year, the command celebrated the Marine Corps Birthday with a traditional grand ball at the Mapes Hotel in Reno, Nevada. Nevada's Lieutenant Governor (and future Gover-

Courtesy of Maj James N. A. Goldsworthy, RM.

Captain James Goldsworthy, Royal Marines, while serving as an exchange officer at the Mountain Warfare Training Center in 1965. Goldsworthy later supervised the Survival, Escape, Resistance to Interrogation, and Evasion course at Marine Corps Base, Camp Pendleton.

nor and U.S. Senator) Paul Laxalt was the Guest of Honor. Shortly thereafter, the notification from Headquarters U.S. Marine Corps that many had been dreading arrived in the form of CMC ltr AO3CLO-mek, dated 27 November 1965. This placed MWTC in a temporary reduced manning status. In addition, it directed the "cancellation of Mountain Operations, Cold Weather Indoctrination and Reserve Training Courses. All facilities to support this training are to be placed in a standby status and prepared to resume operations on short notice."[161]

No one was more disappointed with this sudden turn of events than Captain Jim Goldsworthy, the

---

* The number of students in the September class was made up of three officers and five enlisted.

Royal Marine exchange officer. Several of the RM mountaineering techniques he had introduced in both the summer and winter courses had been widely accepted by his fellow instructor and guides in Mountain Operations and the Unit Training Sections. Colonel Bristow was so impressed with the techniques that Captain Goldsworthy had introduced that he directed they be adopted for use and incorporated into the MWTC standing operating procedures. During the previous May, Captain Goldsworthy had written to his superiors, requesting that his one-year of exchange duty be extended six months.

"My main reason for this request," he explained, "is that having arrived in the middle of a winter season and being due to leave in the middle of the next one, I will not have had sufficient continuity to be of real value to the training center. I am particularly keen to have a full winter season here because I have gained the interest of the staff in certain Norwegian techniques, which I learned on the White Shod Course, and which the colonel intends to adopt next year. Having gained the interest, I would very much like to see and assist in putting them to the test in practice."

This request for an extension received the blessing of Colonel Crockett in the British Embassy and was approved by Royal Marine headquarters in London.[162] But with the cancellation of the 1966 winter courses, this extension was of little value. Colonel Bristow therefore, made every effort to assist his exchange officer in becoming usefully employed. On 19 January, Captain Goldsworthy departed MWTC and on the next day, reported to Staging Battalion at Camp Pendleton. Here, for the next six months, he was tasked with the organization and supervision of a three-day survival, escape, resistance, evasion training program for troops preparing for duty in Vietnam.

In February, 1966, CMC ltr AO1E/bjf of 24 February 1966, published T/O A7670, reducing the manning level of MWTC to seven Marine officers, 89 Marine enlisted, one Navy officer, and three Navy enlisted. The survival escape, resistance evasion program would continue to be the only course offered by the center. Ironically, the Air Force had recently announced that Stead Air Force Base in Reno, Nevada, would close in June, with the base exchange and commissary remaining open only through April. Giving that the training center was brought down to its new manning level, Major John E. Lorzing, the S-4, also assumed duties as the executive officer. Captain Bill Moriarty, the senior instructor and guide of the Survival, Evasion, Resistance, and Escape Section, assumed the additional duty as the MWTC S-3.

On 10 October 1966, Colonel Bristow bade farewell to his few officers and enlisted Marines who remained and turned the command over to his Executive Officer, Major John E. Lorzing. A small, but spirited group from the training center celebrated the Marine Corps Birthday on 10 November that year at the Sahara Tahoe Hotel at Stateline, Nevada. But as everyone suspected, this would be the last birthday celebrated by the training center for some years to come. At the close of the year, MWTC reported that 579 officer and enlisted Marines had successfully graduated from the Survival Evasion, Resistance, and Escape Program.[163]

Deactivation and Caretaker Status

From January through mid-August 1967, 348 students completed the Survival, Evasion, Resistance, and Escape course. In addition, from 21 January through 3 February, the training center provided ski indoctrination training to 230 Marines from Company K, 3d Battalion, 2d Marines, 2d Marine Division, which was preparing for a winter exercise in northern Norway. Company B, 2d Reconnaissance Battalion, also received two weeks of mountaineering training during May of that year.[164] However, with the troop levels in Vietnam approaching the half-million mark, these represented merely the last gasps and vestiges of a command that had once processed over 23,000 trainees in a single year. But as the Commandant of the Marine Corps would soon claim: "Today, there are only three categories of Marines: those who are in Vietnam; those who have just returned from Vietnam, and those who are going to Vietnam."[165]

The official date that the training center was placed in a "cadre status" is not recorded. However, it can be surmised from the final MWTC command chronology report that the decision was probably made in August of 1967. This report, which coincides with the official MWTC closure date of 10 October 1967, describes the flurry and nature of activity during the command's final six weeks of operations:

> Caretaker unit strength has been established as one Marine officer, two Marine SNCOs and two civilian employees.
>
> A steady reduction in personnel has occurred since 1 September 1967 due to command being placed in a caretaker status. Strength has been reduced to zero. Caretaker personnel will be carried on the rolls of Headquarters Company, Service Battalion, Headquarters Regiment, Camp Pendleton, California Correspondence and S&C files have been transferred to Camp Pendleton. Post Of-

Courtesy of *Leatherneck*

Staff Sergeant George Taylor, one of four Marines assigned as caretakers of the training center in 1974, makes regular checks on the MWTC water supply point.

fice has been deactivated. Publications will be retrained at the training center.

Quonset huts have been secured for a period of inactivity. They are denuded of furnishings. Heat is secured.

Many items of food preparation equipment have been removed from the mess hall and sent to Camp Pendleton. Operational rations augmented with fresh milk and coffee was fed from 25 September to 10 October.

All field wire and field telephones were removed. Switchboard and autovon line are secured. Service is now restricted to one commercial line.

Organizational, plant account, special services and property belonging to the Central Service Agency has been returned to Camp Pendleton, with few exceptions. Mountain Operational equipment has been retained. Transfer of cold-weather equipment and clothing is pending and may be sent to Fleet Marine Force, Atlantic.[166]

Although the red and gold sign at the main gate still read "Marine Corps Mountain Warfare Training Center," the entrance would remain barred and locked while the center gradually drifted into five years of inactivity and neglect. During this period, a caretaker unit of 4 to 5 Marines from the base maintenance organization at Camp Pendleton would be the only permanent Marine Corps presence at MWTC for the next nine years.

Use it or Lose it!

By April 1969, over 550,000 American troops had been committed to the defense of the Republic of Vietnam. This included 80,000 Marines then assigned under the III MAF. In July of that year, President Richard M. Nixon announced a change to the policies of the previous six years. In keeping with the president's new doctrine, U.S. ground combat forces would begin to disengage and gradually turn over responsibility for defense of the various battlefronts to the Republic of Vietnam Armed Forces. Among the media and in military circles this became known as the "Vietnamization Program." By early 1971, almost all U.S. Marines had departed Vietnam and returned to their permanent bases in Okinawa, Hawaii, or California. The last Marine infantry battalion to withdraw from Da Nang enclave was the 2d Battalion, 1st Marines, which returned to Camp Pendleton on 26 March 1971. By the middle of the year, only two U.S. Marine units remained in Vietnam: the Marine Advisory Unit and a Detachment of the 1st Air Naval Gunfire Liaison Company, which together numbered less than 250 officers and men.[167]

In the immediate aftermath of its return to Camp Pendleton, the 1st Marine Division soon became but a shadow of its former self; in reality, it was a division in name only. For the next 18 months, under the command of Major General Ross T. Dwyer, Regimental Landing Team 7 (RLT-7) was the only organization that was maintained at a C-2 level of combat readiness and capable of deployment. These were the days when recruiting and standards under the all-volunteer force had dropped to their lowest level and racial tension, discipline problems, and drug use occupied much of the attention of every unit and organizational leader throughout the Corps. In addition, Headquarters U.S. Marine Corps had rightly given priority for manning to the 2d and 3d Marine Divisions using the rationale that those were the two divisions that would have to deploy first to the next likely threat. As a result, the 1st and 5th Marine Regiments and the 1st Division's separate battalions were either largely burdened with conducting three-month on-the-job training courses for individual Marines in approximately 15 military occupational specialties (MOSs). Those Marines were then shipped out to Okinawa or made up "reduced manning battalions/units" with a limited table of organization strength just barely capable of maintaining their organizational equipment.

With the exception of the local Reserve unit in Reno, Nevada, MWTC had remained virtually unused since mid-1967. Then in 1972, the 1st Marine Division Training Exercise and Employment Plan called for the conduct of a summer joint air-mobility exercise. Using Military Airlift Command (MAC) transport aircraft, the plan envisioned that personnel and equipment of one Marine infantry battalion would be airlifted by MAC. Therefore, the division G-3 likely reasoned that rather than remain at Naval Air Station Fallon, why not have the battalion transported to Bridgeport by busses with its rolling stock in trace? This would allow the battalion five days of field training at MWTC. The Commanding General, Camp Pendleton, who for some time had been fielding inquiries from the District Ranger's Office in Bridgeport concerning the Marine Corps' intentions for resuming operations at the training center, was pleased to approve the plan, but with the caveat that no base services would be available to the using battalion. The 2d Battalion, 7th Marines, under the command of Major John I. Hopkins, was selected to be the airlifted battalion and therefore became the first FMF organization to return to MWTC since its deactivation five years earlier. Although the training time at MWTC was judged by the troops as "too abbreviated," the exercise was nonetheless considered worthwhile. Therefore, division planners scheduled three identical exercises for the summer of 1973, but would allow 21 training days at Pickel Meadow for each battalion. Marine Corps Base, Camp Pendleton approved the use of the training center for these exercises, but again reminded the division planners that no support services would be available.[168]

During the early spring of 1973, the personnel situation for the 1st Marine Division improved. The G-1 briefed that by 1 May the division would have sufficient strength to man six infantry battalions with their accompanying combat support and combat service support units. As a result, Brigadier General Adolph G. Schwenk, the division commander, directed that the 2d and 3d Battalions of each of his infantry regiments (1st, 5th and 7th) be brought up to strength, (less one rifle company)* while the 1st Battalions of each regiment would carry on the task of providing entry level MOS skill training. Shortly thereafter, Major General Kenneth J. Houghton, who in 1950-1951 had earned his first Silver Star and Bronze Star Medals with the Reconnaissance Company in Korea, assumed command of the 1st

Marine Division. During the closing days of May, the newly reactivated 2d Battalion, 1st Marines, became the second FMF battalion to be airlifted to Naval Air Station Fallon and thence transported by bus to MWTC with its organizational vehicles following in trace. Because this was to be extended three-week "bare bones" deployment, the battalion was reinforced with a logistic support unit (LSU) from the division's combat service support battalions, which included a truck detachment, an expeditionary shower unit, ration handling and a refueling unit for trucks and aircraft. Moreover, a four-plane detachment of Boeing CH-46 Sea Knight helicopters (on a two-plane rotation between Naval Air Station Fallon and MWTC) was placed in direct support for the purpose of providing troop lifts and emergency medical evacuation to the Naval Hospital located at Naval Air Station Lemoor, California. The commanding officer of the battalion had previously served a tour of duty as the senior instructor and guide of the mountain leadership school at MWTC during the early 1960s. Therefore, in addition to the above logistical support, he also arranged for eight Marines from the 1st Force Reconnaissance Company who were graduates of the Summer Mountain Leadership Course to be attached to the battalion to provide instruction in the basic skills and techniques of military mountaineering. The I Marine Amphibious Force training allowance pool provided sufficient ropes, snap-links, and other climbing gear for this purpose. For a recently reformed infantry battalion, this extended deployment to MWTC was especially beneficial. Here, away from all the distractions of Camp Pendleton, troop leaders could concentrate on "the basics" of maneuvering in terrain that was completely unfamiliar to them. While the battalion headquarters used its time to train in the conduct of field command post operations, the three rifle companies and heavy weapon platoons (81mm mortars and 106mm recoilless rifles) were rotated through five-day blocks of round-robin training stations at different locales. One station, for example, concentrated on day and night map reading; a second on patrolling, while the third emphasized offensive and defensive small-unit tactics. The fourth station, conducted at the Leavitt Training Area, was a centralized block of instruction under the supervision of the force reconnaissance detachment. At this station, the troops received practical application in basic military mountaineering skills such as: balance climbing, knot tying and rope-management,

---

* Under the table of organization and equipment at the time, the Marine infantry battalion was comprised of a headquarters and service company and four rifle companies.

Marines of 3d Battalion, 1st Marines eat chow at the field mess galley while training at the Mountain Warfare Training Center in 1974. They set up tents in the lower Pickel Meadow base camp along Highway 108 and were supported by the logistic support unit.

rappelling, river crossing and the construction of rope installations, including one and two-rope bridges, suspension traverses and vertical hauling lines. Midway through the deployment, commercial busses were chartered for each company to make a 36-hour liberty run to Reno as they completed various phases of training.

At the end of the deployment, the commander of the battalion decided to culminate the exercise with a 50-mile hike. After coordinating with the District Forest Ranger at Bridgeport, a route was approved that ran from MWTC up the Burcham Flat road to a lake located at the 9,000-foot summit of the Sweetwater Range. There, the route meandered northeasterly into Smith Valley, near the town of Wellington, Nevada. The owner of a ranch bordering the state highway that ran south out of Wellington was asked beforehand if he would permit 650 Marines to bivouac in one of his fields for four or five hours, until commercial busses arrived to pick them up. "Sure," he replied, "it's full of rattlesnakes, but go ahead." Thus at 0600 on a cool, cloudless day, the 2d Battalion, 1st Marines, departed from the MWTC airfield in a column of companies that were spaced 15-minutes apart. Eighteen and a half

hours later, the last company arrived intact (there had been no stragglers) at the bivouac site cheered on by an equally exhausted battalion commander and his sergeant major.* As the tired Marines found and crawled into their pre-staged sleeping bags, rattlesnakes were the furthest things from their minds. Four hours later, the busses arrived right on time to transport the foot-sore but proud young Marines to Naval Air Station Fallon. There they loaded aboard the same MAC Lockheed C-141 Constellation aircraft that were in the process of flying in the 1st Reconnaissance Battalion, for the short flight back to El Toro.[169]

During that summer of 1973, the feisty and energetic General Houghton personally visited each of his three battalions during their deployments to MWTC. Based on what he witnessed and the enthusiastic reports of the officers and men he spoke to relative to the value of the training they were receiving at MWTC, he directed his G-3 to schedule four battalions for the summers of 1974 and 1975,

---

* The author was the battalion commander; the battalion SgtMaj was Leland D. "Crow" Crawford who would later become the SgtMaj of the Marine Corps (1979-1983) under Gen Robert Barrow.

Courtesy of *Leatherneck*

A logistics support unit was sent to support the training at center for the first time in 1974. These service and support Marines are performing maintenance on a forklift and a truck.

Marines from 3d Battalion, 1st Marines, erect a AN/RC292 antenna during training at MWTC, in 1974.

Courtesy of *Leatherneck*

In addition to logistic support, helicopter detachments also deployed to the center to support infantry battalions training there. Pictured is a Sikorsky CH-53 Sea Stallion.

but with one modification. Instead of each battalion being burdened with the transportation of expeditionary equipment such as its tactical vehicles, field ranges, refrigerators, shower units and the like, he directed that a logistics support unit be formed and stationed at MWTC from May through October. An logistic support unit, the general said, would add mobility for the training units and provide continuity for support activities. This became the pattern of use at MWTC for the ensuing two years.

In 1975, the 1st Marine Division, then under the command of Brigadier General William L. McCulloch, was tasked by Commanding General, Fleet Marine Force, Pacific, to provide a reinforced rifle company as the landing force for a naval exercise that was scheduled to take place in Alaskan waters during mid-March. The purpose of the exercise was to demonstrate the U.S. Navy's capability to protect the newly constructed oil pipeline and terminal facilities at Prudhoe Bay.

The 7th Marines designated a rifle company to conduct the exercise. The commanding general then gave his division training officer the responsibility of establishing a two-week cold-weather over-snow training program prior to the embarkation of the company. Volunteers from throughout the division who either had previous military, or civilian ski experience formed a 12-man enlisted instructor group. Captain Barry E.C. Fellinger, who had been an infantryman during the Chosin Reservoir campaign and who was recognized as an extremely able rifle company commander, was named as the officer-in-charge of the instructor group. Boxed lesson plans from the former Unit Training Cold-Weather Indoctrination Course were obtained from the files at Camp Pendleton, while skis, snowshoes and cold-weather uniforms and boots were drawn from the I Marine Amphibious Force training allowance pool. Traveling by van, the division training officer and instructor group arrived at Pickel

Meadow on a Sunday night in February to find the base camp under two feet of newly fallen snow. A small instructor base camp was established in the Quonset huts of the old mountain leadership school. For the next several days, the composite instructor group polished up their lesson plans and their own individual techniques for snowshoeing and cross-country skiing. By the time the 7th Marines' rifle company arrived, Captain Fellinger was ready for them. After a nine-year hiatus, MWTC was once again available for winter training operations.[170]

Reactivation of the Mountain Warfare Training Center

Although by the mid-1970s 1st Marine Division had started to make use of MWTC on a more regular basis. Headquarters U.S. Marine Corps had yet to signify to the Department of Agriculture its future intentions for reopening the training center, or even

when that might be. Meanwhile, the District Forest Ranger at Bridgeport began placing an increasing number of restrictions on training by 1st Division using units. In late May of 1974, for example, an incident occurred in the vicinity of Leavitt Lodge involving two off-duty Marines. Although no official complaint was filed, local Forest Service officials decided to suspend Marine units from using the Leavitt Area rock climbing and stream crossing sites for the remainder of the year. As a result, training in rock climbing and mountaineering skills had to be shifted to the much less desirable site located in the vicinity of Grouse Meadow. The G-3 of the 1st Marine Division officially objected to the suspension order of the Forest Service and the Leavitt Training Area was restored as a Marine training site by the time the first deploying battalion arrived at MWTC in June 1975.[171]

It was also in June of 1975 that Major General Charles D. Mize replaced Brigadier General William

Marines of Lieutenant Colonel Matthew Caulfield's 3d Battalion, 5th Marines met the challenge of moving a 106mm recoilless rifle to the top of the peak at Grouse Meadow in 1975.

Courtesy of MWTC

L. McCulloch as the Commanding General, 1st Marine Division. In July of 1950, Lieutenant Mize had deployed with Company M, 3d Battalion, 5th Marines, and had participated in the fighting at the Pusan Perimeter with the 1st Marine Brigade. Following the amphibious assault at Inchon, Lieutenant Mize took command of Company M and was awarded the Navy Cross for extraordinary valor during the heavy fighting to recapture Seoul. For his actions during the Chosin Reservoir campaign and the march out to Hungnam, he was awarded the Bronze Star with Combat "V."[172] Because of his past combat experience in Korea, General Mize quickly recognized not only the value of MWTC as a vital adjunct to his division's overall training program, but especially the readiness of his command to conduct combat operations in snow-covered, mountainous terrain. Based on his initial staff briefings and first on-site visit, he became persuaded that if the Marine Corps did not reactivate the training center in the near future, local Forest Service officials might initiate steps that would in effect repeal the 1951 land use agreement with the Department of Agriculture. Consequently, reactivation of MWTC became one of his early priorities.

General Mize's enthusiasm for breathing new life into the training center was shared by Major General Carl W. Hoffman, the commanding general of Camp Pendleton. However, the response Mize received from the staff at Headquarters U.S. Marine Corps for his reactivation plan was not encouraging. To understand why, one must remember that the mid-1970s were difficult years for the Corps. Serious problems tended to preoccupy the time and energies of the staff at Headquarters U.S. Marine Corps. Racial issues and drug use in the ranks had yet to be brought under control. Moreover, every major command was still reporting a backlog in the number of courts-martial cases awaiting trial, not to mention that local confinement facilities were already filled to the bursting point. General Louis H. Wilson, Jr., who had become the 26th Commandant of the Marine Corps on 1 July 1975, had already initiated several new policies that would raise the existing recruiting standards significantly, and begin a process to clean house of repeated offenders through an "Other Than Honorable" administrative discharge. However, just how much of these programs might cut into the Marine Corps' total end-strength was yet unclear. Furthermore, this was a time when some defense analysts publicly questioned whether the Marine Corps' amphibious doctrine was any longer relevant against the Soviet threat to Western Europe. Therefore, some of these analysts asserted, perhaps the Corps' configuration

of three divisions and wings was no longer valid and should be reduced.[173] Another factor that may have contributed to the reluctance of the staff to reopen MWTC at this time was the major effort that had just been launched by Headquarters U.S. Marine Corps to rebuild the Marine Corps Base at Twentynine Palms, California into a new Air-Ground Combined Arms Training Center. General Wilson himself had first conceived this new mission for the "sleepy" little desert artillery base two years earlier when he was commanding general, FMFPac. Now that he was Commandant, Wilson was determined to give the project a full court press to make it a reality. Within weeks after General Wilson was sworn in as Commandant, planning was underway for the construction of an 8,000-foot expeditionary airfield at Twentynine Palms.[174] Realizing the degree of opposition they faced, Generals Mize and Hoffman decided to counter with an alternate proposal. If Headquarters U.S. Marine Corps would authorize the reopening of MWTC, with the exception of a few key permanent billets, most of the personnel staffing would be provided by Camp Pendleton and its tenant organizations through the Fleet Assistance Program. Moreover, the modest construction improvements and base maintenance would not tap into Marine Corps Military Construction dollars, but over the next several budget years, stay within the bounds and capabilities of west coast Navy and Marine engineer battalions. Under these conditions, the Commandant granted his consent to reopen MWTC.

For over a decade, the organizational colors of the Marine Corps Mountain Warfare Training Center had remained rolled in its brown canvas sheaf and stored in a warehouse at Camp Pendleton. On 10 May 1976, this flag was again finally unfurled and put on parade at a lightly attended reactivation ceremony.[175] Presiding over the ceremony was Lieutenant Colonel George A. Knudson, who had been appointed as the new commanding officer. Knudson was no stranger to the training center. As a rifle platoon commander in 1956, he had deployed to MWTC for a six-week winter field exercise with Colonel "Buck" Schmuck's 5th Marine Regiment. From 1962 to 1964, he had served as the senior instructor-guide of the Escape, Evasion, and Survival Course and had the additional duty of being the post exchange officer.

Lieutenant Colonel Knudson had no illusions about the enormous challenges that lay before him. During the decade of deactivation, maintenance of the plant had of necessity been limited to emergency repairs only. Thus, almost every building required some measure of rehabilitation to make it either functional or livable again. To put the training center back in working order, he had been given a table of organization that called for five Marine officers, 110 enlisted Marines, one Navy officer, and 11 Navy Corpsmen to staff the base medical clinic. Almost all of these personnel were assigned through fleet assistance. During the summer months, rotating engineer units from the Force Engineer Battalion and Navy Construction Battalion were assigned to augment the garrison. The Mountain Warfare Training Center-Bridgeport was back in business.

Chapter 10

NATO's Northern Flank:
A New Imperative, 1979–1983

*I personally believe that mountain warfare train-
ing, whether it's conducted in the summer or the
winter, is a vital ingredient for preparing the Marine
for the kind of warfare that you are discussing here
this week. I believe that mountain warfare leadership and mountain warfare skills are cardinal pre-
requisites to victory. If I had my choice, every
battalion in the 2d Marine Division would go
through Bridgeport every year.*
-Keynote address delivered by Major General Alfred M. Gray Jr., Elverum, Norway, 9-12 March 1982

Strategic Backdrop: From Benign Neglect to
Heightened Awareness

During the first two decades of the Cold War in
Europe, North Atlantic Treaty Organization (NATO)
tended to pay scant attention to its northern flank.
The Soviets simply lacked the capacity to seriously
threaten the combined fleets of the U.S. and its
NATO allies. Although the U.S. Navy, along with
Marine company to battalion-sized landing forces,
did participate in a few combined fleet exercises off
the coast of Norway in the 1960s, these became
smaller in scope as the Commander-in-Chief, Atlantic Fleet was tasked to devote more and more of
his resources to Southeast Asia rather than dealing
with a growing Soviet Northern Fleet. As Dr. David
B. Crist later wrote in a carefully researched strategic background paper for the Marine Corps Historical Division,[*]

> By the 1970s, the Soviets had built up a
> considerable military presence in the Kola
> Peninsula providing them an offensive capa-
> bility to threaten NATO and the U.S. Navy.
> Two motorized rifle divisions were perma-
> nently positioned on the Norwegian border,
> with 10 other divisions designated as rein-
> forcements. In addition, an airborne division
> and two specialized brigades, naval infantry
> and a special forces (*Spetsnaz*) had been
> added to the Soviet forces and appeared to be
> positioned to strike quickly and capture Nor-
> way's northern airfields. Further, the Soviet
> Northern Fleet Air Force alone had over 400
> aircraft, with an additional 450 air defense and
> tactical aircraft. Even more alarming for NATO
> was the rapid growth of Soviet northern naval
> forces. From 1965-1980, they nearly doubled

with over 130 attack submarines and 80 major
warships. The number of ballistic missile submarines rose from 18 to 39 by 1980 and comprised nearly two-thirds of the Soviet ballistic
missile fleet.[176]

As a result of this growing Soviet military threat,
NATO and U.S. planners began an extensive reexamination in the mid-1970s of their respective
strategic plans for defending Norway and, at the
same time, maintaining the integrity of NATO's increasingly vulnerable northern flank. The large air
bases at Bodo and Orland in central Norway
housed all of Norway's fighter aircraft and thus
were critical to NATO's air defense scheme. Moreover, military planners viewed anti-submarine aircraft, both fixed-wing and helicopters, that were
based in northern Norway at Bardufoss and Tromso
as vital for attacking Soviet submarines of the Northern Fleet.

If the Soviets could successfully seize these airfields, their Backfire Bombers would then be capable of bombarding the British Isles, thereby putting
them in position to cut the sea-lanes through which
90 percent of the U.S. reinforcements to NATO's
central front would pass. It would also allow the
Soviets to push their air umbrella well west toward
the Greenland-Iceland-United Kingdom (GIUK)
gap. This in turn could drive NATO naval forces out
of the Norwegian Sea, giving the Soviet fleet unhin-
dered access to the North Atlantic. Conversely, if
NATO could maintain control of the northern airfields, this would not only ensure the safety of the
main sea lines of communications to Germany, but
would permit NATO forces to press forward toward
the Soviet home bases and keep them bottled up
inside the Barents Sea. In short, strategic planners
concluded, "the war in Europe may not be won in
the northern flank, but it could be lost there."[177]

NATO's concern for its northern flank coincided
with the U.S. Navy's internal reexamination of its
own post-Vietnam global strategy. Over time this
led to the development of what in the early 1980s
would become known as the forward maritime
strategy. In essence, this was an aggressive war
strategy which entailed advancing on the Soviets
using submarines and carrier strike forces. This new
strategy was designed to engage the enemy fleet as

close to its home bases as possible, bottle it up, and destroy its offensive capability. Thus, the Soviet build-up of naval and land forces on the Kola Peninsula offered a very plausible scenario upon, which to test and evaluate both the merits and risks of forward maritime strategy. As the Navy began to reassess the threat to the northern flank in the mid 1970s, Marine Corps planners at FMFLant and in Plans and Operations at Headquarters Marine Corps likewise began to study how the Marine Corps could best support the plans of their Navy counterparts to contain the Soviets on the northern flank.

Two areas in the north seemed to hold the most promise. One was northern Norway where Marines could secure valuable airfields. From these, Marine Corps, Air Force, and Navy aircraft could operate as if from a land-based aircraft carrier. The other possible area for employing Marines lay in Denmark's Jutland Peninsula. The narrows constricted by marshes north of the Kiel Canal offered a highly defensible position where Marine reinforcements could provide a secure enclave for NATO air bases, which could either strike at the Soviet Baltic Fleet or threaten the exposed flank of ground forces pushing across the north German plain. In 1975, Major General Philip D. Shutler, the Deputy Commanding General, FMFLant, headed up a Navy/Marine Corps briefing team that was designed to convince NATO officials of the capabilities of Marine air-ground task forces in the north and to persuade them to employ such a force in exercises being scheduled for the following year. The briefings met warm reception from NATO officials and especially from the government of Norway, which had been lobbying the Pentagon for this type of reinforcement for several years.

In the autumn of 1976, the stage was set for the largest Marine Corps deployment to Europe since World War I. Six thousand Marines of the 4th Marine Amphibious Brigade (4th MAB), commanded by Brigadier General Alfred M. Gray, Jr., embarked aboard Navy shipping in North Carolina and headed for two exercise areas that would test the flexible employment and reinforcement capability of projecting a Marine brigade from the sea within the North European Command. On 21 September, air and ground elements of the brigade conducted an amphibious assault with the Royal Marines in central Norway as part of a large naval exercise with the code name Teamwork 76. After back loading from Norway, the 4th MAB headed for Denmark where it participated in a second and much larger exercise known as Bonded Item. The flexibility and air-ground combat capabilities of the 4th MAB pleasantly surprised many NATO observers. With

their foot now firmly in the door, the Marines immediately began planning additional exercises in northern Europe in 1977 and 1978.[178]

Costs and Risks of the New Initiative

Between the two possible employment areas, the Jutland Peninsula and northern Norway, the latter, despite its difficult tactical environment, seemed to Marine planners to offer the most promise and flexibility for Marine air-ground task forces, provided the troops could learn to operate and maneuver in deep snow. This would take time. Post-exercise reports and the evaluations that followed each major exercise in the late 1970s pointed to major deficiencies in this respect. The most serious were attributed to the U.S. Marine Corps' lack of experience in operating in cold weather. In comparison to their Norwegian and Royal Marine counterparts, who were adept at moving their battalions through deep snow on skis, supported by superior over-snow vehicles, U.S. Marine infantry units proved to be far less mobile on the ground. The root causes seemed to be a lack of training and continuity in personnel and the overburdening of the troops with the excessively heavy Korean War—vintage clothing and equipment. Moreover, both proved completely inadequate for the Norwegian winter climate and terrain. As a result, in March 1977, the staff at Headquarters U.S. Marine Corps began to take a serious look at what future investments would have to be made in the 1979 Program Objectives Memoranda to improve the cold-weather capabilities of Marine forces.[179]

Part of the training problem was the lack of a suitable east coast cold-weather training site where the 4th MAB could conduct predeployment training under terrain and climate conditions that would approximate the rigors of a Norwegian winter. The closest it could come up with was the old World War I National Guard facility at Camp Drum near Plattsburg, New York. Unfortunately, Drum* is located on relatively flat ground and while in some years it can be inundated with snow, in others, snowfall may be lacking. This was the case for several of the 4th MAB work-up exercises in the late 1970s. For the 1979-1980 Operation Anorak Express in Norway, the pattern for preparing the force was modified. In this instance, the 36th Marine Amphibious Unit (36th MAU), the exercising Marine force, underwent three weeks of cold-weather training at MWTC, 30 November-20 December 1979. Operation Workup, an amphibious landing on Cape Cod, Massachusetts, followed this training prior to the 36th MAU's deployment to Norway in February

---

* Redesignated Fort Drum in the 1980s.

1980. While evaluators of the exercise could point to some improvement in the mobility of the U.S. Marine contingent, the list of deficiencies in Marine capabilities to operate in deep snow still made it obvious that a significant amount of further work and investment was necessary.[180]

With the commitment of a Marine air-ground task force to reinforce NATO's northern flank (focusing on northern Norway) now a reality, the staff at Headquarters U.S. Marine Corps began to recognize that, until then, exploration of the impact of cold weather on the individual Marine, his weapons systems, and supporting equipment had thus far tended to be piecemeal, isolated, and sporadic. Perhaps no one at Headquarters U.S. Marine Corps appreciated this shortcoming more than the Commandant of the Marine Corps himself. General Robert H. Barrow had replaced General Wilson and was sworn in as the 27th Commandant on 1 July 1979. As a captain, General Barrow had served as the company commander of Company A in Colonel Chesty Puller's 1st Marine Regiment during the recapture of Seoul. His company had also successfully defended the pass at Koto-ri earning him the Navy Cross during the 1st Marine Division's retreat from the Chosin Reservoir in December of 1950. From that first-hand experience, the Commandant was keenly aware of the adverse affects that extreme cold could play on small unit combat effectiveness, if troops are inadequately trained, clothed and equipped. Further, as the commanding general of FMFLant from 1976 to 1978, the exercises of the 4th MAB had given him a unique vantage point from which to study the risks thoroughly, if the Corps did not approach this new mission carefully and deliberately.

As the Assistant Commandant, it is therefore likely that he endorsed the staff view that what was needed was a total overview of cold-weather operations through the mid-range (five year) period. As a consequence, in 1979 Northrop Services Inc., was commissioned to conduct a study to accomplish the following tasks:

(1) Determine and evaluate the capability of a MAGTF to conduct landing force operations during a cold-weather amphibious assault and during subsequent operations ashore; (2) Identify landing force deficiencies in doctrine, tactics, techniques, training, and equipment during a cold-weather amphibious assault, including naval support systems directly involved with ship-to-shore movement; (3) Define individual Marine and MAGTF system requirements to overcome deficiencies;

(4) Provide concepts of operation and techniques, along with concepts of training, which are technologically available; (5) Determine the financial impact of any force structure and equipment program changes.[181]

A draft of the Northrop Study was routed for comment to Headquarters U.S. Marine Corps staff during August of 1980. After considering mission assignments in either northern Korea or Norway, the study concluded with a number of findings and recommendations, a few extractions of which are listed below. First, the study stated that the Marine Corps has the inherent capability to conduct an amphibious assault in dry-cold conditions* (temperatures +20 to –5 degrees F) and in snow depths to 20 inches, provided supplementary training programs are established; the Marine Corps has the inherent capability to conduct limited amphibious assaults in intense-cold conditions (temperature –5 to –25 degrees F) and in an area of snow depth in excess of 20 inches. If snow depths of 20 inches are anticipated, a lightweight all-terrain vehicle and skis for helicopters will be needed. The Marine Corps *does not require a capability to conduct winter warfare operations under extreme-cold conditions** (temperature range –25 to –65 degrees F) in fulfillment of probable assigned missions. Accordingly, the Marine Corps should prepare and promulgate a policy document for guidance of all activities, setting forth levels of cold stress for development, training and acquisition programs.**

Second, the study observed that "the most pressing cold-weather problem facing the Marine Corps" was its effort to develop and maintain a satisfactory state of training readiness for cold-weather operations within the FMF. Present facilities and training programs are inadequate to keep Marines fully trained, conditioned and acclimatized to function effectively under the most severe conditions of weather, terrain and enemy action. Establishment of a brigade-sized, dedicated cold-weather force in II Marine Amphibious Force would enhance the Marine Corps' ability to maintain a high degree of readiness for cold-weather operations.

Third, the study's authors noted the "excessive weight" of cold-weather equipment, clothing, and supplies, which added to the normal load of weapons and ammunition that the infantryman is required to carry and man haul on sleds reduces

---

* Italic by the author.
** The Marine Corps later adopted this finding. In effect, it not only narrowed the scope of training programs, but literally saved millions of dollars when it came time to procure new sets of cold-weather clothing and equipment.

his effectiveness in combat and greatly increases the possibility of cold injury and defeat. There is no simple solution to this problem. It is recommended that a comprehensive program be initiated to develop a holistic approach directed toward increasing the mobility and the combat effectiveness of small infantry units engaged in winter warfare.

Finally, the report offered "a plan for implementation of the recommendations. Initial actions were selected on the basis of affordability in the current budget period and are based on the premise that training and infantry mobility are the *most urgent deficiencies** to be addressed." [182]

A second initiative taken by Headquarters U.S. Marine Corps soon after Commandant Barrow took office was to direct the Commanding General, Camp Pendleton to request Western Division of the Naval Facilities Engineering Command to prepare a master plan for the purpose of providing "a comprehensive guide for the development of the Marine Corps Mountain Warfare Training Center." The scope of the plan was to include a review of existing facilities against the newly established basic facility requirements as well as identification of critical facility deficiencies that need correction to ensure mission accomplishment and a planning base for long-range management of the center.

With respect to basic facility requirement, the Master Plan noted Commandant's direction that for planning purposes, "personnel loading [would] be based on a 260-man permanent party consisting of 11 Marine officers, 217 Marine enlisted men, two Navy officers, 20 Navy enlisted men, and 10 civilians. Also included is a peak load 1,785-man training party, consisting of one 650-man unit, one 1,000-man unit, and 135 individual students." [183]

After completing a preliminary assessment and coordinating its activities with officials at the Forest Ranger Station at Bridgeport, the Western Division team developed three alternative courses of action (1) take no action/minimum maintenance policy, (2) construct permanent facilities at both the permanent and training camp areas, and (3) Construct permanent facilities at the permanent camp only. Ultimately, the Master Plan that was developed recommended pursuing the second course of action on the basis that it would produce a functionally more efficient MWTC. It would also create a more visually aesthetic order while providing a greater protection to the surrounding environment. Noting that training activities and facilities must continue to function with the minimum of interference from the redevelopment, the plan went on to lay out a four-phased plan (Phase 1 FY 1984 through Phase 4 FY 1986) for the demolition of existing buildings as replacement facilities were completed and became available for use. The cost for the entire project in 1983 Military Construction dollars, which did not include demolition of existing buildings, landscaping, construction contingency costs of five percent, or solar heating was estimated to be $22,351,000. [*184]

1981:Year of Decision

A third document that was instrumental in pushing the future use of the MWTC to the forefront was an action paper that was also routed in August of 1980 by Brigadier General Americo A. Sardo, the director of Training, to all of the Deputy Chiefs of Staff at Headquarters U.S. Marine Corps. This document was entitled: Marine Corps Mountain Warfare Training Center, 1985, Training and Development Concept Paper. The purpose of the paper was: "to state the need for a Marine Corps Mountain Warfare Center, define its optimum capabilities, identify resources required, and outline a program to achieve the MWTC of 1985." Each addressee was requested to review the contents of the concept paper and provide appropriate comments, recommendations and their concurrence or nonconcurrence, before going forward to the Commandant. [185]

After making a compelling case for the need of such a training facility, especially in light of the Marine Corps' upcoming commitment to NATO's northern flank, the paper went on to address the comparative financial costs of using Camp Drum vice MWTC:

> Exercise Empire Glacier 1978 and Exercise Alpine Warrior in 1979 cost FMFLant 1.1M and 672K respectively. In both exercises base operating costs of over 200K were paid to Camp Drum. The first exercise was inundated with snow and the second suffered from a lack of it. It is estimated by the Reserve Training Section of Training Division, Headquarters U.S. Marine Corps that at least $2.00 per day for each member of a unit is paid for base operating costs during actual time of departure (ATD) at Camp Drum or Camp Ripley. FY 78 costs for a two-week actual time of departure (ATD) of 142 men at Camp Drum included $20,000 just to open and operate the camp. Using a $2.00 day estimate, an average load of 848 and a permanent staff of 131, it would cost 632K in base operating costs to operate

---

* Italic by the author.

---

* It should also be noted that the scope of the draft master plan did not include the construction of quarters for married personnel other than for the commanding officer and his family.

Courtesy of *Leatherneck*

Colonel John W. Guy, Commanding Officer, Mountain Warfare Training Center from March 1978 to May 1981, presents an award to one of the training center Marines. Colonel Guy is in the center of the picture and at right is First Sergeant Lloyd G. Daniels, the acting sergeant major.

a year round facility at Camp Drum. The current Operations and Maintenance Marine Corps (OMMC) for Bridgeport is 683K. These figures are only presented for comparison as Camp Drum does not provide a mountain environment nor as long and dependable a period of winter conditions.[186]

Drawing from inputs obviously submitted by Colonel John W. Guy and his staff at the Mountain Warfare Training Center, the concept paper went on to visualize in detail what new missions and functions MWTC would be capable of providing by 1985 if certain investments were made. This included establishing a sizable equipment allowance pool, and doubling its 7 November 1979 table of organization to 11 Marine officers and 217 Marine enlisted, two Navy officers and 20 Navy enlisted, and 10 civilian positions over a three year period. Military Construction costs were based on the Draft Master Plan that was still being refined by Western Division of the Naval Facilities Engineering Command. By this time final cost figures in the Master Plan included provisions for the construction of family housing and carried a revised total estimate of 25 million dollars.

By making these investments, the concept paper concluded, the MWTC of 1985 would provide to the Marine Corps:

1. An instructor cadre which will train over 10,000

Marines on site and provide mobile training team support throughout the Marine Corps.
2. A pool of knowledge and experience in cold-weather and mountain operations and logistics.
3. A facility to assist in the development doctrine, tactics and techniques related to cold-weather and mountain warfare.
4. A facility at which the research and testing of cold-weather and mountain clothing, equipment and medicine may be conducted.
5. A yearly product of at least:
Four battalions trained in winter mountain operations.

Five battalions trained in summer mountain operations.

Two Reserve battalions trained in mountain operations.
6. Through formal schools, 540 Marines trained to take an active role in the instruction of their own battalions in cold-weather and mountain operations and in mountain survival.[187]

After the MWTC Concept Paper had been staffed, the director of Training made his refinements and then forwarded it to the Commandant. In mid-March 1981, the staff secretary placed the Concept Paper on the Commandant's schedule for a "decision brief."* Colonel Francis "Frank" Riney, General Sardo's Deputy, gave the brief in the Commandant's conference room that was adjacent to his office. In addition to General Barrow, among those present were his Assistant Commandant, General Kenneth McLennan, the Chief of Staff and all the deputy Chiefs of Staff, or their representatives. General Barrow listened to the one-hour briefing attentively, without raising questions, or making any comment. Following the brief the Commandant sat back in his chair, brought the fingertips of his hands together and started around the table soliciting the opinions of his generals.

The deputy Chief of Staff for Manpower made the opening comment. First, he argued strongly against the MWTC initiative, seriously doubting whether the Marine Corps even needed such a facility; secondly, he objected to its high cost in manpower, money, and materials. As the comments proceeded around the table, Colonel Riney became increasingly disheartened as others expressed similar doubts. Several even recommended that the project should not only be pursued, but that the MWTC base should be abandoned at once. Only the Plans, Policies and Operations Department and

---

* The Director of Training, BGen Sardo suffered a severe heart attack in the latter half of 1980; as a result, the "decision brief" was put on hold for several months. Gen Sardo was still recuperating when the briefing was presented to CMC in March.

a few others made statements strongly in support of the training division's proposal. After going completely around the table, General Barrow turned to the Assistant Commandant and said: "What do you think Ken?" General McLennan proceeded to make a succinct, yet compelling argument for why the Marine Corps could ill afford to give up this valuable training capability, especially with the Corps' growing commitment to the reinforcement of northern Norway. Throughout the briefing and the comments of his generals, Commandant Barrow never said a word. Nor did his face or demeanor ever betray how he personally would come down on the issue. For whatever reasons, he had obviously decided to withhold his final decision until later and simply concluded the meeting by standing up and, after looking at his generals in the eye, announcing: "Whatever we may ultimately decide to do gentlemen, we shall never allow our people to be housed in trailers again."[188]

On 2 May 1981, Lieutenant Colonel (colonel Select) William H. Osgood relieved Colonel John Guy as the commanding officer of MWTC. Like his two immediate predecessors, the newly installed commanding officer was very familiar with MWTC and its unique mission. A native Californian, Bill Osgood graduated from the College of the Pacific and in 1960 was commissioned a second lieutenant in the Marine Corps via the Platoon Leaders Class program. After completing The Basic School in 1961, he was appointed as an infantry officer and saw service with the 1st and 3d Marine Divisions. In the closing months of 1964, he attended Motor Transport Officer's School at Camp Lejeune and was given the additional military occupation specialty of 3502. In April 1965, he was assigned to MWTC as its motor transport officer. Frequently however, he augmented the Unit Training and the Mountain Leadership Sections whenever an additional instructor and guide was needed. He was transferred from MWTC on 1 March 1967 and later found himself as a rifle company commander in the 2d Battalion, 23d Marines, as part of the special landing force. Over the next three years, he continued to serve with that battalion in various capacities until his transfer from Vietnam to the United States in December of 1970. For his actions under fire in Vietnam, Captain Osgood was awarded the Silver Star and Bronze Star, with Combat "V". During the ensuing years, numerous command and staff assignments followed, including instructor duties at the U.S. Naval Academy, a tour at the Manpower Department, Headquarters U.S. Marine Corps, a student at the Air War College, and a short tour with the 3d Marine Aircraft Wing at El Toro, Cali-

Marine Corps History Division

General Robert H. Barrow, Commandant of the Marine Corps, made the critical decision to preserve and modernize the Mountain Warfare Training Center in 1981.

fornia, before his transfer to the training center.[*]

Very shortly after assuming command, Lieutenant Colonel Osgood was notified that the Commandant of the Marine Corps, accompanied by Mrs. Barrow and the sergeant major of the Marine Corps, Leland D. Crawford, would pay a visit to the training center within the next few days. Rather than exposing the Commandant to one more rather standard command briefing, Lieutenant Colonel Osgood and his S-3, Major Edward J. "Ed" Robeson, IV decided that General Barrow would gain a better perspective of the base and its activities by walking about and talking to the troops, or visiting them informally in the field. "That decision turned out the right one," Colonel Osgood would later recall:

> In the beginning, the Commandant was noticeably upset by the run-down condition of the base and its facilities. Nevertheless, as the day progressed and after meeting with some of the troops, his mood seemed to improve and he became more and more animated. The

---

* It was his PLC classmate and former messmate at MWTC during the early 1960s, LtCol Harry Jenkins Jr. (then the LtCol ground monitor at HQMC) who offered Col Osgood the assignment to be the CO at MWTC.

highlight of the day came when we drove up Highway 108, stopping at a granite escarpment just on the west side of Sonora Pass. There we dismounted from our vehicles to observe the Mountain Leadership and Unit Training instructor and guides undergoing refresher rock climbing training before starting the summer season. The Commandant was clearly impressed with the instructor and guides skillful climbing techniques as they negotiated up and down the cliff face. Best of all, he clearly enjoyed the informal banter with the instructors when they came down. There was still quite a bit of snow in the pass and both he and Mrs. Barrow also seemed to be completely taken by the majestic alpine ruggedness of the Sierra Nevada Range.

Throughout the visit, the Commandant made no mention to his host of what the future might hold for MWTC. This suggests that he was likely still mulling over the final decision in his mind. Colonel Osgood did remember, however, that the Commandant was displeased to learn of the number of married personnel who were residing in the government quarters at the Naval Ammunition Depot at Hawthorne, Nevada. "I want you to start moving your people out of that housing area and have them relocate to the Highway 395 corridor," the Commandant told Osgood, as he climbed into his sedan to depart. "Furthermore, you are to call

Colonel William Osgood, Commanding Officer, Mountain Warfare Training Center from 1981 to 1984.

Courtesy of Col William H. Osgood.

my office weekly to let me know how many families are still living there." "He means it," the aide whispered into Colonel Osgood's ear, as he passed to climb into the front seat. By November of that year, Osgood was happily able to report that the daily base bus service to and from Reno had been resumed and that all families had been relocated as the Commandant had directed.[189]

It is unclear exactly when General Barrow finally approved the Marine Corps Mountain Warfare Training Center, 1985, Training and Development Concept Paper. However, every indication suggests that it was probably about mid-May of 1981 after returning from his visit to the West Coast, which included his stop at MWTC. Coincidentally, it was also in mid-May that General Barrow designated Lieutenant General John H. Miller, his deputy Chief of Staff for Plans, Policies and Operations, as the central coordinating authority for all cold-weather issues from training to procurement.[190] The author later had the opportunity to ask General Barrow what the principal considerations were that prompted him to ultimately come down in favor of the MWTC project? Barrow responded

> I deplored the substandard living conditions that our people had to live in; to me the place looked more like a "squatter's camp" than a Marine base. I also believed that if we did not make the investment to upgrade the Pickel Meadow training camp and do it soon, we would have been forced to give it back to the Forest Service and thus lose it altogether. Finally, having been at FMFLant in 1976 and 1977, I had gained some appreciation for the difficulties and complexities associated with our commitment to north Norway. I knew from my own first-hand experience in Korea that mountain training, summer or winter, requires skills that just cannot either be taught or learned "by the seat of the pants."[191]

Unmentioned by General Barrow as a contributing factor, but nevertheless one that must have been of some import, was the timing of his decision. The new Reagan Administration had been in office for five months. Its campaign pledge to rebuild America's armed forces, especially its conventional capabilities, had already been demonstrated with the inclusion of the first set of Maritime Prepositioning Ships (MPS) for the Marine Corps in the revised FY 1981 Department of Defense Budget, with every indication that more investments would be forthcoming. General Barrow was coming to the end of his second year as Commandant. Thus his stature within the defense community was at its peak. Secretary of Defense Caspar Weinberger and Secretary of the Navy John F. Lehman both seemed to earnestly value his views. When he gave military advice on a matter they listened, and more often than not, followed it. Most members of the Senate and House Armed Services and Appropriation Committees also held him in high regard for his forthrightness and professionalism whenever he was called to testify before them. It seems likely, therefore, that the Commandant must have also sensed

that there would never be a better time than the present for the Corps to lay out its case for what he knew would be a substantial investment of taxpayer dollars.

Laying the Foundation for Improvements

By the summer of 1981, Lieutenant Colonel Osgood had learned that the Commandant had approved the Master Plan for the rebuilding of the training center and for doubling the personnel

Courtesy of Col William H. Osgood

Lieutenant Colonel Osgood's quarters before and after the catastrophic natural gas explosion that destroyed it on 23 January 1982.

strength of the command over the next several years. The Fleet Assistance Program for staffing billets at MWTC, he was told, would cease and would be assumed by the Manpower Department at Headquarters U.S. Marine Corps. Other welcome news included the reauthorization for a permanent training center sergeant major. Thus on 31 August 1981, Sergeant Major Charles L. Hayman relieved First Sergeant Lloyd G. Daniels who had been serving as the acting sergeant major since the previous year. Another bit of good news for the personnel staffing of the training center came in the form of Color Sergeant Mahon, Royal Marines, who arrived in 1981 from the Royal Marine Commando Mountain and Arctic Cadre to start a two-year exchange tour at MWTC.

As information on the major changes that were scheduled to take place at Pickel Meadow was circulated, a constant stream of general officers, foreign dignitaries, congressional staffers, budgeters, and facility engineers began descending on the base with increasing regularity. On 11 February 1982, Lieutenant Colonel Osgood and his executive officer attended a meeting at the District Forest Ranger's office to jointly approve the final changes to the MWTC Master Plan and a newly redrafted Memorandum of Understanding. Although the Master Plan promised that the antiquated facilities at MWTC would soon be replaced, it came too late to prevent the accidental destruction of the commanding officer's residence. On 23 January a propane gas leak and subsequent explosion totally collapsed the quarters. Fortunately Lieutenant Colonel and Mrs. Osgood were away in Southern California when the explosion occurred. However, Major Matthew J. "Matt" Heck, the MWTC executive officer, and two staff noncommissioned officers did suffer minor injuries as they tried to extinguish the flames and salvage some of the Osgoods' personal property. [192]

In February 1982, the Commandant approved the comprehensive Cold Weather Combat Operations Study that had been prepared by Northrop Services, Inc. This study made some 40 specific recommendations designed to upgrade Marine Corps cold-weather combat capabilities and would become the blueprint for procurement and training changes within the Marine Corps.

During 9-12 March, the Norwegian Ministry of Defense hosted a joint cold-weather conference at its Terningmoen Camp in Elverum, Norway. Among other things, the purpose of the conference was to determine courses of action for addressing already identified cold–weather operational deficiencies that were of mutual concern to all the parties. Over 100 representatives of major Marine Corps com-

Marine Corps History Division

Major General Alfred M. Gray Jr., Commanding General, 2d Marine Division, believed that training at the Mountain Warfare Training Center played a vital role in preparing division units for deployment to Northern Norway.

mands, selected U.S. Navy and U.S. Army officers, various U.S. civilian cold-weather specialists, members of the Norwegian Armed Forces, and the British and Dutch Royal Marines attended the conference. The meeting was the result of almost a year of planning by Headquarters U.S. Marine Corps, the Marine Corps Development and Education Command, the Office of Naval Research, and Norwegian authorities. The Marine Corps organized the conference while Norwegian authorities provided the logistical support as well as co-chairmen and members for each of the four sub-committees. Major General Alfred M. Gray Jr., the 2d Marine Division, Commanding General, gave the keynote address.[193]

At the start of the second day, the local garrison provided a comprehensive field demonstration to exhibit Norwegian tactics and equipment. During the mobility portion of demonstration, the Norwegian Army particularly impressed the U.S. Marine representatives with its over-snow vehicle (BV-202) that had no difficulty negotiating in 25-30 inches of snow over hilly terrain.* The remaining two days

---

* The U.S. marginal terrain vehicle M116 Husky had been tested at MWTC the previous year and was determined to be unsuitable as an over snow vehicle.

was used for committee working sessions during which more than one hundred agenda items were discussed by the participants regarding training, equipment, combat service support, and standards for battle techniques.[194]

Lieutenant Colonel Osgood and Major Edward J. "Ed" Robeson, IV his S-3, briefed the training committee on the MWTC curriculum of courses for cold-weather combat operations and what new capabilities the base would offer under its Five-Year Training and Development Plan. As a result, the Marine Corps had already decided to shift its pre-deployment training for infantry battalions earmarked for the northern flank from Camp Ripley in Minnesota to MWTC. Once there, these battalions would follow the pattern developed by the British Royal Marines of undergoing two months of intensive cold-weather training prior to departing for the winter exercise in Norway. Moreover, as Lieutenant Colonel Osgood could point out, the training center was already routinely sending its instructors to Nor-

way to attend the Allied Officers Training Course in order to incorporate what they learn into the MWTC training program. It therefore became the conference position that "the MWTC Five-Year Training and Development Plan is sound and well conceived and that an exchange of instructors during the winter months by the MWTC and the Norwegian School of Infantry and winter warfare would benefit both schools and their programs."[195]

The Marine Corps subsequently adopted a number of important recommendations that were jointly discussed at this conference. Among them was the decision to designate 4th MAB as the sole Norway Brigade in order to facilitate institutional knowledge and continuity in planning for cold-weather combat operations. While by 1983 it could be said that the foundations for meeting the major training deficiencies were well on their way toward solution, the same could not be said for the clothing and equipment problem. This would take several more years to resolve.

Chapter 11
Ascending New Heights, 1984-1990

The U.S. Marines are no longer just brave Marines in funny boots. They are true Arctic warriors.

-Brigadier General Lerheim, Norwegian Army
Fall, 1984

Rebuilding MWTC and Expanding Its Capabilities

The year major changes started to take place at MWTC was 1983. Indeed, more initiatives were undertaken that year than in the previous quarter of a century. At the national political level, 1983 also marked the second year of the presidency of Ronald W. Reagan. As the Republican Party had promised before the 1980 election, the build-up of the U.S. military's conventional forces under Secretary of Defense Caspar Weinberger was in full swing. Funding requests that General Barrow believed he needed to begin rebuilding the training center went unchallenged by analysts for the 1983 Department of Defense Budget and were approved with alacrity by the Authorization and Appropriation Committees of the Congress. At the same time, American foreign policy vis-à-vis the Soviet Union became more strident as the president entered into a rhetorical war of words with the Kremlin. On March 8, 1983 at a major speech in Orlando, Florida, the president bluntly referred to the Soviets as an "Evil Empire." Two weeks later, East-West tensions rose further when the president announced to an American television audience his plan to launch a Strategic Defense Initiative (popularly known as "Star Wars."[196] Later, it would become evident that the president's real strategic aim was to rid Eastern Europe of communist domination once and for all. Should the Soviet bloc make an aggressive military response to Reagan's efforts to weaken communism in Eastern Europe, it was likely that sizable Marine and Navy forces would be needed to quickly bolster NATO's northern flank.

From 21 February to 9 March 1983, the staff at MWTC got its first glimpse of a new vehicle that was then being considered for procurement by the Marine Corps. It was the General Dynamics LAV-25 Light Assault Vehicle. This eight-wheeled, lightly armored vehicle had a crew of three and space for four infantrymen in a rear compartment. Its main armament was a 25mm chain gun, and variants were being planned that could mount an 81mm, a

M-220 TOW antitank rocket launcher, or a 105mm howitzer; another variant could serve as a communications vehicle. Its survivability on the battlefield lay in its great speed of 75 to 80 miles per hour. Vehicles were brought to Pickel Meadow to test their capability and performance in freezing cold-weather and under deep snow conditions.

From 27 February to 4 March, MWTC also hosted a new group of trainees. The group consisted of 70 captains who were students at the Amphibious Warfare School at Quantico, Virginia. The purpose was to give these students five days of practical indoctrination training in winter warfare.[197] This training for mid-level officers would be continued and expanded into a winter war game over the next 20 years.

Throughout the early months of 1983, the MWTC Command Chronologies reported numerous visitors who came to the training center. These included (1) site surveyors for conducting Phase I of the rebuilding of facilities; (2) congressional staff members of the Senate and House of Representative Military Construction Committees to receive briefings on the estimated costs of Phase II of the rebuilding master plan; (3) technicians to evaluate prototypes of cold-weather clothing and equipment that were then undergoing testing and development at the U.S. Army Laboratory in Natick, Massachusetts; and (4) medical experts who were assisting the staff in developing the syllabus for a new course in cold-weather medicine for U.S. Navy surgeons and corpsmen.

One initiative that had been directed by Headquarters U.S. Marine Corps in 1981 and that was essentially completed in June of 1983 turned out to be a failure. This was the construction of an 8,000-foot Air Assault Landing Zone just to the north of Bridgeport along Highway 182 in the Toiyabe National Forest at Sweetwater in Lyons County, Nevada. At the time, it was the practice of the USAF Air Mobility Command to annually allocate to the Marine Corps a substantial number of C-130 flight hours for transporting troops and equipment to various training sites around the country. In order to build pilot proficiency, flights that flew into, or out of unimproved dirt strips, were furnished at no cost to the using unit. Therefore, it was reasoned, if such a landing site were constructed in close proximity to the training center, this would provide the means

Courtesy of Col William H. Osgood

Photograph of new quarters constructed for the commanding officer of the training center in 1983. To William H. Osgood it looked "more like a fort on the Maginot Line than living quarters."

for transporting 2d Marine Division battalions to MWTC for winter and summer mountain training at very little expense. Air Force planners at Air Mobility Command enthusiastically endorsed the plan, as did the U.S. Forest Service. In April 1982, Colonel Osgood and representatives from the Forest Service briefed the Lyons County Commissioners on the project.[198] This body also gave its approval to pro-

Major General Kenneth L. Robinson, Commanding General, Marine Corps Base, Camp Pendleton and Lieutenant Colonel Osgood observe the pouring of the cornerstone of the a new bachelor enlisted quarters on 11 August 1983.

Courtesy of Col Col William H. Osgood

ceed. Shortly thereafter, in May 1982, a Naval Construction Battalion from Port Hueneme began clearing ground for the airstrip. By the following spring, Navy engineers declared the work completed and that the Assault Landing Zone was ready to receive aircraft. However, the U.S. Air Force team that arrived to inspect the landing zone refused to certify it because of a small hill mass that was in the flight path. The Construction Battalion tried to remove this obstacle but to no avail. Consequently, the project was abandoned and no plane ever touched down on the air strip.[199]

On 28 June 1983, during ceremonies at an Evening Parade at Marine Barracks Washington, General Robert H. Barrow retired and handed the Corps' battle flag to his successor, the 28th Commandant of the Marine Corps, General Paul X. Kelley. President Reagan himself presided over the ceremony. Having served as the Assistant Comman-

dant for the previous two years, General Kelley was familiar with General Barrow's vision for rebuilding MWTC. Over the next four years, he too would use the influence of his office to ensure that the Master Plan for rebuilding the base stayed on track.

Before General Kelley was sworn in as the new Commandant, Colonel and Mrs. Bill Osgood received the welcome news that they could at last vacate their temporary housing in the officer's club and move into their new quarters that had just been completed on the hill above. Although equipped with new features and appliances, sadly the new structure had none of the charm and warmth of its predecessor. Indeed, Colonel Osgood recalled: "it was so overbuilt and had enough concrete in it that it looked to him more like a fort on the Maginot Line than living quarters.[200]

On 11 August, Major General Kenneth L. Robinson, commanding general of Camp Pendleton was

Topaz Housing Unit in the Coleville area.

on hand at Pickel Meadow to attend the dedication ceremony and to witness the pouring of the cornerstone for the new bachelor enlisted quarters. Shortly thereafter, construction was also started on what would become the new headquarters building for the training center. Phase I of the Master Plan was underway. Also by late 1983, Headquarters U.S. Marine Corps had given its approval to proceed with the construction of a permanent family housing complex for MWTC's married personnel. To achieve this purpose a tract of land was purchased in Antelope Valley on the west side of Highway 395, one mile to the north of the town of Coleville. What subsequently became known as the Topaz Family Housing complex was built under a separate contract. By the summer of 1985 its newly completed dwellings were opened for occupancy to married Marines and sailors who were reporting for duty at MWTC. On 10 October, the Topaz Housing complex was officially opened at a dedication ceremony presided over by Major General Robert E. Haebel, the Commanding General, Camp Pendleton. During the ceremony, each street within the complex was named in memory of eight enlisted Marines who had been posthumously awarded the Medal of Honor during the Korean War.

Major Edward J. Robeson IV, operations officer at Mountain Warfare Training Center during the early 1980s. He played a major role in revitalizing the winter and summer mountaineering courses offered.

Courtesy of *Leatherneck*

Beginning in the early 1980s, commanding officers and their respective operations officers at MWTC gradually began to expand the scope of the formal courses and practical training opportunities being offered at Pickel Meadow. This was done not only to improve the capabilities of units participating in contingency operations in northern Norway, but also to alleviate the lack of mountain and cold-weather experience that was evident throughout the Fleet Marine Force. By mid-summer 1984, the Center had all but reached the peak of its increased capabilities resulting from several new Programs of Instruction. Future annual training plans now called for:

• Three reinforced infantry battalions (1,000 troops each) trained in four weeks of winter mountain operations, one of which could be trained away from MWTC with a mobile training team.

• One infantry battalion highly trained in winter mountain operations through two months of training at MWTC January through February.

• One Reserve infantry battalion trained in two weeks of winter mountain operations at MWTC.

• Four reinforced infantry battalions (1,000 troops each) trained in four weeks of summer mountain operations.

• Two Reserve infantry battalions trained in two weeks of summer mountain operations.

• Four Winter Mountain Leadership Courses of two-week duration (Grade B) for 30 students; designed to enable small unit leaders to serve as assistant instructors for their own battalions upon deployment to MWTC for winter training.

• One Winter Mountain Leadership Course of four weeks duration (Grade A) for 30 students; designed to qualify small unit leaders (officers, staff noncommissioned officers (SNCOs) and noncommissioned officers (NCOs) in winter skills at the "master" level, thereby permitting them to serve as instructors for their parent unit. Successful attainment of the Grade B course served as a prerequisite.

• Six Summer Mountain Leadership Courses of two-weeks duration (Grade B) for 30 students; designed to enable small unit leaders to serve as assistant instructors for their own battalions upon deployment to MWTC for summer training.

• Two Summer Mountain Leadership Courses of four-weeks duration (Grade A) for 30 students; designed to qualify small unit leaders (officers, SNCOs and NCOs in summer skills at the "master" level, thereby permitting them to serve as instructors for their parent units. Successful attainment of the

Courtesy of Col William H. Osgood

In January 1984, two former instructor-guides from the 1960s reunited at Mountain Warfare Training Center. Lieutenant Colonel William H. Osgood, on the left, and on the right is Colonel Harry W. Jenkins Jr., Commanding Officer, 2d Marine Regiment, while visiting the training center.

Grade B summer course served as a prerequisite.

• Two Senior Officer Winter Planning Courses of two-weeks duration for 20 field grade officers; designed to enable staff officers to incorporate cold-weather and mountain warfare considerations into tactical planning.

• Two Winter and two Summer Mountain Survival Courses of two-weeks duration for 30 students; designed primarily for aircrews and reconnaissance personnel who may unexpectedly find themselves in a survival situation in a mountainous or cold-weather environment.

• Two Cold Weather Medicine Courses of two-weeks duration for 40 students; designed to enable FMF medical personnel to prevent, recognize and treat cold-weather illnesses and injuries and provide advice to commanders on the medical aspects of cold-weather and mountain operations.

• Mountain Flying Training. In addition to the foregoing, helicopter units could use MWTC and its environs to conduct cold-weather and mountain "terrain flying" flying exercises either in conjunction with survival courses for aircrews, or in support of battalion field exercises.[201]

This increase in base loading, or training activity, placed a heavier demand on both the training center's facilities and its instructor staff. These added requirements came as no surprise. As early as 1980, they had been outlined in detail in the training division's original Marine Corps Mountain Warfare Training Center, 1985, Training and Development Concept Paper. In 1981, General Barrow had given his approval to meet these anticipated requirements. As a result, initiatives in the 1983-1984 Headquarters Program Objective Memorandum calling for the modernization of water, power and sewage systems, for example, had managed to keep pace with this expected growth. The personnel strength lagged behind what had been expected. Albeit the personnel strength of the base was gradually on the rise, Camp Pendleton was slow in endorsing the training center's request for much needed increases in its table of organization. By January 1984, it would still only number 11 Marine officers and 162 Marines and one Royal Marine enlisted, two U.S. Navy officers and 11 Navy enlisted, and six civilians. Indeed, it would take another two and a half years (July 1986) before the new authorized strength would finally be achieved at 15 Marine officers and 211 Marines and one Royal Marine enlisted, three U.S. Navy officers, 15 Navy enlisted, and nine civilians.[202]

On 25 July 1984, Colonel Bill Osgood turned over the command of MWTC to his successor, Colonel John I. Hopkins. Colonel Hopkins was a decorated combat veteran who had served two tours of duty in Vietnam: first as a battalion advisor to the Vietnamese Marine Corps in 1965-1966 and during 1967-1968 as the operations officer in 1st Battalion, 4th Marines; and later in the 9th Marines. In the late summer of 1972, as a major he commanded the 2d Battalion, 7th Marines, 1st Marine Division. This had been the first infantry battalion to return to Pickel Meadow for field training since its closure in 1967. Prior to assuming command at MWTC, from August 1982 to June 1984, Hopkins had served as the Chief of Staff, I Marine Amphibious Force at Camp Pendleton.[*]

Since the beginning of the combined NATO winter exercises, Royal Marine Commandos had consistently demonstrated a far greater proficiency in over snow movement than their U.S. Marine counterparts. Furthermore, British forces tended to be better prepared to withstand the rigors of the harsh winter climate inside the Arctic Circle. What gave British troops this edge? The principal reason given was the almost two months of intensive individual and collective training in both Scotland and in North Norway prior to the exercise. In fact, one of the recommendations that came out of the Joint Cold Weather Conference conducted in Norway in March of 1982 urged that U.S. Marine maneuver bat-

---

[*] Cols Hopkins and Osgood literally switched assignments, as the latter immediately became the Chief of Staff at I MAF.

talions adopt a policy that would give them that same level of pre-deployment training.[203] However, it was not until 1985 that components of the 4th Marine Amphibious Brigade (4th MAB) actually began to implement this recommendation into their annual training plans. In preparation for Operation Cold Winter 1985, the commanding officer of the 2d Marine Regiment, Colonel Harry Jenkins, Jr., himself a former instructor-guide at the training center, had scheduled his reinforced 1st Battalion, 2d Marines, to receive five weeks' winter mountain operations training at MWTC during January and early February. Marine Aircraft Group 40, the air component of 4th MAB, likewise sent Marine Medium Helicopter Squadron 266 (HMM-266) to MWTC for most of the same period. Then in early February, the balance of the 4th MAB, including its artillery, amphibian tractor company, combat engineers, and other air and combat service support units deployed from Camp Lejeune to Camp Drum, New York. Upon completion of its training at MWTC, the 1st Battalion, 2d Marines, and HMM-266 rejoined the brigade for three more weeks of collective training in cold-weather operations. After conducting a force-on-force field exercise, the entire 4th MAB was airlifted to northern Norway. Thus for the first time, the primary air and ground units did acquire almost two months of training in cold-weather operations before their deployment to Norway. Post exercise comments that year confirmed that the proficiency and readiness of Marine units to conduct combat operations in extreme cold and deep snow were so dramatically improved that the 4th MAB made this pattern of pre-deployment training a standing operating procedure for all future NATO winter exercises in North Norway.[204]

It was during this time that another source of assistance for establishing these new procedures turned out to be none other than Major Jim Goldsworthy, the Royal Marine exchange officer who had served with Colonel Jenkins as an instructor at MWTC 20 years earlier. Goldsworthy would later recall:

> In the mid-1980s, I was assigned to the amphibious planning staff of SACLant* to foster common understanding of cold-weather operations between our two corps. As the role of the USMC expanded to include support of north flank operations in time of war, with annual training and joint exercises with the Royal Marines and the Norwegian Army Brigade North, this understanding proved to

---

* Supreme Allied Commander, Atlantic (SACLant) Headquarters was located at the U.S. Naval Operating Base, Norfolk, Virginia.

be a very useful contribution to overcoming problems and establishing common procedures. The bond was strengthened when Colonel (later Major General) Harry Jenkins, Jr., a great friend and fellow instructor with me at MWTC, commanded the BLT deployed for training in Norway with the 3d Commando Brigade, Royal Marines, commanded by Brigadier Andy Keeling, also a friend with whom I had served in 42 Commando in the Far East. I have no doubt that my time spent at Pickel Meadow was of value to the USMC and the Royal Marines both professionally and personally building a bond of understanding and mutual respect that prevails to this day.[205]

Colonel Hopkins' tenure as commanding officer at MWTC turned out to be short-lived. Within five months the new commander was selected for promotion and on 7 May 1985, Colonel Hopkins was advanced to the rank of brigadier general, with orders to Camp Lejeune to serve as Assistant Division Commander, 2d Marine Division. His 10 months as commander at MWTC were not, however, without their challenges. In May 1985, shortly before Colonel Hopkins's departure, MWTC received a visit and inspection by the Inspector General (IG) of the Marine Corps. A month prior to the inspection, the command had identified several problem areas that required higher headquarters' attention before the IG's visit. One issue pertained to an unresolved Memorandum of Understanding between MWTC and Naval Air Station Fallon involving search and rescue and medical evacuation support. Another spoke to the matter of a 20 percent shortfall in the MWTC staffing goals. A third related to how the Lahotan Water Control District had effectively blocked construction on the new mess hall because of concerns over contaminated soil found during the initial excavation. However, it was an interpretation of the Wilderness Act and Forest Service policy by local USFS officials (Reno Supervisor and the Bridgeport and Carson District Rangers) that potentially offered the most serious challenge to the future capabilities of the training center's mountain operations program.

Since the creation of the Mountain Leadership Course in 1957, instructor-guides had been authorized to use the alpine terrain around Matterhorn Peak for the summer courses on a joint use basis. The purpose was to develop individual skills in mountain walking, snow and ice climbing techniques, and in practical methods of glacier crevasse rescue. Use was generally limited to 30 students, 12

The Matterhorn Peak region had been the site of useful mountaineering training since 1957. In 1985, the U.S. Forest Service closed the area to military training. It is now known as the Hoover Wilderness Area.

instructor-guides for four days, six times a year. Similarly, beginning in March, 1959 at the direction of Lieutenant Colonel Averill, a team from the Operation and Training Section had pioneered a 60-kilometer cross-country ski and snow shoe trek route on the western side of the Sierra divide starting at the upper reaches of Silver Creek at MWTC and ending on Highway 4 below the town of Markleville in Alpine County. This trek route was periodically used, also on a joint use basis, as a route for a non-tactical ski march during the winter Mountain Leadership Course. Sometime in the early 1980s, the Matterhorn Peak area was designated the Hoover Wilderness and later, the area to the north of MWTC was designated as the Carson-Iceberg Wilderness. In response to two requests by the commanding officer of MWTC to use Hoover Wilderness area for individual mountaineering instruction, both requests were denied by the District Ranger at Bridgeport. In his letters back to the commanding officer the District Ranger stated: "Contests such as physical or mental endurance of a man or animal, foot races, canoe or boat races, competitive trail rides, survival contests or exercises and other activities of this nature will not be permitted in wilderness and primitive areas."[206]

In response to Colonel Hopkins's request for a permit to gain access to the trek route located in the Carson-Iceberg Wilderness during the winter

months, this too was similarly denied by the Carson District Ranger, who stated: "The proposal is clearly a structured military exercise and is prohibited by Forest Service policy."[207] Before the Inspector-General Marine Corps' visit, Colonel Hopkins had already appealed the decisions of both District Rangers to their supervisor in Reno. However, the latter refused to reverse the decision rendered by his two subordinates. Subsequent to the IG's visit, a final appeal by Headquarters U.S. Marine Corps to The Honorable John R. Block, secretary of agriculture, also failed to alter the positions taken by the local U.S. Forest Service Rangers.[208] Some type of alternative to these restrictions would therefore have to be found, especially to make up the loss of the Hoover Wilderness area. Resolution of these and other issues would fall into the lap of Colonel John F. Stennick, who on 28 June 1985 relieved Lieutenant Colonel Earnest Van Huss as the training center's new commander.

Improvements in Cold-Weather Clothing and Equipment

By mid 1985, all of the major deficiencies that had been identified during the March 1982 Joint Cold Weather Conference in Norway were well on their way toward resolution. All, that is, save the clothing and equipment issue. Since the mid-1970s, mountaineering outfitters such as North Face, Mar-

Courtesy of MGen Harry W. Jenkins Jr.

The 2d Marines command post group packing up at Pickel Meadow prior to deploying to Northern Norway in 1985. Regimental commander Colonel Jenkins is second from left wearing a white cap. The Marines have not yet been issued modern Gore-Tex clothing.

mot, Patagonia, Helle Hansen, and others had been introducing a host of new lightweight winter garments, sleeping bags load-bearing pack systems, and mountain tents. Initially, this gear was offered in limited quantities to a small clientele at high prices. By 1980, however, these companies were pushing out from their high-end, technical niche markets into the mass market. The recreational industry was steadily improving its capability to produce high quality, durable clothing and equipment

General Paul X. Kelley, Commandant of the Marine Corps, and his aide Lieutenant Colonel Frank Libutti visit Jenkins's field command post during Exercise Cold Winter in Northern Norway in 1985. Captain James T. Kenney, the headquarters commandant, stands second from left.

Courtesy of MGen Harry W. Jenkins Jr.

Courtesy of MGen Harry W. Jenkins Jr.

Marines from 2d Marines training in Northern Norway during Exercise Cold Winter. They are carrying wooden Northland skis.

using synthetics and new manufacturing processes at reduced costs. The Gore-Tex Company was at the center of much of the latest clothing because of its novel method of producing waterproof breathable lining laminated to many types of outer fabrics. Nonetheless, when the troops of the 4th MAB flew off to north Norway to participate in exercise Cold Winter 1985, their bulky cold-weather clothing "kits" were still basically the same items that their Marine counterparts had worn during the Korean War, with the one exception that most of the brigade had been outfitted with a set of the new

Marines of 1st Battalion, 2d Marine Regiment skijoring behind a BV-206 in Northern Norway during Exercise Cold Winter.

Courtesy of MGen Harry W. Jenkins Jr.

Gore-Tex outer jacket and trouser shells.[209]

In August 1985, Captain Jeffrey W. "Jeff" Bearor was in the process of transferring to MCB Quantico, after completing a two-year tour as an exchange officer with the Royal Marines. Between his four weeks as a student in the Winter Mountain Leadership Course at MWTC in 1982, and the two winters he deployed with 45 Commando inside the Arctic Circle, Bearor had accrued a total of seven months of valuable experience in the previous three years operating under conditions of extreme cold. Little did he realize that it was this experience that would soon become the pretext for his next three-year assignment. When he reported to the G-1 at Quantico, Captain Bearor already had in hand orders slating him to be an instructor at The Basic School. A quarter of a century later, Bearor could still vividly recall the day he reported for duty at Quantico:

Courtesy of MGen Harry W. Jenkins Jr.

An M198 155mm howitzer of 1st Battalion, 10th Marines emplaced for firing during Exercise Cold Winter. White camouflage netting used in winter terrain to conceal the howitzer from enemy aircraft and chains on the tires.

> Despite my protests, the G-1 seemed determined to assign me to the Development Center, a place I had never heard of. I politely excused myself, told her I was not checking in, and that I would return tomorrow. I proceeded to call everyone I knew to find out what the Development Center was and what it was I was going to do there. What I found out was that the Director, Brigadier General Robert F. "Bob" Milligan, was looking for a company-grade officer with cold-weather experience to take over the mountain and cold-weather project that had been languishing since the retirement of the previous billet holder six months before. So, very shortly I found myself the Cold Weather Combat Clothing and Equipment officer at the Development Center. Brigadier General Milligan had been the commanding officer of 2d Marine Regiment[*] and had first-hand knowledge of the woeful state of our cold-weather clothing and equipment inventory. He wanted it fixed, now.[210]

What Bearor found was a nascent program still struggling to get off the ground. With the Army's help, it had produced prototypes of first-generation

extreme cold-weather clothing based on synthetic materials, for operational tests and evaluation. This included outer garments of waterproof Gore-Tex fabrics. But that, as Bearor, remembers, was just about the extent of the entire program.

Over the next three years, Bearor would spend much of his time at MWTC gathering information and using members of the training centers schools to test and evaluate clothing and equipment. The insights he gained from these visits, along with the personal contacts he made with members of the 2d Marine Regiment and the 4th MAB staff proved invaluable as the clothing and equipment program was sped up and expanded. In addition, the Development Center started to host regular conferences and coordination meetings at MWTC with representatives of the U.S. Army operating forces from Alaska, the Army Natick Laboratory, and Special Operations Forces. Canadian, British, Dutch, and Norwegian representatives were also frequent participants at these meetings. "The more we learned the better our efforts to improve the Marines' individual kit, which now included the water repellent Nomex underwear," remembers Bearor. Moreover, the Marine Forces Atlantic commanders, Lieutenant Generals Alfred M. "Al" Gray Jr., and Ernest T. "Ernie" Cook, 4th MAB commanders Brigadier Generals Carl Mundy Jr., and Matthew P. "Matt" Caulfield, and 2d Marine Regiment commanders Colonels Harry W. Jenkins Jr., and Michael J. "Mike" Byron were all intensely engaged and supportive in moving the cold-weather and equipment program forward as rapidly as possible. "Through these combined efforts," said Bearor, "we improved every piece of cold-weather clothing in the Corps inventory while at the same time taking 35 pounds off

---

[*] May 1982-May 1983

the back of the individual Marine."[211]

Efforts to equip Marine forces, as well as clothe them, also proved successful. For several years, Marine ground forces had wanted a tracked vehicle, such as the Swedish built Volvo BV-202 and its successor the BV-206, to enhance moving troops and supplies in deep snow. These were the vehicles that were commonly used by the Norwegian and British combat formations during winter exercises in northern Norway. Before Fiscal Year 1985 funds ran out, the Marine Corps was able to make an initial purchase of what would later become hundreds of BV 206s. The vast majority of these vehicles were stored with the prepositioned stocks of equipment being placed in central Norway; but approximately 20 were also directly delivered to MWTC in the early months of 1986. Once there, they replaced the aging Thiokol snow-cats and were put into use of driver training and to support both the formal schools and winter mountain operations training. Other equipment improvements included a new metal cross-country ski to replace the old 1943, high-maintenance Northland hickory skis; and an entirely new load-bearing system of lightweight packs of the latest design. Thus by the time Bearor left the Development Center in 1988, all of this new cold-weather clothing and equipment was in the process of being stocked in the Marine Corps' three Marine expeditionary forces training allowance pools, with priority going to II MEF.[212]

Land Prepositioning in Norway

Up until Exercise Cold Winter 1985, the 4th MAB had arrived in Norway by traditional amphibious shipping. For years planners on both side of the Atlantic had been acutely aware of the major flaw of this plan. In the event of hostilities with the Soviet Bloc, by the time the Marine reinforcing formations arrived, the enemy might have already seized control of the strategic northern airfields. If, however, they could arrive by aircraft instead, with most of their heavy equipment and ammunition already pre-staged, they could rapidly reinforce Norway, eliminate the need for scarce amphibious shipping, and realize an 80 percent reduction in the amount of airlift required.

As early as 1976, the Norwegian government had begun pushing for negotiations on the prepositioning of equipment in Norway. But it would take five years of give and take discussions as to where these stocks would be located and whether "all-weather" Marine aircraft would be included in the task organization before an agreement could be worked out. Under the working terms of reference, the government of Norway was adamant that the Marine

brigade's equipment should be stored in the vicinity of Trondheim. The fact that this was some 400 miles south of the brigade's expected area of employment became a major sticking point for Marine planners. Reluctantly however, the Marine Corps finally accepted this location and on 16 January 1981 at a ceremony in the Pentagon, representatives of both nations signed a draft Memorandum of Understanding Governing Pre-stockages and Reinforcement of Norway. [213]

In October 1982, the storage agreement was completed, providing for 30 days of supplies and enough equipment for a Marine brigade of up to 13,000 troops and 155 aircraft—now designated the Norway Airlanded Marine amphibious brigade. In describing the principal features of pre-positioned stocks in Norway, Dr. Crist has noted:

> The equipment was tailor made for operating in the confines of north Norway. No tanks were included, but it did have an artillery battalion, engineer equipment, and Swedish-built over-the-snow vehicles, and a large number of infantry antitank weapons. All the equipment needed to fight, except the men and communications gear, would be ready and waiting in climatically controlled caves, hollowed out into the sides of a mountain. The first of the equipment began arriving in November and was placed in old World War II German bunkers until the first pre-positioning facility could be completed in 1985.[214]

The plan for airlifting the brigade was simple in theory, but difficult in execution. It involved deploying the Marines by chartered aircraft to airfields in north Norway, while Norwegian "Ro/Ro" (roll on, roll off) ships ferried the brigade's heavy equipment and ammunition from Trondheim, north through the Norwegian Leeds to the vicinity of Bardafuss. Once men and equipment were married up, they would be incrementally employed north and east to their battle positions. The plan, however, was fraught with a host of "what ifs," any one of which carried the potential for throwing the entire scheme into a logistical nightmare.

Therefore, a number of steps were taken to ensure that there would be a smooth logistical flow between an arriving Marine combat formation and the equipment earmarked for its use. For example, the climate-controlled caves where the preloaded vehicles were permanently stored were especially designed to allow easy access to a specific organization's equipment, no matter when that unit may arrive. Moreover, the Center for Naval Analysis was

Colonel John Stennick, Commanding Officer, Mountain Warfare Training Center, 1985-1988, on one of the several snowmobiles used at the time.

contracted to develop a detailed model for the movement of the air-landed Marine amphibious brigade from arrival to the movement of its combat positions. Two years in the making, the model examined every aspect of movement from aircraft off-load rates, how long it would take to move to assembly areas, to even where hot food would be provided to the troops along the route. This model was rigorously tested beginning with the first exercise using prepositioned equipment in February 1985, and was further refined and updated during exercises over the next several years.[215]

In the meantime, by the mid-1980s, U.S. Atlantic Fleet's forward maritime strategy of aggressively deploying carrier strike forces off the coast of Norway had also become a reality. As a major component of this strategy, Marine air-ground task forces from II MAF were now participating annually in two major combined exercises on NATO's northern flank. In September the 4th MAB would deploy in ships and conduct amphibious operations, usually in central Norway. Then in late February and early March the Norway air-landed Marine amphibious brigade (also 4th MAB and later 4th MEB) would take part in an AFNorth combined winter exercise, usually conducted in the north. Therefore, to add a little more weight and strength to the growing U.S. Marine Corps commitment to the region, beginning in 1985 the commander of Allied Forces North was

happy to accept a permanently assigned U.S. Marine brigadier general to his NATO headquarters at Kolsas, outside of Oslo. The first Marine officer to hold this billet (Assistant Chief of Staff Operations) was the former Commanding General, 4th MAB, Brigadier General H. Norman Smith. His successor was Brigadier General Jarvis D. Lynch Jr., who served in the same billet from February 1986 to July 1987.[216]

Picking up the Pace in Operations and Modernization of the Training Center

Colonel John F. Stennick was born and raised in northern Oregon. He graduated from Oregon State University with a bachelor of science degree in wildlife management and was commissioned a second lieutenant in December of 1962. He was designated an infantry officer after graduating from The Basic School in July 1963. During the ensuing 22 years before taking command at MWTC, he served two tours of duty in the Republic of Vietnam (was seriously wounded in action during his first tour in 1965) and had held a number of important command and staff assignments within the 2d and 3d Marine Divisions; at Marine Corps Development and Education Command , Quantico, Virginia; and at MCB, Twentynine Palms California. Prior to coming to the training center he was the Head, Manpower Control Branch at Headquarters U.S. Marine Corps.[217]

Mules purchased in 1985 by Colonel Stennick and entrusted to Lieutenant Colonel Earnest Van Huss, the center executive officer. Special saddles were acquired that were suitable for mounting mortars and heavy machine guns assigned to a Marine weapons company. Select Marines received special training in packing the mules.

Even before assuming command at the training center, Colonel Stennick recognized that one of his first tasks was to heal the strained relationships that had been widening between the Mountain Warfare Training Center and the District Ranger's Office in Bridgeport. Later, he would remark:

> As I took command at MWTC, I made it clear that I had a deep and abiding appreciation for the alpine environment and intended to do right by it. Major General Robert Haebel (who was CG, MCB, Camp Pendleton and in attendance at the change of command ceremony) picked up on my remarks and subsequently backed me on funding for a full-time U.S. Forest Ranger to serve on the MWTC staff, paid for by the U.S. Marine Corps. This arrangement rapidly turned the cool attitude of the District Forest Ranger one hundred and eighty degrees into a supportive partner. To further improve this relationship, we volunteered Marine Corps assets to benefit the area by developing a "joint trash exercise" to include helicopter lifts from wilderness areas to remove old mining equipment that otherwise could not be reached without leaving a footprint in the delicate alpine meadows. An early snow in September of 1985 gave the Pickel Meadow cadre some real live survival training with 9-foot drifts of snow and won over the Forest Service when we removed junk that had been a blight for years in the adjoining wilderness area.[218]

The second initiative taken by the new base commander was the purchase of four mules and a bell mare for the purpose of reintroducing animal packing into the syllabus at MWTC. This project was entrusted to Colonel Stennick's executive officer, Lieutenant Colonel Earnest A. "Ernie" Van Huss, who was a horseman. The stable located in the flat was remodeled to accommodate the stock and special saddles, upon which to mount the mortars and heavy machine guns of a infantry weapons company were fabricated. Also, a small cadre of permanently assigned Marines from the training center was sent to Jackson Hole, Wyoming to receive instruction in animal packing at a professional packing school. A third initiative was the establishment of a course in which to train snipers in the techniques of high altitude shooting. The course was conducted in the vicinity of Hawthorne Naval Ammunition Depot.

With the base table of organization now up to strength, the first quarter of calendar year 1986 found the training center operating at full capacity. From early January to late February, MWTC hosted two winter Mountain Operation Courses for two infantry battalions of the 2d Marine Division, plus the tactical headquarters of Colonel Harry Jenkins's 2d Marine Regiment as part of their advance training for Exercise Anchor Express 1986 in Norway.* In addition, two other Mountain Operation Courses were conducted for two infantry battalions of the 1st Marine

---

* This NATO winter exercise ended up being cut short after an avalanche tragically killed a squad of ski troops from Norway's Brigade North.

Marine sniper training at the Sniper Range near Hawthorne, Nevada in the 1980s.

Division; three Mountain Leaders Courses; four Cold-Weather Survival Courses; five Cold Weather Medical Courses; a Field Grade Planning Course (a 10-day orientation course for 75 officers from the Amphibious Warfare School at Quantico, Virginia) and a series of rotating helicopter support detachments.[219]

As 1986 turned into spring and summer, MWTC personnel continue to provide the Mono County Sheriff's with a ready-made capability for emergency search and rescue operations. In May of that year some 60 Marines and Navy corpsmen assisted the Sheriff's department and the California Highway Patrol when a chartered bus returning from a Nevada gambling casino lost control heading south on Highway 395 and plunged into the fast moving waters of the West Walker River. During the next month, Staff Sergeant Kern from the Mountain Leaders Course and Petty Officer Richards from the Mountain Medicine Course were sent to Alaska to join a team of 14 U.S. Army Rangers for an ascent of Mount McKinley. Funded by the U.S. Army, the purpose of the climb was to determine the requirements for developing a high altitude rescue capability. The peak was successfully scaled and the team returned safely.

With respect to modernization of base facilities, 1986 saw the completion of the headquarters building, the fire station, the maintenance/communication

electronics shop, the bachelor officers' quarters, two water storage tanks, and finally, after the Western Division, Naval Engineering Facilities Command had corrected a number of design flaws, the bachelor enlisted quarters. Once the bachelor enlisted quarters was opened for occupancy, demolition of the Quonset huts that had housed bachelor-enlisted personnel for the past 35 years began. This allowed excavation to begin on the multi-purpose training facility/post exchange complex building. Similar to the case with the bachelor enlisted quarter, construction of the new mess hall building had also fallen behind schedule because of initial "over building" flaws in its design. Therefore, it would be a year before this facility would open. Conversion of the former officer's club (Pickel Lodge) into distinguished visitor quarters and special events reception room, a project started by Colonel Hopkins, was also completed in 1986.

During 1987 the operational tempo at Pickel Meadow continued at the same hectic pace as the previous year. Before the year would close, over 13,000 passengers would be transported and 886 tons of cargo hauled to the base in support of the training center's missions.[220] In contrast to previous years, however, Colonel Michael J. "Mike" Byron's 2d Marines tactical headquarters group and the two reinforced infantry battalions from the 2d Marine Division who came for pre-deployment winter mountain operations training in January and February arrived completely outfitted in the new light-weight Gortex/Nomex winter clothing uniforms drawn from the II MAF training allowance pool. By the following year, these uniforms would be stocked in the training allowance pool in each of the three Marine amphibious forces. The Sierra snow-pack that year was com-

Marines of 3d Battalion, 4th Marines, training in Operation Anchor Express, 1986, conducted at Brostabotn, Norway. Troops at this point were completely outfitted with Gore-Tex clothing and metal skis.

Courtesy of MGen Harry W. Jenkins Jr.

For Operation Anchor Express, 4th Marine Amphibious Brigade was flown to Norway. All major end items and equipment including BV-206s, amphibian tractors, artillery, trucks, and tentage had been prepositioned in caves in the vicinity of Narvik, Norway.

paratively lighter than normal. As a result, winter mountain operations training and the other MWTC courses of instruction had to be conducted at the higher elevations. Furthermore, because of the reactivation of the U.S. Army 10th Mountain Division at Fort Drum, New York in 1986, the 4th MAB, now commanded by Brigadier General Matthew Caulfield, shifted its last phase of winter pre-deployment training to the Army National Guard installation at Fort McCoy, Wisconsin before being air-lifted to Norway.

In March, Colonel Stennick was on hand to observe the 4th MAB's combined winter exercise in northern Norway. He returned to Oslo in the latter part of June to brief the Joint U.S. Norwegian Cold-Weather Conference on MWTC's current status and capabilities and returned just in time to host a visit to the training center by Major General Henry Beverly, Royal Marines.

Shortly after the Beverly visit, tragedy struck. At the end of June, Mountain Leaders Class 1-87 was nearing the end of its training program. Because the previous winter was unusually dry, the instructor staff determined that it was infeasible to do snow and ice climbing training at any of the usual locations close to the training center. Therefore, a one-day excursion to Mount Whitney was organized to allow this routine training and, at the same time, af-

ford the students the opportunity to ascend the highest peak in the lower 48 States. Thus during the predawn hours of July 1, 1987, some 38 students from the Summer Mountain Leader's Class boarded a base bus for the drive to the trail head west of Lone Pine, California. The 22-mile one-day trek up and down the windswept 14,000-plus foot peak proved as challenging a test as the students had been led to believe. The peak was successfully summited, however, and all students and instructors made it back to the trailhead before dark. Kurtis P. "Kurt" Wheeler, one of several NROTC Midshipmen who was a student in the class, relates what happened next:

The entire class of junior officers, staff noncommissioned officers, and NROTC midshipmen boarded the bus at dusk and most fell asleep immediately after such a long grueling day. The instructors boarded a 12-passenger van and began to lead the way down the switched-backed mountain road. Like most of my classmates, I leaned forward onto the daypack on my lap and prepared to get some shut-eye. Just minutes into the trip I recall hearing the bus driver express alarm. He seemed to be attempting to pump the brakes. We were noticeably accelerating down the mountain

Aerial photo of the modernized Mountain Warfare Training Center in 1986. At the far right, the new bachelor enlisted quarters are almost ready for occupancy. The headquarters building and the bachelor officer quarters at the top of the picture have been completed.

and soon shot past the van in front of us. The driver struggled valiantly to keep the bus under control but it was clearly a losing battle. We seemed to be shifting to two wheels with each gut-wrenching curve on the S-shaped mountain road. Gravity won out and I can vividly recall seeing the world turn on its side as the swath of desert lit up by the headlights shifted before us. Time seemed to slow down as we veered off the road and rotated 90 degrees. There was incredible violence as we hit the rocky desert ground. The side of the bus opened up like a tin can and the windows immediately smashed. I can still feel the sensation of the sand, rocks and broken glass rushing past my head and hands. In a few seconds it was over. The bus lay still and it was totally silent. No one screamed or cried out. The next hour was a blur as instructors (who had been safe in the van) and able bodied classmates worked to evacuate the wounded from the bus. Someone contacted emergency services and the area soon swarmed with rescue personnel.

Of the 38 students who were on the bus, two were killed, 19 were hospitalized and eight, including Midshipman Wheeler, miraculously walked away with virtually no injuries. The remainder were treated and released. Twenty-two years after the accident,

Wheeler would still painfully remember it as "a tragic end to what I still consider one of the best months of my life-in the beautiful Sierra Nevada Mountains."[221]

In the spring of 1987, the mess hall was officially dedicated and began serving permanent personnel, students and battalions there for field training. This permitted the old mess hall to be demolished and allowed construction to begin on the new medical/dental clinic. Construction was also begun on a new motor transport building and a new ski lift located at the higher elevations of upper Wolf Creek Canyon.

In addition to meeting the demands of a full schedule and overseeing the flurry of activity taking place at the training center, at the request of Headquarters U.S. Marine Corps, Colonel Stennick was also tasked to send a field-grade officer to Chile to observe Chilean Marines conduct mountain operations in the Andes. An added request asked that he send a cadre of noncommissioned officers to Columbia to instruct Drug Enforcement Agents in mountaineering skills.[222]

In the summer of 1988, the training center underwent a number of personnel changes. On 1 July, Colonel Stennick turned over the reins of command to his executive officer, Lieutenant Colonel William Healy, and proceeded to his next duty station at Camp Pendleton. It had been a busy three years and much had been accomplished. During the last months of his tenure the new ski lift had become operational in time for use by the 2d Marine Division battalions, which came for winter mountain operations training in January and February 1988. The training facility post exchange complex and the new Medical and Dental building were both completed and accepted for occupancy on 12 April and an addition was being made to the commanding officer's quarters. The contract for Milcon Project P-954 Chapel and Recreation Center was in the process of being awarded. When these two structures were completed in the next year, it would mean that the Master Plan had been essentially built out. In addition to an exchange of Commanders, Major James "Jim" Snell, the S-3, also departed on 1 July. His relief was Major Rodney C. "Rod" Richardson, who reported to the training center after completing a two-year exchange tour with the Royal Marines. During July, General Alfred M. Gray Jr., 29th Commandant of the Marine Corps, paid a visit to the training center. Everything he saw from training programs to people to the new base facilities impressed him. The Commandant praised the MWTC staff for all of its efforts, but in particular for substantially improving the capability of Marine forces to fight and win under arctic conditions.[223]

Reaching the High Water Mark

Colonel Phillip E. Tucker assumed command of the MWTC on 18 August 1988. An Alabambian by birth, he graduated from the Virginia Military Institute with honors in 1964 and accepted a regular commission in the Marine Corps. As a lieutenant colonel, Tucker had served for a year in the Republic of Korea (ROK) as the emergency action officer with the ROK U.S. Joint Forces Command. After graduating from the National War College in 1985, he served three years in Hawaii. Prior to being assigned to MWTC, Tucker was the Fleet Marine Officer, U.S. Pacific Fleet, Pearl Harbor.[224]

Also in the summer of 1988 at another ceremony, this one at Camp Lejeune, North Carolina, Colonel John W. Ripley relieved Colonel Mike Byron and assumed command of the 2d Marine Regiment. Ripley was a recognized combat leader who had distinguished himself by almost single-handedly destroying the bridge at Dong Ha during the North Vietnamese Army Easter Offensive in the Republic of Vietnam, thereby stopping an enemy tank attack. Ripley had also served a two-year exchange tour with the Royal Marines. The experience had given

Marines of the 2d Marine Regiment are being instructed in downhill ski techniques at the new ski lift constructed in upper Wolf Creek Canyon. The ski lift was completed in January 1988.

Courtesy MWTC

Courtesy MWTC

Marines training at Pickel Meadow, late 1980s, outfitted with the new Gore-Tex clothing and tentage.

him a keen appreciation for conducting combat operations in deep snow and extreme cold. By now, though, Ripley was not the only cold-weather warrior in the regiment. For the past year it had been the policy of the 2d Marine Division to purposely staff battalions of the 2d Marines with officers and staff noncommissioned officers who had extensive experience in cold-weather operations. This included anyone who was a former instructor, a graduate of a Mountain Leadership Course at MWTC, an exchange officer with the Royal Marines, or anyone who could claim down-hill or cross-country ski ex-

Colonel John W. Ripley, here in Vietnam, was also a veteran of service in Northern Europe. His regiment used the MWTC to prepare for assignment to Norway.

Marine Corps History Division

perience. As early as December, therefore, the troops who were scheduled to deploy to north Norway as part of Ripley's regiment in March, could already be seen practicing their cross-country ski techniques on roller blades with ski poles around Camp Lejeune, North Carolina's broad avenues.[225]

On 4 February 1989, Ripley's tactical headquarters group and his 2d Battalion, 2d Marines, completed their four weeks of cold-weather training at Pickel Meadow and returned to Camp Lejeune for a week of rest. Meanwhile, Brigadier General Matthew P. Caulfield's 4th MEB* was in the process of deploying to Fort McCoy, Wisconsin for Exercise Alpine Warrior. One Reserve infantry battalion had already arrived at McCoy and was undergoing cross-country ski and snowshoe training administered by a mobile training team of instructors from MWTC. As each major component of the MEB arrived from Camp Lejeune or Cherry Point, it was quickly integrated into an air-ground brigade, eventually numbering some 9,000 Marines and sailors. After two more weeks of unit training, Alpine Warrior concluded with a three-day force-on-force tactical field exercise. The Tactical Exercise Control Group then conducted a rigorous critique, emphasizing both shortcomings and strengths that were observed. On the 25th of February, the troops began embarking aircraft for the flight to Norway.[226]

Among the U.S. observers who were on hand during the opening phase of Exercise Cold Winter

---

* In 1988 CMC Al Gray directed that the word "Expeditionary" vice "Amphibious" be reinstituted when referring to Marine air-ground forces.

89 in Norway was Lieutenant General Carl Mundy Jr., a former commander of both the 2d Marines and the 4th MEB and now the Assistant Chief of Staff, Plans and Operations at Headquarters U.S. Marine Corps. Accompanying him on the same plane was the Commanding General, 2d Marine Division. Witnessing the components of the 4th MEB arrived by air and quickly marry up with pre-staged equipment and then move off toward their battle positions was an impressive sight. Well outfitted in their new winter uniforms and lightweight equipment, the troops looked fit and eager to give a good account of themselves as they prepared to take on the British and Norwegian units playing the role of the opposing force. While comparing notes during their flight back to Washington, both generals were of the same opinion that with respect to the Norwegian contingency, everything had at last seemed to come together. They also agreed that most, if not all, of the major deficiencies that had severely reduced the mobility and combat effectiveness of U.S. Marine forces to operate in deep snow and extreme cold over the past decade, had either been solved or close to resolution.[227]

The remainder of 1989 would prove to be another banner year at the training center. In addition to the instruction provided by the mobile unit training team at Fort McCoy, almost 11,000 Marines underwent training at MWTC. In April, HQMC approved a request to add an additional 15 Hägglunds BV-206 vehicles to the training center's inventory, with a projected delivery date of September

Marine training with M249 5.56mm squad automatic weapon in the small-arms range at Wolf Creek Canyon, late 1980s.

Courtesy MWTC

1990. For FY-1990, Congress authorized 2.3 million dollars for minor repair and improvements of the base; sufficient funds for 33 additional houses to be constructed at the Topaz base housing facility, and eight million dollars for FY 1991 for billeting students and battalions at the lower base camp. And in August, construction was begun on a new equipment support facility, also located in the lower base camp.[228]

During May of 1989 an eight-man team from MWTC traveled to Denali Park in Alaska to make an ascent of Mount McKinley's 20,320-foot peak. This was the first Marine sponsored assault led by the S-3, Major Rodney "Rod" Richardson.* "Our mission involved testing some of the new clothing and equipment that had been developed for use in extreme cold-weather," recalled Denhoff 20 years later. "We also tested medications like Diamox, which was supposed to help fight high altitude cerebral edema."[229]

U.S. Army aircraft from Fort Wainwright flew the team to the 14,000-foot level, where the U.S. Army had established a camp to conduct tests and experiments. After spending several days acclimatizing, the party began its ascent to higher elevations. However, Richardson and Varmette soon contracted acute mountain sickness and were forced to retreat back to the Army base camp at 14,000 feet.** The six remaining members of the party then moved to 17,200 feet to stage for an assault on the summit. Once there, a storm kept them tent-bound at that level for several days before they could proceed and reach the summit. When the team descended back to the 14,000-foot base camp, they were asked to help recover the bodies of three British climbers who had fallen to their death.[230]

In November of 1989, the Berlin Wall, one of the major symbols of the Cold War, came crashing down. Thereafter, the U.S.S.R. began to disintegrate from within. Ironically, these events took place just as Marine capabilities to wage a successful campaign in north Norway were reaching their peak. Then in August 1990, Iraq invaded Kuwait. As a result, a substantial number of NATO and U.S. forces were shifted to the Persian Gulf to conduct Operation Desert Shield and Desert Storm. As a conse-

---

* The team included Capts Thomas M. "Tom" Varmette and Timothy C. "Tim" Wells, Lt Gregg McAninch, MC, USN, Royal Marine Color Sgt Martin Wilkin, SSgts Alejandro G. Bello and Richard N. Denhoff, and Sgt Wesley D. Clark. (Col Wells would later return to MWTC as its commanding officer 2005-2006).
** In June of the following year (1990) Maj Richardson led a second assault on McKinley accompanied by MWTC members: Capt Fargrave, and Sgts Sommers and Estes. The team successfully reached the peak and returned safely.

Courtesy MWTC

Swedish-built Hägglunds BV-206, an extremely useful over-snow vehicle for moving troops and supplies. The Mountain Warfare Training Center acquired a handful of these in 1986, and an additional 15 in 1990.

quence, exercises at MWTC and Norway were suspended for the coming year.

Dr. Crist's paper concluded with the following observation:

> While the entire debate over the defense of NATO's northern flank may be reduced to a footnote of the Cold War, it provided some

At right, Major Rodney Richardson, MWTC Operations Officer, 1988-1990.

Courtesy MWTC

lasting effects on the Marine Corps. It established the Marines as the premier service within the DOD in cold-weather operations, providing invaluable training for all the armed forces in an area where few had looked since the early 1950s. In a purely parochial view, the Marines obtained an entire brigade's worth of equipment over and above what was required in the Fleet Marines; with the funding provided by supplemental appropriations. This does not include the additional money obtained to purchase new Gortex and other cold-weather clothing, replacing those designed three decades earlier.

The use of the Marines in northern Europe provided valuable lessons on how the Marine Corps can be used to support the fleet in the littorals. By using the Marines to secure airfields, which served to supplement carrier aircraft, while not a new concept, added a new dimension to how NATO could fight the Soviets in confined waters of the Norwegian Sea. The ability to alter the organization of the marine amphibious brigade, was instrumental in supporting the naval campaign, be it against the Soviet fleet or attacking the flank of the Soviet Army in Germany. For the Marine Corps specifically, deployments to Norway offered the chance to find solutions to problem the other were slow in seeing. In the process this afforded the opportunity for the Marine Corps to, once again, provide an example of its ability to innovate and adapt to changing defense concerns.[231]

Although the U.S. Marines would continue to exercise in Norway with small-size forces up through the early 1990s, these were of lesser imperative and urgency than those of the previous decade. As the Marine Corps moved on to other more pressing contingencies in the 1990s, so too would the leaders at MWTC have to examine what new tasks and missions might now come their way.

Chapter 12

The 1990s: A Post-Cold War World

The influence of mountains on the conduct of war is very great; the subject, therefore, is very important for study.
-Carl von Clausewitz, On War, *Book V*

Introduction

Ever since Hannibal led his Carthaginian army over the Alps to invade the heart of the Roman Empire in 218 BC, generals have sought to overcome or to exploit mountainous terrain in pursuit of military victory. The tactical and logistical considerations for mountain warfare have evolved over time—and continue to evolve. But many of the solutions to the challenges associated with mountain operations remain timeless. Hannibal, for example, utilized 37 war elephants to great effect. Today's Marines train with pack mules at the Marine Corps Mountain Warfare Training Center. In fact, the March 2009 *Marine Corps Gazette* featured a Marine and a Bridgeport pack mule on its cover. Despite some of the timeless aspects of mountain warfare, however, the Marine Corps Mountain Warfare Training Center spent much of the 1990s trying to define its continued relevance and continued mission in the immediate post-Cold War era. The Mountain Warfare Training Center (MWTC) had its origins in the early days of the Cold War, and had thrived and grown in its demonstrated ability to prepare Marines for combat against Communist aggression in Korea and operations on NATO's (North Atlantic Treaty Organization) northern flank in Norway. The fall of the Berlin Wall in 1989, followed by the disintegration of the Soviet Union in 1991, marked the end of that defining conflict, and left the U.S. military as well as the MWTC adjusting to a new world order.

Operation Desert Storm, another defining event for the U.S. military, demonstrated the continued utility of the Marine aircraft group task force. However, following an overwhelming victory in the first Persian Gulf Conflict, the United States accelerated a drawdown of its military forces that affected every branch of military service—and every base, including Marine Corps Mountain Warfare Training Center, Bridgeport. Still, it would take a while for American and NATO planners to redirect their focus from a threat that had been greatly diminished. For example, the Marine Mountain Warfare Training Center provided a mobile training team to support Operation Battle Griffin in March of 1991—a NATO oper-

ation in northern Norway that focused on how to counter an invasion of that Scandinavian country by Soviet forces above the Arctic Circle. Marine Corps—and MWTC—support for NATO operations in Norway would continue for several more years, despite the reduced threat in that potential theater of operations.

Continuing Operations While Dealing with Future Uncertainties

With the Pentagon cutting budgets and personnel while also eliminating bases, the Marine Corps had to contend with the Defense Base Closure and Realignment Commission. Eventually, a number of Marine facilities and bases would be closed, including major installations such as the air station at El Toro, California. Even though 1991 marked the 40th Anniversary of the MWTC at Pickel Meadow, the Corps would have to spend considerable time throughout the 1990s making the case as to why the Bridgeport base was still needed.

In the meantime, mountain and cold-weather training would continue. With the preponderance of Marine forces having been deployed with two Marine expeditionary forces during Operations Desert Shield and Desert Storm, much unit training had been cancelled at Pickel Meadow during 1990-1991. With the return of these units to the United States, however, activity at MWTC increased. Regular unit training resumed and specialized courses were again filled with students. As the training tempo increased, the dining facility served over 270,000 meals in 1992. The 3d Battalion, 6th Marines, and 2d Marine Division headquarters element arrived on 11 January 1993 to spend over a month in pre-deployment cold-weather training in preparation for Operation Battle Griffin in Norway in March. Not only Marines, but service members from other branches and other countries would journey to northern California and make the final four-mile drive up Route 108 to the mile-high Pickel Meadow base camp and its unique training opportunities. In August 1991, for example, U.S. Navy SEALs arrived at Pickel Meadow for specialized training. In October 1995, 30 French Legionnaires arrived for two weeks of mountain training, which continued a Marine Corps Mountain Warfare Training Center tradition of hosting military training for foreign service members.[232]

High-level officers exhibited an interest in the

Small parties of Mountain Warfare Training Center personnel often made Mount McKinley expeditions in the 1980s and 1990s. From left to right are Lieutenant Commander Sitler, USN (MC); Captain Malay; Staff Sergeant Miller, and Sergeant Lamar at the summit in 1992.

base. In July 1991, Major General J. Michael Myatt (commander of 1st Marine Division in Operation Desert Storm) conducted a Commander's Conference at MWTC. The base additionally hosted numerous visits from assorted very important persons, including General Carl Mundy, Commandant of the Marine Corps, on 18 October 1993. The following month, the base hosted Vice Air Marshal Dodworth of the British Royal Marines and Commander Paranhos of the Brazilian Marine Corps.[233]

Pickel Meadow continued also to serve as a focal point for the gathering and dissemination of knowledge on cold-weather and mountain warfare. Some of this involved research—in January and February 1993, 3d Battalion, 2d Marines, spent six weeks testing new field gear, including the North Face Tent, extended wear gloves, the Minnesota sled, ski march boots, and the vector pack. In October, four MWTC survival instructors attended the Canadian Forces Survival Training School at Edmonton, Al-

berta. In June 1994, Marine Corps Mountain Warfare Training Center sent a six-member Mount McKinley expedition team to Alaska. This group of instructors would be testing new equipment and techniques on the 20,000 foot plus mountain also known as Denali, North America's highest peak. Three members would successfully summit the mountain on 23 June. These were typical examples of how Pickel Meadow personnel might be deployed—anywhere from Norway to Alaska—in the interest of professional development in the areas of cold-weather or mountain warfare training. The base also continued its longstanding tradition of providing considerable support and a military presence at community functions. MWTC provided color guards, mule teams, and static displays at no less than 21 civic events during 1993.[234]

A succession of able base commanders and dedicated staff continued to oversee infrastructure improvements and challenging training at MWTC. On

31 July 1991, Colonel Russell W. Schumacher Jr., assumed command of the base from Colonel Phillip E. Tucker. After three years of supervising training and growth of the base, Schumacher turned command over to Colonel Raymond L. "Skip" Polak in June 1994.[235] Infrastructure improvements continued through 1995. The mess hall repair project was completed in April, which provided upgrades to the facility at a final cost of $447,000. Construction of the Project 9-797 Training Billeting Support Facilities was completed on 9 August at a final cost of $10,027,000. This project added 91,484 square feet of facility space to Marine Warfare Training Center—a 75 percent increase.[236]

On 9 July 1996 Colonel Polak turned the command over to Colonel Paul W. O'Toole Jr. (Two days later three Marines were struck by lightning on the mountaintop known as 9494.[237] A successful medical evacuation operation rescued all three, but the incident was another reminder of the hazards of training in the mountain environment—even in the summer.) Under Colonel O'Toole's watch, infrastructure and base activities expanded. For example, the year 1996 was a busy time for religious activities at MWTC. A base chapel had earlier been constructed to replace the original structure. This building matched the design of most of the newer buildings, as the older structures and Quonset huts which marked the older camp gradually disappeared. On 4 February, Catholic mass was reinstated at the chapel. From 12-13 September the chapel held the first base-wide Relationship Enhancement Program for married personnel. Then, on 24 December, the annual Christmas Eve Ecumenical Candlelight Service provided the base with a spiritual glow.[238]

In 1997, Colonel O'Toole and base personnel had to make some short-term adjustments when sections of Highway 395 were destroyed by flooding—cutting off MWTC from points north.[239] This was yet another reminder about the fragility of man-made structures in that harsh, mountain environment. Air operations remained integral to base operations as they had been since its first 1951-1952 winter when transport planes dropped food and supplies to Marines cut off in Pickel Meadow by extraordinary snowfall. In 1997, Helicopter Marine Medium 466 deployed to Bridgeport to provide CH-46 helicopter support for winter mountain operations from 27 January through 24 March. The CH-46 unit included Captain Sarah M. Deal, the Marine Corps first female naval aviator.[240]

Trapper Ted's Full Moon Saloon was completely painted and decorated.[241] While the new facility lacked the informal, rustic charm of its predecessor, which was built by Marines and still stands above the base fishing hole, the current club features panoramic views of mountain vistas that are unmatched by any other U.S. Marine Corps club. The facility provided quality service for Pickel Meadow patrons, even though not recognized as the Marine Corps Best Small Club for several years running.

At the end of 1998, the MWTC personnel report featured 13 Marine officers and 207 enlisted, as well as five naval officers and 17 enlisted sailors. These numbers were generally consistent with staffing levels throughout most of the decade. Seventeen Navy Achievement Medals were awarded during the course of the year and there was only one court martial.[242]

The medical clinic continued to upgrade its facility and assigned naval personnel continued professional education on and off base during the course of the year. The clinic specialized in treating the injuries and conditions peculiar to a mountainous environment. For example, nine patient casualties were treated in January 1998. All were the result of severe cold and exposure.[243] The Command Education Program also continued to grow as classes were established on base and other courses were made available via the internet. The Mountain Warfare Training Center established academic affiliations with Barstow College and Central Texas College.[244] The base exchange continued to provide service to the MWTC community, and in addition to special monthly sales also sponsored a fishing sale, a garden and outdoor sale, a physical training sale, a sportsman's sale, and a toy sale.[245]

Demonstrating MWTC Value During Peacetime

Despite all the good things happening on board Marine Corps Mountain Warfare Training Center, its leaders were very much aware of base realignment and closure (BRAC) and the need to raise awareness about the value of the base. One of the commanders attuned to this issue was Colonel Polak, who served as base commander from 1994 to 1996. A graduate of the University of Wisconsin, Polak was no stranger to cold weather. He later served as commanding officer at Marine Barracks, Adak, Alaska. Earlier he had also served as an artillery officer during the Vietnam conflict.

Polak was serving as an instructor at the Command and Staff School in Quantico, Virginia, when he received a telephone call from his monitor, Colonel James T. Conway (later the 34th Marine Corps Commandant.) "Have I got a deal for you," said Conway to Polak.[246] "Colonel Conway told me about the CO's position at Bridgeport," recalled Polak. "I'd been up there to go hunting in the 80s with John Stennick [MWTC commanding officer from 1985-1988]. I was intrigued."[247] Polak remembered, "It was a quiet time, post-Desert Storm. We worked on a five-year plan, put in streetlights, did barracks improvements, upgraded sewage treatment, and improved the roads. We also developed a 'Search and Rescue' capability to help civilian authorities when required. We helped save some hikers, including a guy who broke his back."[248]

Polak connected well with local neighbors and ranchers and also spent considerable time mollifying Forest Service officials, with whom good relations were a priority, as MWTC-Bridgeport operates on leased Forest Service land. Although live fire has always been a challenge to arrange for Mountain Warfare Training Center personnel, Polak did set up a winter live fire "range" in Sonora Pass, featuring a snowmobile towing a target across a 100 meter kill zone. And yet despite all these positive developments, Polak was always quite aware of BRAC and its possible implications for MWTC. "We knew we needed to make a case for the base," said Polak. "While the Korean scenario has always been with us, with the reduction of the Norway threat, people were asking reasonable questions as to whether we needed to invest in Bridgeport." Polak felt that there was intangible value to training at a base like Pickel Meadow. "It's a great place for leadership assessment," he explained. "You learn about yourself and you learn about leadership. The cold, the mountains, and the altitude all combine to create real physical and emotional stress that can't be replicated elsewhere."[249]

The challenge for Polak and his successors, Colonel O'Toole and Colonel Robert W. Strahan—at least until 2001—was to make the case for the base's existence, so that the excellent training occurring there could continue, both for U.S. Marines and for their allies. As an example of this training, on 8 January 1997, the Winter Mountain Leaders Course convened with 56 students. Included in the class were six U.S. Army Special Forces personnel. The group also included five foreigners—two noncommissioned officers from France, two noncommissioned officers from formerly Communist Croatia, and one officer from Kyrgyzstan. The presence of the latter—coming from a former Soviet Union Republic—was a reminder that the Cold War was indeed over.[250]

A second course followed the one that convened in January. Other MWTC courses of instruction offered in 1997 included four cold-weather survival courses, five cold-weather medicine courses, three mountain survival courses, four wilderness medicine courses, two summer mountain leader courses,

one winter and one summer instructor qualification course. This menu of specialized Cold Weather and Mountain Warfare Courses is typical of what was offered at MWTC throughout the 1990s. Additionally, very important persons and foreign visitors continued to come to review the Pickel Meadow experience. On 3 March, a company from the Canadian Army's Princess Patricia's Battalion arrived for a three week training package. (Five years later this unit would later serve alongside American forces in Afghanistan.) On 17 June, the commanding officer of the 12th Austrian Mountain Regiment, Colonel Steinwender toured MWTC.[251]

Colonel Strahan took over commanding officer duties from Colonel O'Toole on 25 August 1999, and he too, along with his staff, gave serious thought to how Marine Corps Mountain Warfare Training Center could best serve the interests of the Marine Corps. In a March 2001 article in the *Marine Corps Gazette*, Strahan both outlined his thinking and invited input from others around the Corps. Strahan first reiterated MWTC's mission statement:

The wartime origins of the Mountain Warfare Training Center come bull circle with the deployement of Marines as part of Operation Enduring Freedom in Afghanistan. Lieutenant Colonel Mike Moffett, co-author, was present as a field historian documenting the centers continued value in training Marines for harsh climates.

Courtesy of author

Courtesy of author

Retired Major General Harry Jenkins Jr., Colonel John Guy, and Major General Orlo K. Steele, at the 50th Anniversary Celebration at the Mountain Warfare Training Center on 6 September 2001.

"To prepare Marines and sailors to develop doctrine and to test equipment for MAGTF operations in mountainous and cold-weather environments."[252] Strahan and his staff believed that the means to accomplishing this mission included unit training, individual training, mobile training teams, equipment evaluation, and authorship of doctrinal publications.

In terms of unit training, Strahan noted that, traditionally, seven Active and two Reserve battalions trained at Pickel Meadow every year. He invited his readers, however, to ask what kinds of units should train there, and at what point in their "life cycle" or "training, exercise, and employment plan." He suggested his own answers, of course, and also demanded consideration of what the purpose of MWTC training actually was:

> Is it MAGTF operations in a mountainous/cold-weather environment? Is it unit cohesion training in a stressful environment? Is it small unit leadership? "Is it adventure training (skiing and mountain climbing)? We think it should be MAGTF operations, with the other things being natural byproducts of the environment.[253]

As part of accomplishing this mission, Colonel Strahan described the desired progress of unit training, including "the neglected skill [of] logistics training in mountains and cold weather . . . We need to be more realistic about moving rolling stock, casualties, ammo, water, and chow by using organic equipment [in such environments]."[254] In terms of individual training, which Strahan considered a "supporting attack" to the primary mission, he advertised the Mountain Leader's Course, the Staff Officer Cold Weather Orientation Course, Wilderness Cold Weather Medicine Course, and the Survival Course. Other "supporting attacks" included the training of mobile training teams which could subsequently train units that did not or could not deploy to Marine Corps Mountain Warfare Training Center as well as the evaluation of equipment for the Warfighting Laboratory or the Marine Corps Systems Command. Another supporting effort was the six publications in the *Marine Corps Warfighting Publications* 3-35 series authored by MWTC. Strahan stressed that those operating forces that deployed to cold-weather exercises and to the mountains of Korea played or should play, a vital

John Marjanov

Throughout its first half century, the Mountain Warfare Training Center could usually claim more than its fair share of certified Marine "characters" serving among its ranks. Arguably however, perhaps none was quite as colorful, or became more legendary than did the unconventional and rather irascible Master Gunnery Sergeant John Marjanov.

John was born and raised in Pittsburgh, Pennsylvania. His formal schooling did not go beyond the 8th grade. He enlisted in the U.S. Navy in 1944 and served in a SeaBee Construction Battalion in the Pacific and Shanghai, China until his discharge in May of 1946. Thereafter, he immediately enlisted in the U.S. Army Air Corps; following his discharge from the Air Corps in July of 1949, he enlisted in the Marine Corps and after completing recruit training at Parris Island, Marjanov started a 25-year career a Marine combat engineer.

John was a staff sergeant in a replacement draft preparing for duty in Korea in 1952 when he first underwent training at Pickel Meadow under the Cold Weather Battalion. In 1953, while assigned to the 1st Shore Party Battalion, 1st Marine Division in Korea, John was a dozer operator in support of British Commonwealth Forces when he was nominated to receive the British Empire Medal. This award was presented to him at the British Embassy in Washington D.C., in 1955. Although knighthood was never part of this award, nevertheless, from that point on, to his fellow staff noncommissioned officers he was always: "Sir John."

John was a bachelor gunnery sergeant serving with the 7th Engineer Battalion at Camp Pendleton in 1964 when he submitted a personnel request to be assigned to MWTC. This was granted and in December he became the chief of the heavy equipment section. In June of 1966, as the training center began its drawdown toward caretaker status, Marjanov was transferred to Republic of Vietnam where he served continuously for the next two years. For his meritorious service as Operations Chief of the 1st Engineer Battalion and subsequently as equipment chief with the 7th Engineer Battalion, Master Sergeant Marjanov was awarded the Navy Commendation Medal with Combat "V."

Master Gunnery Sergeant Marjanov was serving at Camp Pendleton when he retired on 30 September 1974 after more than 30 years of active military service. Soon thereafter, he was hired by the California Department of Transportation as a heavy equipment repairman and assigned to work on Highway 395 corridor in the vicinity of Bridgeport, California. It was then that John took up residence at the dormant training center by simply parking his trailer behind the staff noncommissioned officers (SNCOs) Club Quonset hut. After the training center was reactivated in 1976, one of the base commanders attempted to have John and his trailer evicted. But Sergeant Major Leland D. Crawford, Sergeant Major of the Marine Corps at the time interceded in John's behalf and the trailer stayed put. Crawford also paved the way for John to apply for one of the civilian maintenance positions when it became available in the late 1970s.

As facilities at MWTC were modernized and training programs expanded in the 1980s, "Top" Marjanov's service and value to the training center rose steadily. Unofficially, he became the continuity between what was best about the old ways and how to weave them into the new. When there was a problem, Sir John would have a practical solution for fixing it. A typical story described how one of the Thiokol Trackmasters had become stuck in a snow-covered pass at the higher elevations and the rescue vehicle that was sent to snake it out ended up slipping into a ravine. It became questionable whether both vehicles could be salvaged. John appeared on the scene and through an improvised and intricate system of blocks, tackles and pulleys, he managed to extricate both vehicles.

Active participation in three wars and a host of overseas deployments to the Far East had given Master Gunnery Sergeant Marjanov more lessons in practical leadership skills than most people ever gain in a lifetime. Marjanov was kind and decent to everyone; his most enjoyable off-duty past time was cracking a few cans of beer and swapping tales with the young troops. Nightly, Sir John would "hold court" sitting in his old barber's chair down at the Motor Pool, or later at the heavy equipment repair facility at the lower base camp, answering their questions about this and that and regaling them on what it was like to "soldier" in the old Corps. Without ever claiming it, to the thousands of Marines and sailors who served at MWTC during the last two decades of the 20th century, officer and enlisted alike, retired Master Gunnery Sergeant John Marjanov was the esteemed patriarch and conscience of the command.

In October 1995, Colonel Ray Polak, the Commanding Officer, MWTC presented Master Gunnery Sergeant Marjanov with an award commemorating his 50 years of federal service.

---

role in providing "essential feedback to the publication review process."[255] Indeed, Strahan, noted, MWTC was "a clearinghouse for mountain/cold-weather issues," not only within the Marine Corps but also with the U.S. Army and allies such as Argentina, Canada, and the United Kingdom.[256] Strahan concluded that "we think the MWTC is an interesting laboratory for training and thinking about combat readiness because it operates at the confluence of individual training, unit, training, doctrinal development, and equipment evaluation." Rarely, he noted, does one "see all those things intersect in a cross-functional way at the unit level . . . . As one of the premier training centers in the Marine Corps, we want our evolution to be guided by the genuine needs of the Operating Forces. We look forward to hearing your ideas."[257]

Golden Anniversary

On Thursday, six September 2011, Colonel James M. Thomas, who on 10 August had just relieved Colonel Strahan as the commanding officer of MWTC, welcomed numerous dignitaries, special guests, former Marines and their families to Pickel Meadow to participate in the training center's 50th Anniversary celebration and open house.

Some of the guests and visitors had trained at the MWTC years before—in some cases decades earlier. Those who had not been to Bridgeport for many years remarked that while in the terrain hadn't changed much, the infrastructure sure had. "Where did all the tents go?" was an oft-heard refrain.[258] Many former Marines, particularly from the early 1950s, had never seen the base bereft of snow.

Several static displays were set up on the parade deck, which included winter operations clothing and equipment, stables operations, a communications display, and some of the specialized vehicles peculiar to a place like Pickel Meadow. The fitness center was open so that visitors could see the climbing wall and the climbing gear. Inside the multipurpose building were displays on survival operations and historical photographs. There was also a movie presentation.[259]

The open house ran from 1000 to 1400 hours. The anniversary ceremony itself commenced at 1100 hours. Speakers included: Col James M. Thomas; Major General Thomas S. Jones, Commanding General, Training and Education Command; Major General David F. Bice, Commanding General, Camp Pendleton; and Major General Orlo K. Steele, (Retired), a former staff officer and mountain leader at Pickel Meadow.[260]

The speakers reflected on the beauty of the base, as well as its history, as approximately 400 guests and visitors listened. It was noted that the base had been in a cadre status for nine years (1967-1976) and that while the country was at peace, there was a still need for what the Mountain Warfare Training Center had to offer. Reminiscences were shared, both poignant and humorous. When the ceremonies were completed, attendees mingled, or went to the mess hall.[261]

It was 6 September 2001. Five days later, on 11 September, the world would change and things would never be the same again. As had been the case 50 years earlier, Marines would soon be preparing to fight in a remote Asian land with forbidding mountains and extreme temperatures. Now, instead of Korea, the thoughts of those who would train at Pickel Meadow would focus on a different place—Afghanistan.

Epilogue

Cold Weather and Mountain Operations in the 21st Century

Our realistic training and education system will prepare Marines for complex conditions and to counter the unexpected. Our noncommissioned and junior officers will be prepared for greater responsibility in an increasingly complex environment while potentially operating in a decentralized manner.
-General James T. Conway
Commandant of the Marine Corps

Strategic Backdrop

In less than 30 days following the September 11, 2001 attacks on the United States, President Bush ordered General Tommy Franks, the commander at U.S. Central Command, to launch combat operations to eradicate the Taliban regime in Afghanistan and to destroy Osama bin Laden and his al-Qaeda network. Operation Enduring Freedom relied heavily on Afghan opposition forces known as the Northern Alliance, with substantial support from U.S. airpower, special operation forces and unconventional warfare Central Intelligence Agency operatives.[262]

By the middle of November, Taliban's forces had been driven from most of Afghanistan's larger cities. At the same time, stationed in the Arabian Sea were two Navy amphibious ready groups with the 15th and the 26th Marine Expeditionary Units (15th and 26th MEUs) with approximately 4,400 combat-ready Marines. This naval task force, designated TF 58, was under the operational control of the naval component commander of Central Command and was commanded by Brigadier General James N. Mattis, who thus became the first Marine to command a naval task force in combat. As the situation on the ground became more fluid, General Franks decided it was time to deploy this brigade-size force of Marines. On 25 November, traveling over 400 nautical miles using its sea-based helicopters, elements of the 15th MEU flew in to seize a landing strip in Afghanistan that became known as Forward Operating Base Rhino. This stunning display of flexibility and operational reach was later followed up with the 26th MEU's seizure of Kandahar Airfield on 14 December.[263] By the end of December the remnants of the Taliban army that had managed to escape entrapment, along with the al-Qaeda fighters, had been pushed back toward the Tora Bora redoubt and other strongholds near the Pakistan border.

Operation Enduring Freedom highlighted the relevance of the Mountain Warfare Training Center in ways unseen since the Korean War in the 1950s and the Norway contingency of the 1980s.

Five days after combat operations began in Afghanistan, a *San Diego Union Tribune* story published on 12 October 2001, carried the headline: "Marines . . . hone their mountaineering skills at a Marine Corps training center in the Eastern Sierras."[264] The article went on to list the various venues where U.S. armed forces conducted mountain combat training. It described training operations at Pickel Meadow and how the terrain approximated that found in Afghanistan, with 11,000-foot peaks and restricted lines of communication.

The same issue of the *Union Tribune* also ran a feature story specific to the Mountain Warfare Training Center. A battalion from the 6th Marine Regiment from Camp Lejeune was training at Pickel Meadow and the article included quotes from several troops from the battalion.

"This would be very good training for a workup to Afghanistan," said Corporal Brandon J. Beardsley.

Colonel Jim Thomas was quoted as well:

"Since the activities of September 11th, it's a revalidation of what we've been doing here for 50 years," said the MWTC commanding officer.[265]

An Associated Press story datelined: "Bridgeport, Calif." Appeared in the *Tahoe Daily Tribune* on 16 October and described how Marines at Pickel Meadow were training hard at high altitude while thinking of Afghanistan.

"If called to go there for whatever reason, I'd go, no problem at all," said Sergeant Alan Quartararo, 26, as he prepared to slide upside-down along a 100-foot rope strung more than 60 feet above the West Walker River.[266]

In December of 2001, *Outside Magazine* sent its "reconnaissance agent," Mark Jenkins to take a look at what the Marine Corps was doing "to condition its troops to fight in extreme environments like Afghanistan." The columnist spent his first several days at the training center observing students in the Winter Mountain Leader's Course and an infantry battalion undergoing practical field exercises. Jenkins was escorted at various times by the S-3, Major Craig Kozeniesky, Captains Mike Andretta, Clinton

Culp, Justin Anderson and Royal Marine Color Sergeant Steven Tooby. Jenkins's subsequent comments lauded the training environment and the scope and quality of the instruction. In his article, Jenkins noted that:

> Every year approximately 10,000 Marines undergo training at MWTC. By comparison, the Army Northern Warfare Training Center in Fort Wainwright, Alaska, sees fewer than 500 servicemen annually, and the Army National Guard Mountain Warfare School, in Jerhico, Vermont, trains several hundred soldiers, National Guardsmen reservists each year. The Army's 10th Mountain Division, despite its name and history has not trained units in mountaineering, avalanche work, or cold-weather survival since World War II.[267]

Jenkins went on to relate his MWTC observations directly to Afghanistan, by stating: "Among the members of the 15th and 26th Marine Expeditionary Units deployed near Kandahar in late November were a number of mountain leaders and assault climbers who have received advanced training at the MWTC, while hundreds of other Marines who were sent to Afghanistan have also been trained at the Center."[268]

Jenkins followed up his visit to the MWTC by accompanying Major Kozeniesky, the Mountain Leader's instructor staff, and some 60 Marines to the "Texas Range" at the Fort Greely Military Reservation in central Alaska. Forty of the Marines were graduates of the advanced Winter Mountain Leaders Course and were ranked "Tier Two," or experienced mountain men. Twenty were graduates of the basic Winter Mountain Leader's Course and were identified as "Tier One" beginners. All aspired to become instructors at MWTC and were there to pass the Instructor's Qualification Course. Jenkins shadowed this group and the Mountain Leader Course instructors through seven days and nights of maneuvering in deep snow, patrolling, executing tactical problems and bivouacking in bone-chilling cold temperatures that seldom rose above–15 degrees.[269] In the end, Jenkins summarized his total time with the Marines by writing:

> With all the talk of fighting in extreme environments like Afghanistan, I wanted to explore the connection between military challenge and the outdoor world. Worried about the combat readiness of these backcountry warriors, instead I found chiseled soldiers hiking 3,000 feet up a mountain fully loaded with state-of-the-art equipment. They

have a sense of duty and honor that is rarely this intense in the civilian world. It was gratifying to see that some people still hold these things in high esteem.[270]

On 3 December 2001, the commanding general at Marine Combat Development Command hosted a one-day Quantico seminar of "Graybeards" to examine the special warfighting capabilities that the Corps might contribute to the campaign taking place in Afghanistan. Former Assistant Secretary of Defense Francis J. "Bing" West chaired the seminar. Participating were a number of former civilian defense policy-makers and retired Marine senior officers including Lieutenant Generals Bernard E. "Mick" Trainor, and Norman H. "Norm" Smith and Major Generals Ray L. Smith and Orlo K. Steele. Also invited to attend the seminar was a former S-3 at MWTC, retired Lieutenant Colonel Rodney C. "Rod" Richardson. Over the previous several years, Richardson had been engaged in guiding climbing expeditions into the Hindu Kush out of Peshawar, Pakistan. Among the proposed recommendations that the group briefed to the commanding general was Richardson's concept for creating a company-sized unit which would include a score of six to eight man high altitude strike teams (HASTs). This concept, which had been previously blessed by Colonel James M. "Jim" Thomas at MWTC, envisioned that the high altitude strike team unit be organized, trained and specially equipped at Bridgeport, deployed in-theater for acclimatization training and then employed in a fashion similar to the "Stingray" operations that were used in Vietnam. A weekly rotation of several teams to the 14,000-15,000 thousand foot elevations would seek to interdict al-Qaeda and the Taliban lines of communications between Pakistan and Afghanistan by directing fire from drones and attack aircraft against identifiable targets. The commanding general strongly endorsed the concept and asked that West, Smith, Steele and Richardson brief the plan to Lieutenant General Emil "Buck" Bedard, the Deputy Chief of Staff for Plans and Operations at Headquarters U.S. Marine Corps early the next morning. After hearing the briefing, Bedard said he believed the concept had merit. However, he went on to share that "We just received word that the Marines will be pulled out of Afghanistan in the next few weeks."[271]

The Mountain Warfare Training Center stood ready to play an increased role in the post 9/11 schemes of things, particularly with regard to preparing forces slated for deployment to Afghanistan. But by early 2002, the initial keen interest in mountain operations had begun to fade. Several factors caused this to happen. First, the rapid collapse of the Taliban had reduced the need for major combat formations to be dispatched to Afghanistan. Second, Secretary of Defense Donald H. Rumsfeld and other Department of Defense policy-makers had embraced a doctrine that emphasized lightness and mobility, while minimizing the number of troops assigned to the area of operations. U.S. Central Command planners were cautioned to hold the force numbers to a level deemed necessary to keep the Taliban at bay and to provide security for Afghanistan's fledging national government, led by Hamid Karzai, but no more than that. Thus the pressure from the Pentagon to minimize the number of American "boots on the ground" in the Afghan theater was significant.[272] And third, as hostilities in Afghanistan started to scale down, the Bush Administration almost immediately began to shift its focus to Iraq and the Saddam Hussein regime.

Mountain Warfare Training Center Shifts with the Tides of War

By mid 2002, it was clear that the next phase of the Bush Administration's "War on Global Terrorism" would focus on establishing a U.S. presence into the heart of its Middle East antagonists. This new endeavor would require enormous resources. I MEF, based at Camp Pendleton, was earmarked to provide the backbone of the Marine forces that would be initially committed, if the decision was made to invade Iraq. Consequently, the spotlight that had briefly shined on Pickel Meadow as being the prime training venue for future operations swung south to the desert training base at Marine Corps Air Ground Combat Center, Twentynine Palms.

Pickel Meadow's venerable old warrior, Master Gunnery Sergeant John Marjanov, however, did not live to witness these events. In the spring of 2002, John became seriously ill. Upon hearing of his condition, former commanding officer, Colonel Russell W. "Russ" Schumacher, Jr., immediately drove down from Moscow, Idaho to visit "Sir John" at his bedside. Colonel John Stennick likewise came from Oregon to spend time with his crusty old friend. On 24 May, 2002, John died quietly in his sleep.

Many of John's new, as well as his friends of longstanding were on hand at the base chapel memorial service to bid their legendary hero farewell. Former base commander, Colonel Raymond L. "Skip" Polak gave the eulogy.[273]

The long anticipated invasion of Iraq, code named Operation Iraqi Freedom, was launched in March 2003. Within 30 days the Iraqi army had ceased to be an effective fighting force, Saddam Hussein was in hiding and Coalition forces occupied Baghdad. Colonel Joel G. Schwankl replaced Colonel Thomas and assumed command of MWTC on 17 July 2003. Immediately, the new commander was confronted with units and individuals canceling scheduled training at Pickel Meadow. The situation was similar to what had occurred during Operation Desert Shield and Desert Storm in 1990-1991. The 2003 Command Chronology showed that the mess hall reported a total of 126,207 meals served during the year,[274] down from 301,344 meals served during the previous year.[275] But there were no indications that any caretaker status was ever seriously considered for the MWTC, as had occurred during the war in Vietnam.

Combat operations and the casualty figures from the Iraq Theater would dominate the news for the next several years. Not all Marine combat forces however, were destined to deploy to Iraq. From 2003 onwards the troop levels of U.S. and NATO forces in Afghanistan were slowly increased beyond the limits once envisioned by Secretary Rumsfeld. Therefore, battalion landing teams from both the 2d and 3d Marine Divisions soon became part of the mix of U.S. forces being rotated to Afghanistan for six-month deployments. As a result, training in mountain operations once again began to take on a higher priority for battalions that perhaps might find themselves headed for Operation Enduring Freedom. Consequently the training tempo at MWTC during 2004 gradually began to rise once again.[276]

From 8-10 June 2004, the training center hosted a Joint Conference on Warfighting in Afghanistan. Over 85 military officers and civilians attended. Many who were present had just completed recent tours of duty in support of Operation Enduring Freedom (OEF). Although U.S. Army and Marine Corps representatives dominated the conference, all of the military services were represented with the exception of the Coast Guard. The purpose of the conference was to serve as a clearinghouse for "lessons learned" from those who had recently been in direct contact with the Taliban militants that were attempting to reclaim control of the Afghan rural countryside. What worked and what didn't work? What were the best practices in tactics? What was the most effective weaponry in the high mountains? What clothing and equipment was valued? These were the types of questions that the presenters shared with one another that ultimately would be summarized in a conference report. One of the presenters from the Marine Corps, for example, was a rifle company commander from a battalion in the 2d Marine Division, whose company had been routinely in contact with the insurgents at elevations ranging from 10,000 to 12,000 feet. Interestingly, and perhaps prophetically, at the close of the conference there was strong consensus among those participating that the United States would likely still be engaged in Afghanistan, long after our forces had been withdrawn from Iraq.[277]

Throughout the midyears of the first decade, the insurgencies and violence taking place in both Iraq and Afghanistan intensified. Like its Army counterparts, Marine regular and reserve air-ground forces became increasingly stretched thin. Consequently, turnaround times between unit deployments to one theater or another were shortened. This meant less time at home bases for these organizations to recuperate and rebuild their personnel strength and combat readiness before making their next deployment. Furthermore, division and wing tactical exercise employment plans (TEEPs) were constantly being altered to meet unexpected contingencies. Thus, an organization that may have devoted a month of its work-up time to training in the desert at Twentynine Palms in anticipation of its deployment to Iraq might be informed on short notice that it was now headed for Afghanistan. Or in some cases, the situation might be the reverse.

The challenge that confronted Battalion Landing Team 1/6 was a prime example. During 2004, it conducted combat operations in Afghanistan in support of OEF. Between 1 April and 10 July, it was credited with killing over 100 enemy fighters, capturing over 131 more, and for conducting over $300,000 worth of civil affairs activities.[278] However, BLT 1/6 had only been formed for three weeks before it was deployed overseas. Thus, it did not have the customary six months in which to integrate its attachments, send its Marines to special courses of instruction and accomplish the desired ramp-up training at either Pickel Meadow or Twentynine Palms. Ultimately, the organization managed to adapt to its surroundings and overcome this handicap. But its after-action report stressed that pre-deployment training at the MWTC would have proven very desirable and beneficial.[279]

Colonel Schwankl's tour as commanding officer ended on 15 July 2005. The training centers' executive officer, Lieutenant Colonel Robb Etnyre would serve as the acting commander until the arrival of Colonel Timothy C. Wells on 1 September. Soon after Wells arrived the Base Realignment and Closure Commission issued its final report and recommendations to the secretary of defense. The Commission had been sitting throughout the year,

considering what military bases nationwide were no longer of value and should be closed or reduced. The Commission found the Marine Corps Mountain Warfare Training Center as offering "nationally recognized training for high desert, mountainous operations" and recommended that it be retained.[280]

Colonel Timothy C. "Tim" Wells was no stranger to MWTC and its core training programs. As a captain during the mid 1980s he had served a two-year tour of duty as an instructor-guide in the Mountain Leaders Course. Therefore, he could recall the special relationship that had evolved during those years between MWTC, the 2d Marine Division, its 2d Marine Regiment and the 4th MEB in preparing troops to meet the rigors of a winter Norway campaign. Reflecting on this previous experience, he quickly recognized that the same level of coherency and consistency that had proven so successful during the decade of the 1980s, was seriously lacking with respect to pre-deployment training for battalions, or regimental headquarter elements being sent to fight in Afghanistan. Accordingly, in October 2005, Colonel Wells drafted a concept paper proposing a new Notional USMC Order of Battle for Cold Weather/Mountain Operations with a special focus on Afghanistan. Specifically, Wells recommended the 4th MEB based at Camp Lejeune be designated the principal coordinator and force provider, with the 3d Marines, based at Kaneohe, Hawaii fulfilling the role the 2d Marines had assumed for the Norwegian contingencies of the 1980s. In addition to other forms of training support, he proposed that "MWTC would provide small teams (6-18 Marines) to augment 3d Marines or 4th MEB capabilities as required. The MWTC teams would be assigned reconnaissance recon and search and rescue missions at high altitudes (above 14,000 feet) and in extreme weather conditions where advance climbing, survival or mobility skills were needed."[281]

However, Colonel Wells elected to retire in mid-2006. Therefore, implementation of the foregoing concept, or developing other ways of how MWTC might best support the Operation Enduring Freedom effort was left to his successor, Colonel David B. Hall. Colonel Hall assumed command of the training center on 14 August 2006.

Debates over Deployments

The balance of forces between Iraq and Afghanistan became a campaign issue even before the 2008 national elections when Senator Barack Obama accused the Bush administration of having left the Operation Enduring Freedom campaign unfinished from the very outset. Senator Barak H.

Obama claimed that the war in Iraq "allowed us to neglect the situation in Afghanistan. We know . . . that al-Qaeda is hiding in the hills between Afghanistan and Pakistan. And because we have taken our eye off the ball, they are stronger now than any time since 2001."[282]

Lessons from Afghanistan

U.S. Marine Corps History Division field historian Lieutenant Colonel David Benhoff visited Afghanistan in 2009 and interviewed numerous Marines about lessons learned.

Interviewee: Palazzo

Lieutenant Colonel Louis J. Palazzo, was the mentor to the commanding officer of the 2d Brigade, 201st Corps, Afghan National Army: "I think one thing the Marine Corps needs to look at is the pre-deployment training program. Twentynine Palms is probably not the right venue for embedded training teams coming to this part of Afghanistan. There is no desert. There is no flat, drivable land in this area. It's all mountains. And we did about four days at Mountain Warfare Training Center in Bridgeport. Honestly, that's where we need to do the whole pre-deployment training. We did four days at Bridgeport and 21 days at Twentynine Palms. It probably should have been reversed. Twentynine Palms is great for the live-fire aspect, which we really can't do in Okinawa. We're very limited as far as especially crew-served live-fire training, but Bridgeport, humping those mountains, learning that terrain, learning the restrictions that are placed on you because of that terrain was more instrumental than the 21 days we spent at Twentynine Palms. I know part of—we brought this up while we were there. Part of the problem is that there is no structure really to support that at Mountain Warfare Training Center, but if this is the way of the future for the Marine Corps in the next five to 10 years, then probably something needs to be done to make it supportable, because that's where we should train."

Interviewee: Sanchez

Lieutenant Colonel Eleazar O. Sanchez was the 3d Brigade senior adviser with the Afghan National Army. He also lauded the Bridgeport pre-deployment training experience: "Bridgeport was probably the best training we had during the entire pre-deployment training portion. It was extremely tough, because one day we were in Hawaii and then within 24 hours we were up at altitude. And then in less than 48 hours we were 10,000 feet up in the mountains, where every day was about 15 hours a day and you're humping all day, setting up ambushes, going on patrols, doing those kinds of things. But, you know what? The Marines loved it, though, because it not only challenged them physically, it challenged them mentally. I think for the mental toughness aspect of it, that was probably the most valuable lesson we learned . . . if I could do it all over again, if there was something that I could recommend for the future Marine teams, is to conduct training up in the mountains, . . . if I could recommend [training] to the Marine Corps embedded training teams that are coming here, especially in the mountainous regions, Bridgeport is the place to do it."

Interviewee: Wester

Lieutenant Colonel Sean D. Wester was the officer-in-charge of Embedded Training Team 6-4, which operated in the mountains of northeast Afghanistan. He concurred with regard to the value of Bridgeport: "There's probably still some debate out there, about training at Bridgeport, California, at Mountain Warfare Training Center, versus going to Twentynine Palms. We did a mixture of both. We spent a little over seven days initially at Bridgeport. I think we should have spent more time there. I think the split between the two is good, but the value of Bridgeport was that we were immediately thrust into a mountainous environment. We went from Okinawa's near-sea level environment to an environment where the elevation was 6,000 feet and higher. We were in great physical shape and we discovered immediately that 6,000 feet and above robs all of it from you . . . That week at Bridgeport, as painful as it was for the team, was the thing that began to cement us. I mean, we were coming together before then, but going through the grueling physical aspects of marching, land navving, conducting tactical operations, tactical exercises, in the mountains at Bridgeport . . . When we made it through that week at Bridgeport, when we got to Twentynine Palms, it was a piece of cake, because the bonding and cementing process happened there, under that sharp physical slap in the face of Bridgeport. So I would say working, conducting training in a place like Bridgeport, at elevation, up and down mountains and doing the small unit leadership things in that rugged terrain, absolutely essential, absolutely."

A resurgent Taliban did result in a growing commitment of American forces in support of Operation Enduring Freedom. By 1 June 2008, according to Department of Defense figures, the United States had 48,250 troops stationed in Afghanistan–37,700 active component and 10,550 National Guard or Reserves.[283] One month after taking office, President Barak H. Obama followed up on his campaign pledge by ordering an additional 17,000 U.S. troops to the Afghan theater in support of OEF.[284] In December of 2009, the President would commit 30,000 more American troops to Afghanistan. These developments caused some to ponder whether MWTC again assuming greater responsibility for readying and conditioning Marine forces for counterinsurgency operations in a harsh climate and steep mountainous terrain. But most of the Marine units would be deployed in Afghanistan's Regional Command South, in the flat desert of Helmand Province.

On 1 July 2008, Colonel Norman L. Cooling took command of the training center. A graduate of the U.S. Naval Academy, he had been born and raised in Texas. Cooling began his Marine career as a rifle platoon commander in the 2d Marine Division in 1987. As a lieutenant colonel, he commanded the 3d Battalion, 3d Marines, leading his infantrymen through two separate six-month overseas deployments, one in Iraq and the other in Afghanistan. Based on those recent experiences, Cooling came to his new command with a clear view of just what skills offered at the training center needed greater attention, and conversely, which were of a lesser value and therefore should be de-emphasized.

Furthermore, six days after Cooling assumed command, the Commandant of the Marine Corps, General James Conway paid a visit to the MWTC. Cooling later recalled that the Commandant: "directed me to develop an alternative block IV (battalion to regimental headquarters sized) mission rehearsal exercise in the event that the then emerging operations in Afghanistan positioned the in complex, mountainous terrain."[285] Following through on groundwork inherited from his predecessor and guidance he received from both Commandant and the Training and Education Command, Colonel Cooling immediately challenged his staff to develop a new strategic vision for MWTC.

A Strategic Vision for MWTC's Second Half-Century

In November of 2008, Colonel Cooling and his staff completed their recommendations for Mountain Warfare Training Center's future. The centerpiece of their new concept involved a new

capability for MAGTF organizations to greatly expand the scope of their Operation Enduring Freedom pre-deployment training by not being confined to the Pickel Meadow maneuver area. Instead, under a revised scheme of operations, using units would be able to extend the distances of their exercises to the surrounding environs as well. The stated goal of the command now became "to ensure that each of the Center's formal schools courses and its unit training programs impart MAGTF units and their leaders with the skills to fight and win in complex terrain."[286] The fundamental challenge of mountain warfare, their document emphasized, is that all operations are conducted in highly complex terrain-similar in some respects to urban warfare. Rapidly changing and extreme weather conditions only added to the challenge.[287]

Before reaching this conclusion, the MWTC staff had conducted an extensive review of after-action reports and operational analyses from Operation Enduring Freedom. Their review highlighted how complex mountainous terrain affects planning and execution within each of the six functions of war fighting: maneuver, fires, intelligence, command and control, logistics and force protection. They acknowledged that applying the lessons learned associated with each function to the unique dynamics associated with every potential area of operations presented a daunting challenge for the trainers. For example, aside from Afghanistan, the Marine Corps Intelligence Activity Mid-Range Threat Estimate had identified 19 other states or locales of particular interest, which featured mountainous terrain to some degree.[288] Nonetheless, they believed that given the right resources, there was enough flexibility in the training programs inherent to the MWTC that most of these challenges could be met successfully using all the local terrain that could be made available.

As Cooling and his staffed looked ahead to the next step, it now became an "operational imperative" to leverage the strengths of greater Bridgeport as a training venue, while at the same time seeking ways to mitigate its two historic weaknesses: land management constraints that inhibit combined arms live fire training and a shortfall in training enablers such as training allowance pools and exercise control groups for the conduct of major air-ground exercises. The term "greater Bridgeport" rightly implied that some aspects of a Marine air-ground task force exercise would be conducted away from Pickel Meadow proper with its restricted fire limitations. Nonetheless, by taking advantage of the Hawthorne Army Depot and the Naval Air Station in Fallon Nevada, together with the Bureau of Land Management, private land owners and U.S. Forest

Service corridor that lay in between, these appendages cumulatively created a highly desirable and relevant venue for both maneuver and combined-fire Marine air-ground task force exercises.*

In order to convert this vision into reality, Colonel Cooling and his staff initiated action to achieve the following six objectives to:
1. Enhance and expand access to ranges and training areas
2. Enhance range control capabilities
3. Enhance exercise support capabilities
4. Acquire new targets and training systems
5. Develop installation facilities and infrastructure
6. Establish a Marine air-ground task force training range as part of MWTC.[289]

As a result of its efforts, the MWTC experienced a 238 percent increase in training throughput between fiscal years 2008 and 2009. By the following year the base was operating at full capacity, training just under 14,000 troops. Meanwhile, all of the formal school courses had been adjusted from the old cold war templates to new programs of instruction based on the current situation and operations taking place in Afghanistan. Having also forged a special relationship with the Marine Special Operations Command located at Camp Lejeune, troops from that command also began arriving in greater numbers then ever before.[290]

As of May 2010, it was too early to tell whether all these initiatives could be fully implemented. As already noted, since its founding, the fortunes of the Mountain Warfare Training Center have ebbed and flowed, depending on which threat was most pressing at the time. Nevertheless, the 2010 Department of Defense announcement that declared that U.S. troop strengths in Afghanistan would exceed those of Iraq suggested that the MWTC will continue to be a very active place and operating at full capacity for at least the near term.[291]

Finally, if there is any validity to the axiom "past is prologue," then one can assume it is likely that there are Marines, yet unborn, who will one day arrive at Pickel Meadow as either individual students, or part of a battalion and find themselves trudging uphill under arms with a full pack to bivouac sites such as Grouse Meadow, or at the upper reaches of Silver and Wolf Creeks. Doubtless, they too will

contend with adversity and experience the unexpected and just like their predecessors, learn by doing just what it takes to successfully fight and survive in a mountain/cold-weather campaign. Since that summer day in 1951 when Lieutenant Colonel Donald B. "Don" Hubbard and First Lieutenant Richard M. Johnson first surveyed Pickel Meadow as a potential training area and had the "Eureka" moment described in Chapter 3, over 500,000 troops have undergone some form of instruction at Bridgeport and have found themselves doing exactly the same. It should also be noted, that the half-million figure does not represent just U.S. Marines. Included therein are: U.S. Navy Seals, U.S. Army Special Forces, Marines from the Republic of South Korea, Marines from Chile, British Royal Marines, Dutch Marines from The Netherlands, Canadian Army and other military officers from a number of allied nations. And, with very few exceptions, each one of those half-million troops has, in some fashion, benefited from the experience.

Major General Thomas S. Jones, the former commanding general, training and education command, and one who has had wide, personal experience in leading troops through a number of mountain and cold-weather operations, perhaps explained the real value of MWTC best, and implicitly the reason it should be preserved for generations of Marines to come, when he told columnist Mark Jenkins:

> Training in a cold mountainous environment is the closest thing we have to approximating the stress a soldier undergoes in combat. If a Marine can learn to fight in the cold of the mountains, he can fight anywhere-desert, jungle, anywhere. Yet the reverse is not necessarily true. Severe cold and rugged terrain forces soldiers to work together, to share and eventually overcome incredible adversity. It builds cohesiveness. You can't simulate humping a 70-pound pack to 11,000 feet. You can't simulate climbing and skiing. You can't simulate cold. You can't simulate fear. You have to experience these things—experience them and learn from them. That's how to make a soldier. Even if we never fought another day in the cold or the mountains, we would still train there because it teaches Marines how to handle extreme conditions. That is the real power of the Mountain Warfare Training Center, and the brass knows it.[292]

---

* The first series conducted in 2009 became known as Exercise Mountain Warrior. In June 2010 the base played host to a MEB-sized exercise named Exercise Javelin Thrust, which evolved into the largest maneuver of Marine combat forces in the history of the training center.

.

Notes

Chapter 1

1. Mary Hill, *Geology of the Sierra Nevada* (Berkeley: University of California Press, 1975), pp. 169-70.
2. Ibid., p. 162
3. Ibid., pp. 172-77
4. T.H. Watkins, *California: An Illustrated History* (New York: American West Publishing Co., 1973), p. 30.
5. Eugene L. Conrotto, *Miwok Means People* (Fresno, CA: Valley Publishers, 1973), p. 4.
6. Ruth Herman, *The Paiutes of Pyramid Lake: A Narrative Concerning a Western Nevada Indian Tribe* (San Jose, CA: Harlan Young Press, 1972), p. 169
7. Phil Townsend Hanna, *California Through Four Centuries* (New York: Farrar & Rinehart, 1935), pp. 4, 10.
8. Robert L. Reid, ed., *A Treasury of the Sierra Nevada* (Berkeley, CA: Wilderness Press, 1983), p. 2.
9. Frank S. Wedertz, *Mono Diggings* (Bishop, CA: Chalfant Press, 1978), p. 13.
10. Reid, ed., pp. 18-24.
11. Ernest Lewis, *The Fremont Cannon: High Up and Far Back,* (Western Trails Press, 1981).
12. John C. Fremont, *The Exploring Expedition to the Rocky Mountains, Oregon, and California* (Buffalo, NY: Derby, Orton, and Mulligan, Publishers, 1853), p. 321.
13. Lewis, The Fremont Cannon, p. 13.
14. Irving Stone, *Men to Match My Mountains* (Garden City, New York: Doubleday & Co., 1956), p. 46.
15. Ibid., p. 47.
16. Wedertz, *Mono Diggings*, pp. 21-22.
17. Ibid., p. 23.
18. J. S. Holliday, *The World Rushed In: The California Gold Rush Experience* (New York: Simon and Schuster, 1981), pp. 39, 48.
19. Stone, *Men to Match My Mountains*, p. 131.
20. Dan De Quille, *The Big Bonanza* (New York: Alfred A. Knopf, 1947), p. 76.
21. Ella M. Cain, *The Story of Early Mono County* (San Francisco: Fearon Publishers, 1961), pp. 4-9.
22. Ibid., pp. 10-14.
23. Mining Books D, 1861-1862, pp. 457, 512 and 578, Mono County Recorders Office, Bridgeport, California.
24. Assessor book entries for 1863, p. 46; Aug1867, p. 162; 1869, p. 144, Mono County Assessor's Office, Bridgeport, California.

Chapter 2

25. Maj M.S. Hall, "Cold Weather Combat Clothing," *Marine Corps Gazette* May48, p. 56.
26. Murray Morgan, *Bridge to Russia* (New York: E.P. Dutton Co., 1947), p. 47.
27. Maj Orlo K. Steele, "For Special Duty in Bering Sea," USMC Command and Staff College Individual Research Paper, 1972, MCU Archives, Quantico, Va., p. 50.
28. Col James A. Donovan, *Outpost in the North Atlantic: Marines in the Defense of Iceland* (Washington, D.C.:Hist&MusDiv, HQMC, 1992), pp. 6-7
29. Bailey, Thomas A. and Ryan, Paul B. "Hilter vs. Roosevelt The Undeclared Naval War" p. 156.
30. Donovan, *Outpost in the North Atlantic*, p. 10.
31. Ibid.
32. Ibid., p. 25
33. LtGen William K. Jones, *A Brief History of the 6th Marines* (Washington, D.C.: Hist&MusDiv, HQMC, 1987), p. 44.
34. "CinCPacFlt Exercise MICOWEX 49A," 1949, Box 1 (labeled "Cold Weather Operations, 1949-1977"), Studies and Reports, MCU Archives, Quantico, Va.
35. "Observers Report, Exercise MICOWEX 49A," Kodiak, Alaska, Feb49, Box 46 (labeled "Exercises"), Studies and Reports, MCU Archives, Quantico, Va.

Chapter 3

36. Clay Blair, *The Forgotten War: American in Korea, 1950-1953* (New York: First Anchor Books, 1989), p. 363.
37. Lynn Montross and Nicholas A. Canzona, *U.S. Marine Operations in Korea, 1950-1953*, vol. III (Washington, D.C.: HistBr, G-3 Div, HQMC, 1957), p. 119.
38. CMC letter AO-3-SNA, 9Nov50 to CG, Marine Barracks, Camp Pendleton, Cold Weather Training Correspondence File, HD RefSec, Quantico, Va.
39. CG, Tra&Repl Comd ltr 5942 of 12Nov50 to CMC, Cold Weather Training Correspondence File, HD RefSec, Quantico, Va.
40. Col Walter "Mu Mu" Moore intvw with MajGen O.K. Steele, 26Feb02, hereafter Moore intvw.
41. MSgt G.E. Burlage, "Cold Weather Training," *Leatherneck* (Apr51), pp. 15-16.
42. Moore intvw.
43. BGen E.H. Simmons, *Frozen Chosin: U.S. Marines*

at the Changjin Reservoir (Washington, D.C.: Hist&MusDiv, HQMC, 2002), p. 122.

44. CG, Tra&Repl Comd ltr 18492 of 15Jun51, Cold-Weather Training Correspondence File, HD RefSec, Quantico, Va.

45. CMC spdltr AO-3-jb of 7Jul51 to CG Marine Barracks, Camp Pendleton, Cold Weather Training Correspondence File, HD RefSec, Quantico, Va.

46. CG Tra&Repl Comd ltr to CMC of 31Jul51, Cold-Weather Training Correspondence File, HD RefSec, Quantico, Va.

47. Col Richard Johnson intvw with MajGen O.K. Steele, 11Apr02, hereafter Johnson intvw.

48. Bridgeport District Forest Ranger Office, "Toiyabe National Forest Fact Sheet, 1907-Present."

49. *Bridgeport Chronicle-Union*, 17Aug51.

50. CG, Marine Barracks, Camp Pendleton, MSG 250022Z Aug51 to CMC, Cold Weather Training Correspondence File, HD RefSec, Quantico, Va.

51. Official Marine Corps Biography of Col Donald B. Hubbard Sr., 25May67, HD RefSec, Quantico, Va.

52. Mr. John Schneider intvw with MajGen O.K. Steele 6Sept01, hereafter Schneider intvw.

53. Cold Weather Training Report of Fleet Marine Force, Pacific Troops 1951-1952," 17May52, p. 2, Cold Weather Training Correspondence File, HD RefSec, Quantico, Va.

54. Schneider intvw.

Chapter 4

55. First endorsement by CO, Staging Regiment, Tra&Repl Comd, Camp Pendleton, on Cold Weather Battalion, "Activity Report," ltr ser 970, 26May52, Cold Weather Training Correspondence File, HD RefSec, Quantico, Va., p. 1.

56. Burke Davis, *Marine! The Life of Chesty Puller* (Boston: Little, Brown, and Co., 1962), p. 348.

57. *Bridgeport Chronicle-Union*, 28Oct51, Mono County Public Library.

58. CO, Cold Weather Battalion, "Activity Report," ltr to CMC, 26May52, in Cold Weather Training Correspondence File, HD RefSec, Quantico, Va., hereafter, 'Activity Report,' 26May52."

59. Johnson intvw, and Johnson, exchange of e-mails with MajGen O.K. Steele, 4Oct02.

60. James Brady, *The Coldest War* (New York: Simon and Schuster, 1990), p. 7.

61. Mr. Harold Haberman, intvw with MajGen O.K. Steele, 6Sept01 (at MWTC 50th Anniversary Celebration), hereafter Haberman intvw.

62. MajGen O.P. Smith to CMC, 29Jan52, Personal Correspondence File of LtGen O.P. Smith, MCU Archives, Quantico, Va.

63. "Activity Report," 26May52, p.4.

64. LtGen Bernard E. Trainor, *On Going to War: A Marine Lieutenant's Korean War Experiences* (Quantico, Va.: Marine Corps Association, 1998), p. 4.

65. Haberman intvw.

66. First Endorsement of CO, "Activity Report." 26May52, p. 2.

67. Ibid., p. 4.

68. Mr. Elliot Chassey to CO, MWTC, Bridgeport, California, 23Sept00, in MWTC S-3 Office.

69. See Appendix A, which is Annex "C" of 'Activity Report,' 26May52."

Chapter 5

70. Enclosure (7) of Staff Study of Continued Training at Cold Weather Battalion and Development of a Permanent Camp, 13Mar52, in CO, Cold Weather Battalion Activity Report, ltr to CMC of 26May52, Cold Weather Training Correspondence File, HD RefSec, Quantico, Va,. p. 1 (This report, not the enclosure itself, is hereafter cited as Hubbard Report).

71. Cold Weather Training Report of Fleet Marine Force, Pacific Troops personnel during 1951-1952," 17May52, Cold Weather Training File, HD RefSec, Quantico, Va., pp.14, 16 (hereafter Ryffel Report).

72. Hubbard Report, p. 5.

73. Ryffel Report, p. 15.

74. Hubbard Report, p. 8

75. Ibid.

76. Ibid., p. 8; Ryffel Report, p. 11.

77. Hubbard Report, p. 8.

78. Ibid., p. 7.

79. Ibid., 8.

80. Ryffel Report, pp. 14-15.

81. Enclosure 7 of Hubbard Report.

82. Hubbard Report, p. 8.

83. Cold Weather Training Center Staff Study, 24Oct57, CWTC Briefing Folder, MCU Archives, Quantico, Va., pp. 7-9, hereafter CWTC 1957 Staff Study.

84. CMC Report to the Secretary of the Navy for FY 1956-1957, HD RefSec, Quantico, Va., p. 49.

85. Official Biography of BGen Donald M. Schmuck, 1Nov59, HD RefSec, Quantico, Va.

86. Maj Bruce Norton and SgtMaj Maurice J. Jacques, *Sergeant Major, U.S. Marines* (New York: Ballantine Books, 1995), pp. 86-87.

87. Head Training Section ltr AO3c-1jv, 27Jan53, to Assistant Chief of Staff, G-3, HQMC, Cold Weather Training File, HD RefSec, Quantico, Va.

88. BGen Donald Schmuck intvw with MajGen O.K. Steele, 1Aug02.

89. Martin Russ, *The Last Parallel* (New York: Rinehart & Co., 1957), pp. 23-24.

90. Official Biography of BGen Clayton O. Totman, 14Dec59, HD RefSec, Quantico, Va.

91. CMC Report to the Secretary of the Navy for FY

1954-1955, HD RefSec, Quantico, Va., p. 17.

92. Heinl, *Soldiers of the Sea*, p. 589.

93. CMC Report to the Secretary of the Navy for FY 1955-1956, HD RefSec, Quantico, Va., pp. 63, 64.

94. *Hold Back the Night* Correspondence File, HD RefSec, Quantico, Va.

95. Lawrence H. Suid, *Guts and Glory: The Making of the American Military Image in Film* (Lexington: University Press of Kentucky, 2002), pp. 140-41.

96. Jack Lewis, "Camp Cloudburst," *Leatherneck* Oct58, p. 52.

97. Pickel Lodge History, Command and Historical Summary File, MWTC, Bridgeport, Ca.

98. Lineage of Marine Corps Mountain Warfare Training Center, 1951-1997," 31Mar98.

Chapter 6

99. Cold Weather Training of Fleet Marine Force, Pacific Troops Personnel During 1951-1952, Cold-Weather Training File, HD RefSec, Quantico, Va., p.14.

100. Official Biography of BGen Donald M. Schmuck, USMC,1Nov59, HD RefSec, Quantico, Va.

101. BGen Donald M. Schmuck, phone intvw with MajGen O.K. Steele, 1Aug02.

102. CWTC 1957 Staff Study.

103. Code of Conduct Executive Order 10631 for Members of the Armed Forces of the U.S., Federal Register, 20 FR 6057, 20Aug55.

104. CWTC 1957 Staff Study.

105. Biographic Data Sheet on LtCol Sidney F. Jenkins, n.d., HD RefSec, Quantico, Va.

106. CWTC 1957 Staff Study, p. 6.

107. CMC ltr AO-3c-mjr to CO, CWTC, 23Aug57, Cold Weather Training Correspondence File, HD RefSec, Quantico, Va.

108. CWTC 1957 Staff Study.

109. MSgt Carl H. Raue intvw with MajGen O.K. Steele, 17Sept03. Raue formerly served as Mountain Leader Courses Unit Chief.

110. Ibid.

111. CWTC 1957 Staff Study

112. MSgt H.B. Wells, "Rope and Piton," *Leatherneck* Dec57, pp. 17-18.

113. CWTC 1957 Staff Study

114. Annex D to CWTC 1957 Staff Study.

Chapter 7

115. Gerald P. Averill, *Mustang: A Combat Marine* (Novato, CA.: Presidio Press, 1987), pp. 281-82.

116. CWTC 1957 Staff Study, p. 23.

117. Averill, *Mustang*, pp. 273, 275.

118. "In Memoriam," obituary of LtCol Gerald P. Averill, *Mestengo* (a quarterly newsletter of the Marine Corps Mustang Association) Spring94, p. 14.

119. Averill *Mustang*, p. 273.

120. Ibid., pp. 275-76.

121. Ibid., p. 281.

122. SgtMaj Bill Conley, intvw with MGen O.K. Steel, 3May06, hereafter Conley intvw.

123. Averill, Mustang, p. 278.

124. Col James Knapp, intvw with MGen O.K. Steele, 15Jan07, hereafter Knapp intvw. Knapp was senior instructor-guide of the Mountain Leadership Course at CWTC, 1959-1961.

125. Averill, *Mustang*, p. 278.

126. Ibid., pp. 283.

127. Conley intvw.

128. LtGen Ernest C. Cheatham, Jr. intvw with MGen O.K. Steele, 12May02; Col Warren Wiedham intvw with MGen O.K.Steele, 27Feb06, hereafter Wiedham intvw.

129. Raue intvw, 17Apr06; Wiedham intw, 27Feb06.

130. Averill, *Mustang*, p. 284

131. Official Biography Col Glen E. Martin, 28Jun68, HD RefSec, Quantico, Va.

132. Col Glen E. Martin intvw with MGen O.K. Steele, 1Jul02.

133. Ibid.

134. Ibid.

135. Ibid.

136. Ibid.

137. Personal knowledge of the author, who served at MWTC as senior instructor and guide of the Mountain Leadership Course, 1963-1964.

Chapter 8

138. Knapp intvw, Col Knapp was present and witnessed this event.

139. Mr. Wiley Clapp intvw with MGen O.K. Steele, 1Jul02.

140. Anthony Milavic, A Ski Story, Washington, DC, 11Jan96, document in possession of the author. For another detailed description of this unique combat leader, see "The Life and Times of Stan Wawrzyniak," *Leatherneck* (Apr92), pp. 26-31. LtCol Stanley Wawrzyniak died of a heart attack at his home in Swansboro, NC, on 26 October 1995, just a few weeks shy of his 68th birthday. He is interred in the Veterans Cemetery in Jacksonville, NC.

141. Personal Record File of MGySgt John Marjanov furnished by Retired Records Section (Pers-313E) Navy Personnel Command, St. Louis, MO.

142. Col Gerald H. Turley, e-mail to MGen O.K. Steele, 3May06.

143. Maj Anthony Milavic, e-mail to MGen O.K. Steele, 11Nov08.

144.Maj Anthony Milavic, A Sea Story, posted on internet 20Mar07.

145. Personal knowledge of the author, who served

at MWTC, 1963-1964.

146. Ibid.

147. Official Biography of Col Frank R. Wilkinson, Jr., 1969 HD RefSec, Quantico, Va.

148. Personal knowledge of the author who was part of the S-3 briefing team for Gen Shoup and later participated in the afternoon rock climbing demonstration.

149. Paul B. Fay, Jr., *The Pleasure of His Company*, (Popular Library, 1977), "Foreword" page.

150. Lineage of Marine of Corps Mountain Warfare Training Center, Bridgeport, CA., 31Mar98.

151. Personal knowledge of the author, who was standing between the two principals in the Leavitt Training Area when this conversation took place.

152. Personal knowledge of the author.

153. Article in *Last Outpost* (MWTC newspaper) vol. 4, no. 3 (11Feb65).

154. Maj James Goldsworthy, OBE, RM, intvw with MGen O.K. Steele, Jan01; also "Goldsworthy File," a collection of written personal written accounts and document, kindly forwarded to the author by Maj Goldsworthy on 20Feb01.

Chapter 9

155. Pentagon Paper, vol. 3, p. 236.

156. *The Irony of Vietnam: The System Worked*, Leslie H. Gelb with Richard K. Betts, published by the Brookings Institution, Washington, DC. 1979, p. 373.

157. Personal knowledge of the author who at the time of this incident was senior instructor and guide of the Mountain Operations Course and participated in the search for the three drowned Marines.

158. MWTC Semi-Annual ComdC Rpt for the period 1Jul65-31Dec65 dated 25Jan66, and 9Mar07 personal telephone interview with MajGen Harry Jenkins, Jr., who had been a witness to this incident on 7 June 1964.

159. Official Biography of LtCol John P. Bristow, Mar64, HD RefSec, Quantico, Va., encl. 1, p.5.

160. MWTC Semi-annual ComdC, 1Jul-31Dec65, HD RefSec, Quantico, Va., encl. 1, p. 5-encl. (1).

161. Ibid., p. 4

162. Goldsworthy File.

163. MWTC ComdC Rpts, 1Jan-30Jun66, and 1Jul-31 Dec66, HD RefSec, Quantico, Va., p. 1 of each report.

164. MWTC ComdC, 1Jan-30Jun67, HD RefSec, Quantico, Va., p.1

165. Comment made by Gen Wallace Green Jr., Commandant of the Marine Corps, in address to the combined Amphibious Warfare School (AWS) and Command and Staff College students, Feb67. The author was in attendance as an AWS student.

166. MWTC Final ComdC Rpt, 10Aug67, HD RefSec, Quantico, Va., pp.1-3.

167. Col Gerald H., Turley, USMCR, *The Easter Offensive: The Last American Advisers, Vietnam, 1972* (Novato, CA: Presidio Press, 1985), p. 23.

168. CG, MCB Camp Pendleton ltr BT3/JCD/jeg to CG, 1st Marine Division, 16Feb73, in CWTC 1956-1963, historical file located at MWTC Bridgeport.

169. Bob Dietrich, "Marines and Airmen Team to Test Force-in-Readiness," *San Diego Evening-Tribune*, 23Jun73.

170. Personal knowledge of the author, who served as training officer, 1st Marine Division, 1974-1975.

171. CG, 1st Marine Division, ltr 3/OKS/mg 1500 to CG, Camp Pendleton, 21May75, author's personal MWTC file.

172. Official Biography of the late MajGen Charles D. Mize, revised Aug76, HD RefSec, Quantico, Va.

173. Martin Bikin and Jeffery Record, *Where Does the Marine Corps Go from Here?* (Washington, D.C.: Brookings Institute, 1976).

174. Col Verle E. Ludwig, *U.S Marines at Twenty-nine Palms*, California (Washington, DC: Hist&Mus-Div, HQMC, 1989), pp. 67-70.

175. U.S. Marine Corps Lineage of Mountain Warfare Training Center, 1951-1997, 31Mar98.

Chapter 10

176. David B. Crist, Strategic background paper on NATO's northern flank, Marine Corps Historical Center, 1999, in MCHC Archives, p. 3, hereafter Crist Paper.

177. Ibid., p. 2.

178. Ibid., pp. 12-13.

179. HQMC Staff Status Report on the Attainment of Cold Weather Capabilities 1977, located in Box 1, Cold Weather Operations file, MCU Archives.

180. Northrop Services, Inc., Executive Summary of Preliminary Report on USMC Cold Weather Combat Operations Study, Aug80, MCU Archives, sec 2, p. 6.

181. Ibid., p.xvii.

182. Ibid., pp. xviii-xx.

183. Western Division Naval Facilities Engineering Command, Draft Master Plan for USMC Marine Corps Mountain Warfare Training Center, 1981, p. 17.

184. Ibid., p. 64.

185. Marine Corps Mountain Warfare Training Center, "1985 Training and Development Concept Paper," Aug80, HD RefSec, Quantico, Va., p. 1

186. Ibid., p. 5

187. Ibid., p. 19.

188. Personal knowledge of the author, who represented DC/S, Plans, Policies, and Operations at this

briefing.

189. Col William H. Osgood intvw with MajGen O.K. Steele, 5Jul09.

190. Crist Paper, p. 16.

191. Gen Robert H. Barrow intw with MajGen O.K. Steele, 5Jun03.

192. MWTC ComdC, Jan82, HD RefSec, Quantico, Va., encl (1), p. 5.

193. Northrop Services, Inc., Executive Summary of Final Report on the Conference on Cold Weather Combat Operations, Jun82, MCU Archives, Quantico, Va., pp. 1-2, 1-3.

194. Ibid., p. 1-4.

195. Ibid., p. 4-10.

Chapter 11

196. Edmund Morris, *Dutch: A Memoir of Ronald Reagan* (New York: Random House, 1999), pp. 472, 475.

197. MWTC ComdC, Feb83, HD RefSec, Quantico, Va., encl. (1), p. 4.

198. MWTC ComdC, 1Jan-30Jun82, HD RefSec, Quantico, Va., encl (1), p. 4.

199. Col William H. Osgood, intvw with MajGen O.K. Steele, 30Jul09.

200. Ibid.

201. Marine Corps Mountain Warfare Training Center Courses of Instruction. 1980-1985, MWTC Historical File, S-3 Office, MWTC, Bridgeport, California.

202. MWTC ComdC, Dec83, encl (1), p. 1; MWTC ComdC, 1Jan-30Jun86, encl (1), pp. 1-2, HD RefSec, Quantico, Va.

203. Northrop Services, Inc., Training Committee Report, in Final Report on the Joint Cold Weather Combat Operations Conference, 8-12 March 1982, MCU Archives, Quantico, Va., p. 4-12.

204. MajGen Harry Jenkins, Jr., intvw with MajGen O.K. Steele, 30Oct09, hereafter Jenkins intvw.

205. Goldsworthy File.

206. Bridgeport Ranger District to CO, MWTC, 22Feb84, on file in S-3 Office, MWTC.

207. Carson Ranger District to CO, MWTC, 4Jan84, on file in S-3 Office, MWTC.

208. MCB, Camp Pendleton Inspector, Memo on Command Matters/Problem Areas, 10Apr85, on file at S-3 Office, MWTC.

209. Jenkins intvw.

210. Personal Recollections of SES Jeffrey Bearor, C/S TECOM, MCCDEC who served as project manager for the acquisition of Cold Weather Clothing and Equipment at the Development Center 1985-1988, hereafter Bearor Recollections.

211. Ibid.

212. Ibid.

213. Crist Paper, pp. 19-20.

214. Ibid., p. 20.

215. Ibid., pp. 22-23.

216. MajGen Jarvis Lynch, intvw with MajGen O.K. Steele, 9Jan10.

217. Official Biography of Col John F. Stennick, undated, furnished to the author on 28Jul09.

218. Personal recollections of Col John F. Stennick, undated, furnished to the author Jan2010, hereafter Stennick Recollections.

219. MWTC ComdC, 1Jan-30Jun86, HD RefSec, Quantico, Va., sec. 2, p. 4.

220. MWTC ComdC, 1Jul-31Dec87, HD RefSec, Quantico, Va., sec. 2, p. 4.

221. Personal recollection of LtCol Kurtis P. Wheeler, submitted to authors in Sept09.

222. Stennick Recollections.

223. MWTC ComdC, 1Jan-31Dec88, HD RefSec, Quantico, Va., encl (1), p.3.

224. Official Biography of Colonel Philip E. Tucker, MWTC Historical Summary File, Section. E, former commanding officers.

225. Personal knowledge of the author, who was CG, 2dMarDiv, 1987-1989.

226. Ibid.

227. Ibid.

228. MWTC ComdC, 1Jan-31Dec89, HD RefSec, Quantico, Va., encl (1), p. 5.

229. Personal recollections of GySgt Richard Denhoff, furnished to authors Sept09; "Conquering McKinley—Testimony of Strength," *Camp Pendleton Scout*, 22Nov89.

230. Ibid.

231. Crist Paper, 35.

Chapter 12

232. MWTC ComdC, 1991, p. 9; MWTC ComdC, 1992, p. 5; MWTC ComdC, 1993, p. 4; MWTC ComdC, 1995, p. 7.

233. MWTC ComdC, 1993, p. 14.

234. Ibid., pp. 4, 14; MWTC ComdC, 1994, p. 4.

235. MWTC ComdC, 1994 p. 4.

236. MWTC ComdC, 1995, p. 7.

237. MWTC ComdC, 1996, p. 22.

238. Ibid., p. 24.

239. MWTC, ComdC, 1997, p. 31.

240. Ibid., p. 13.

241. Ibid., p. 28.

242. MWTC, ComdC, 1998, p. 4.

243. Ibid., p. 18.

244. Ibid., p. 20.

245. Ibid., p. 22.

246. Col Raymond L. "Skip" Polak, intvw, 9Jan09, Tape DSS_FLDA, hereafter Polak intvw.

247. Polak intvw.

248. Polak intvw.
249. Polak intvw.
250. MWTC, ComdC 1997, p. 7.
251. Ibid., pp. 9, 32, 33.
252. Col Robert W. Strahan, "What Good is the Marine Corps Mountain Warfare Training Center?" *Marine Corps Gazette* (March 2001), p. 23.
253. Ibid.
254. Ibid., 25.
255. Ibid., 25.
256. Ibid., 26.
257. Ibid.
258. Polak intvw.
259. MWTC 50th Anniversary Program, 6Sept01.
260. Ibid.
261. MWTC ComdC, 2001, Narrative summary, p. 1.

Epilogue

262. Col Nicholas E. Reynolds, *"U.S. Marines in Iraq, 2003 Basrah, Baghdad and Beyond*, History Division, U.S. Marine Corps Washington D.C. 2007, p.1.
263. Ibid., pp. 6-7.
264. Gidget Fuentes, "Harsh Weather, Rugged Terrain Will Challenge Troops," *San Diego Tribune*, 12Oct01, p. A5.
265. Jeanette Steele, "High Mettle: Mountain War Games Offer Marines Taste of Afghanistan Terrain," *San Diego Tribune*, 12Oct01.
266. Brendan Riley, Associated Press Writer, "Sierra Troops Preparing for Mountain Battle," Tahoe Daily Tribune, 16Oct01, p.1A.
267. Mark Jenkins, "Winter to the Corps," *Outside Magazine*, Feb02, p. 66.
268. Ibid.
269. Ibid., pp. 65, 68-69, 96.
270. Ibid., p. 11.
271. Personal knowledge of author O.K. Steele who participated in this seminar and the briefing for LtGen Emil Bedard.
272. Personal knowledge of author Michael I. Moffett, who served with the CentCom J3 (operations) branch, 2001-2002.
273. Polak intvw.
274. MWTC ComdC for CY 2003, p. 4
275. MWTC ComdC for CY 2002, p. 4.
276. MWTC ComdC for CY 2004, p .4.
277. Personal knowledge of author O.K. Steele who was invited by the CO, MWTC to sit in and observe this conference.
278. "Ready to Fight" *Marine Corps Gazette*, Nov04, p. 14.
279. Ibid., p.16.
280. Personal knowledge of author O.K. Steele, who served on Governor Schwarzenegger's California council on base support and retention from 4 November 2004 to 17 November 2005.
281. Col Timothy Wells, Concept Paper on USMC Order of Battle for Cold Weather Mountain Operations dated 6 October 2005 held in MWTC S-3 office.
282. Senator Barak Obama, AFL/CIO Democratic Presidential Candidate Forum, Chicago, IL, 7Aug07.
283. JoAnne O'Bryant and Michael Waterhouse, U.S. Forces in Afghanistan, Congressional Research Service, Library of Congress, 15 July 2008.
284. David S. Cloud and Mike Allen, "Obama Shifts Focus to Afghanistan," *www.politico.com* 17Feb09.
285. Col Norman L. Cooling e-mail messages to LtCol Michael I. Moffett dated 6Feb10.
286. Command and Staff, MWTC, "A Training Complex for Complex Training," *Marine Corps Gazette*, Mar09, p. 56.
287. Col Norman L. Cooling, Strategic Vision and Commanders Planning Guidance for Mountain Warfare Training Center, November 2008, p. 1.
288. Ibid., p. 6.
289. Ibid., p. 15.
290. Col Norman L. Cooling e-mail message to LtCol Michael I. Moffett dated 6Feb10.
291. Figures reported on the PBS News Hour by Jim Lehr on 23 May 2010.
292. Mark Jenkins, "Winter to the Corps," *Outside Magazine*, Feb02, pp. 66-67.

LINEAGE

OF

MARINE CORPS MOUNTAIN WARFARE TRAINING CENTER
BRIDGEPORT, CALIFORNIA

1951-2001

ACTIVATED 31 AUGUST 1951 AT CAMP PENDLETON, CALIFORNIA, AS
COLD-WEATHER TRAINING BATTALION, PROVISIONAL STAGING
REGIMENT, TRAINING AND REPLACEMENT COMMAND

REDESIGNATED 11 SEPTEMBER 1951 AS COLD WEATHER BATTALION,
STAGING REGIMENT TRAINING AND REPLACEMENT COMMAND, CAMP
PENDLETON, CALIFORNIA, AND RELOCATED TO BRIDGEPORT,
CALIFORNIA

REDESIGNATED 28 MAY 1952 AS COLD WEATHER BATTALION,
BRIDGEPORT, CALIFORNIA, MARINE BARRACKS CAMP, PENDLETON

REDESIGNATED 1 SEPTEMBER 1953 AS COLD WEATHER BATTALION,
BRIDGEPORT, CALIFORNIA, MARINE CORP BASE, CAMP PENDLETON

REDESIGNATED 15 SEPTEMBER 1956 AS MARINE CORPS COLD-
WEATHER TRAINING CENTER, BRIDGEPORT, CALIFORNIA

REDESIGNATED 1 NOVEMBER 1963 AS MARINE CORPS MOUNTAIN
WARFARE TRAINING CENTER, BRIDGEPORT, CALIFORNIA

REDUCED TO ZERO STRENGTH 10 OCTOBER 1967 AND COMMAND
PLACED IN CADRE STATUS

REACTIVATED 10 MAY 1976 AT BRIDGEPORT, CALIFORNIA, AS MARINE
CORPS MOUNTAIN WARFARE TRAINING CENTER

31 MARCH 1998
_____
DATE

C. C. Krulak
COMMANDANT OF THE MARINE CORPS

HONORS

AWARDED

MARINE CORPS MOUNTAIN WARFARE TRAINING CENTER
BRIDGEPORT, CALIFORNIA

MERITORIOUS UNIT COMMENDATION STREAMER

1990-1991

NATIONAL DEFENSE SERVICE STREAMER WITH THREE BRONZE STARS

GLOBAL WAR ON TERRORISM SERVICE STREAMER

31 MARCH 1998
_____
DATE

_____
COMMANDANT OF THE MARINE CORPS

Appendix B

Chronological List of Commanding Officers
1951 to Present

Lieutenant Colonel Donald B. Hubbard	30 August 1951–24 August 1952
Major Roger D. Peterson (Acting)	25 August 1952–21 September 1952
Lieutenant Colonel Donald M. Schmuck	22 September 1952–26 March 1954
Colonel Clayton O. Totman	27 March 1954–16 July 1955
Lieutenant Colonel Sidney F. Jenkins	17 July 1955–30 March 1957
Lieutenant Colonel Keigler E. Flake (Acting)	31 March 1957–2 June 1957
Lieutenant Colonel Alexander W. Gentleman	3 June 1957–6 July 1958
Major Richard F. Dyer (Acting)	7 July 1958–2 August 1958
Lieutenant Colonel Gerald P. Averill	3 August 1958–30 June 1960
Colonel Glen E. Martin	1 July 1960–6 June 1962
Lieutenant Colonel Nathaniel H. Carver	7 June 1962–10 July 1963
Colonel Frank R. Wilkerson Jr.	11 July 1963–6 June 1965
Lieutenant Colonel Lester V. Swenson (Acting)	7 June 1965–15 July 1965
Colonel John B. Bristow	16 July 1965–10 October 1966
Major John E. Lorzing	11 October 1966–10 October 1967
Lieutenant Colonel George A. Knudson	10 May 1976–28 March 1978
Lieutenant Colonel John W. Guy	29 March 1978–1 May 1981
Colonel William H. Osgood	2 May 1981–24 July 1984
Colonel John I. Hopkins	25 July 1984–7 May 1985
Lieutenant Colonel Earnest A. Van Huss (Acting)	8 May 1985–27 June 1985
Colonel John F. Stennick	28 June 1985–1 July 1988
Lieutenant Colonel William E. Healy (Acting)	2 July 1988–17 August 1988

Colonel Phillip E. Tucker   18 August 1988 – 31 July 1991

Colonel Russell W. Schumacher Jr.   1 August 1991 – 31 May 1994

Colonel Raymond L. Polak   1 June 1994 – 8 July 1996

Colonel Paul W. O'Toole Jr.   9 July 1996 – 25 August 1999

Colonel Robert W. Strahan   26 August 1999 – 10 August 2001

Colonel James M. Thomas   11 August 2001 – 17 July 2003

Colonel Joel G. Schwankl   18 July 2003 – 15 July 2005

Lieutenant Colonel William Etnyre Jr.   16 July 2005 – 1 September 2005
  (Acting)

Colonel Timothy C. Wells   1 September 2005 – 13 August 2006

Colonel David B. Hall   14 August 2006 – 1 July 2008

Colonel Norman L. Cooling   2 July 2008 – 11 June 2010

Colonel Phillip W. Chandler   12 June 2010 -

Appendix C

Chronological List of Sergeant Majors
1958 to Present

Sergeant Major James Westerman	1958–1959
Sergeant Major William J. Conley	1959–1961
Sergeant Major Harry A. Stoneburner	1961–1964
Sergeant Major Richard R. "Big Red" Ebert, Jr.	1964–1966
First Sergeant Lloyd G. Daniels (Acting)	1 May 1980–31 July 1981
Sergeant Major Charles L. Hayman	1 August 1981–3 April 1984
Sergeant Major Edward O'Leary	13 June 1984–10 February 1988
Sergeant Major Ronald S. Newman	11 February 1988–23 February 1990
Sergeant Major Henry S. David Jr.	24 February 1990–11 September 1992
Sergeant Major Raymond W. Jones	12 September 1992–31 August 1994
Gunnery Sergeant George A. Welsh Jr. (Acting)	1 September 1994–17 January 1995
Sergeant Major Richard F. Boyler	18 January 1995–22 May 1998
Sergeant Major Harold D. Bressler Jr.	23 May 1998–27 June 2000
Sergeant Major Johnny D. Matlock	28 June 2000–3 August 2003
Sergeant Major Daniel J. Fierle	4 August 2003–12 May 2006
Sergeant Major Michael W. Redmyer	13 May 2006–18 November 2008
Sergeant Major Douglas E. Power	19 November 2008–Present

Department of the Agriculture and Navy Joint Policy

<u>COPY</u>

DEPARTMENT OF AGRICULTURE

Washington 25, D. C.

February 19, 1952

The Honorable
The Secretary of the Navy

Dear Mr. Secretary:

Reference is made to your letter of February 4, with which you enclosed two signed copies of "A Joint Policy between the Department of the Navy and the Department of Agriculture Relating to the Use of National Forest Lands for Defense Purposes."

We are returning to you herewith the signed duplicate of this Joint Policy.

Copies of this agreement are being sent to local field officers of the Forest Service and you may be assured that forest officers will deal expeditiously with requests made by your Department for the use of national forest lands.

We hope that you will advise your field commanders of the importance of preventing unnecessary damage to national forest lands and improvements which the Department of the Navy may be using for training or defense purposes, and that restoration of damages to lands and improvements should be given current attention.

Sincerely,

/s/ Charles F. Brannan

Secretary

Enclosure

<u>ANNEX "C"</u>

A JOINT POLICY

Between the Department of the Navy and the Department of
Agriculture Relating to the Use of National Forest Lands
for Defense Purposes

A. The Department of Agriculture recognizes:

1. That the Department of the Navy needs varied terrain for
   maneuver and training purposes, and that it may be necessary
   in the interest of national defense to use national forest
   land.

2. That immediate availability of land is often of prime importance to the defense effort.

3. That defense use of lands will inevitably result in some
   damage, despite all efforts to protect the land.

B. The Department of Agriculture will therefore:

1. Give full recognition to the defense program and meet, as
   expeditiously as possible, the requests of the Department of
   the Navy for the use of national forest lands when it has been
   determined that such use is essential for the defense effort.

2. Delegate the authority to issue permits to regional foresters
   so as the facilitate speedly local action on the requests of
   Commandants of Naval Districts and the Commandant of the Marine
   Corps.

3. Instruct regional foresters to consider fully the defense
   requirements before imposing objections to use of national
   forest land and in setting up restrictions on its use.

4. Instruct local forest officers to cooperate fully with representatives of the Department of the Navy in all matters
   relating to the use and administration of national forest
   land needed for defense purposes.

C. The Department of the Navy recognizes:

1. That national forests are intensively managed lands which are
   of vital importance to the economy and defense production of
   the United States.

2. That the use of national forests for maneuvers and training
   will inevitably result in damage to important natural resources
   and frequently inflict damages of an irreparable nature.

3. That it may be often in the public interest and consistent
   with the national defense to select other lands for maneuvers
   and training.

D. The Department of the Navy will therefore:

1. Request the use of national forest lands for maneuver and training purposes only when it has been determined that the lands are essential for the defense effort.

2. Make every effort, consistent with defense requirements, to obtain the use of other lands which are less intensively managed, less susceptible to damage, and are less valuable to the national economy.

3. Instruct Naval shore establishment and Marine Corps commands to take all reasonable precautions to protect national forest lands from damage. Repair damages done to the extent permissable from annual maintenance appropriations of the Navy and Marine Corps, taking into consideration improvements made within the area that would have normally been made by the Forest Service. Also, to cooperate with local forest officers on problems of fire protection, erosion control, and other land management functions, and to provide such services, direct or through reimbursement of personnel, and the defense use may necessitate.

4. Authorize Naval shore establishment and Marine Corps commands to negotiate with local forest officers for the use of national forest lands.

5. Budget for restoration moneys, to the extent mutually agreed upon between the Departments of Agriculture and Navy.

6. Return national forest areas to the administration of the Forest Service as soon as practicable after the need for them has ceased.

Approved February 19, 1952

/s/ Charles F. Brannan
Secretary of Agriculture

Approved 4 Feb. 1952

/s/ Dan A. Kimball
Secretary of the Navy

- 2 -

Index

Afghanistan, 130, 134-141
    2d Brigade, 201st Corps, Afghan National
Army, 139
Aggressor Platoon, 23, 27, 31, 44, 57, 59, 61-62, 65
Aircraft types
    Boeing CH-46 Sea Knight, 90
    Cessna OF-2, 65
    Constellation, C141, 91
    Sikorsky CH-53 Sea Stallion, 93
    Sikorsky HO3, Dragonfly, 45
    Sikorsky UH-34 Seahorse, 65
Air Force Commands and Units
    Air Force, 52, 83, 87-88, 98, 108-109
    Air Force National Guard C-119, 32-33
    Air Mobility Command, 107-108
    Stead Air Force Base, 52, 69, 88
Alacron, de Hernando, 3
Almond, Major General Edward M., USA, 19
Anderson, Justin, 136
Andretta, Captain Mike, 135
al-Qaeda, 136-135, 139
Alexis, Godey, 4
Aleutian Islands, 11-12, 17-18
Alta, California, 3
Army Commands and Units
    7th U.S. Army Division, 19
    Eighth Army, 19
    10th Mountain Division, 18, 21, 54, 69,
121, 136
    X Corps, 19
    38th Infantry Regiment, 1st Battalion, 21
    Rangers, 120
    Special Forces, 130, 141

Army Field Manual, 20
Army Laboratory, Natick Massachusetts, 107
Army Schools and Training Centers
    Arctic Survival School, 17
    National Guard Mountain Warfare School,
136
Averill, Lieutenant Colonel Gerald P., 61-68, 71,
77, 84, 113
Azores, 12, 14
Barrow, General Robert H., 91, 99-104, 107, 109,
111

Barstow Supply Center, 49, 70

Beardsley, Corporal Brandon J., 135
Bearor, Captain Jeffrey W., 116-117
Bedard, Lieutenant Colonel Emil "Buck," 136
Bello, Staff Sergeant Alejandro G., 125
Benhoff, Lieutenant Colonel David, 139
Benton, Senator Thomas H., 4
Beverly, Major General Henry, 121
Bice, Major General David F., 133
Big Bear Civilian Conservation Corps, 20
Black Mountain, 21
Block, Honorable John R., 113
Bonesteel, Major General Charles H., USA, 14
Boyd Major Vernon D., 38
Brady, Lieutenant James, 32
Brannan, Charles F., 36
Bridgeport, California 25-26, 37, 44, 46, 53, 76-77,
80, 132, 139
Bridgeport Chronicle-Union, 25, 30
Bristow, Colonel John B., 86-88; major, 87; cap-
tain, 86
British 79th Division, 13-14
British Royal Marines
    3d Commando Brigade, 112
Brown, Lieutenant Joseph P.S., 53
Buchanan, Secretary of War James, 7
Buck, Lieutenant Billy B., 53
Burcham Flat, 5, 91
Bureau of Land Management, 140
Burtsell, Gunnery Sergeant Ronald L. "Ron," 74, 83
Bush, President George W., 135, 137-138
Byron, Colonel Michael J., 116, 120, 123

Cabrillo, Juan Rodriguez, 3
California Fish and Game Law, 68
Camps
    Drum, 98, 100-101, 112, 121
    Elliot, 14
    Hale, 18, 21, 52-53
    Lejeune, 56, 102, 112, 123-124, 135, 138,
141
    Pendleton, 18, 20-24, 26-27, 29-30, 33, 34-
42, 44-45, 48-49, 56, 58-59, 61, 65, 67-68, 75-77,
80, 82, 87-90, 93, 95, 100, 108-111, 119, 122, 132-
133, 137
    Ripley, 100, 106
    San Onofre, 29, 44
Carson, Christopher "Kit," 4, 6

Carson Pass, 9
Carver, Colonel Nathaniel H., 69-70, 77, 79
Cascade Range, 1
Cates, General Clifton B., 19-20
Caulfield, Lieutenant Colonel Matthew P. "Matt,"
94, 116, 121, 124
Chassey, Elliot W., 36
Cheatham, Captain Ernest C., Jr., 65-66
Chinese Communist Forces, 16, 19, 75
Chinese People's Army
        124th Division, 19
Churchill, Prime Minister Winston S., 12-13
City of San Francisco, 32, 35
Clapp, Lieutenant Wiley M. Jr., 73
Clark, Sergeant Wesley D., 125
Clipper, Captain Charles H., 61, 64, 67, 71
Cochrane, Captain Henry C., 11-12
Cold Weather Battalion, 26-30, 32-44, 46-47, 132
Cold-Weather Indoctrination Program, 21, 22, 27,
30, 36, 38, 41, 42, 48,
Cold Weather Training Battalion, 26, 33, 36, 47-48
Cold Weather Training Center, 46-49, 53, 59, 61,
63-64, 67, 69, 72, 76, 80, 82
Cook, Ernest T., 116
Cooling, Colonel Norman L., 140-141
Conley, Sergeant Major William J., 63, 65
Connors, Chuck, 45
Conway, Colonel James T., 129, 135, 140
Crawford, Sergeant Major Leland D. "Crow," 91,
102, 132
Crespi, Juan Fray, 3
Crist, Dr. David B., 97, 117, 126
Crockett, Colonel A. J. S., RM, 80, 88
Culp, Clinton, 136
Curtis, Major General Henry O., 13-14
Curtis, Major James, 61
Cushman, Major General Robert E., Jr. 81-83

Da Nang, 85, 89
Daniels, First Sergeant Lloyd G., 101, 105
Deal, Captain Sarah M., 129
Denhoff, Richard N., 125
Department of Agriculture, 25, 36, 94-95
Department of Interior
        Bureau of Reclamation, 58-59, 79
Deptula, Major Edwin A., 78, 82
Devil's Gate Pass, 5
Donovan, Colonel James A., Jr., 13-17
Donner Pass, 32, 35
Douse, Captain George, 81
Dwyer, Major General Ross T., 89
Dyer, Major Richard F., 61
Ebert, Sergeant Major Richard R. "Big Red," Jr., 76

Eggers, Captain Robert F., 52, 73
Eisenhower, President Dwight D., 48, 68
Escape, Evasion, and Survival (EE&S) Course, 48-
49, 52, 57, 64-65, 69, 73-74, 95
Estes, Sergeant, 125
Etnyre, Lieutenant Colonel William "Robb," Jr., 138
Ewing, Staff Sergeant Eugene "Gene" L., 74-75
Exercises
        Alpine Warrior, 100, 124
        Anchor Express 1986, 119-121
        Cold Winter 1985, 89, 112, 114-117, 124
        Empire Glacier 1978, 100
        Javelin Thrust, 141
        MICOWEX 49A, 18
        Mountain Warrior, 141
        Teamwork 76, 98

Fales Hot Springs, 9
Fales, Samuel, 9
Fargrave, Captain, 125
Fay, Paul B., Jr. USN, 79-80
Fellinger, Captain Barry E.C., 93-94
Fitzpatrick, Thomas "Broken Hand," 4-6
Flynn, Sergeant Major Daniel J., "Dan," 76
Font, Pedro, 3
Forts
        Benning, Georgia, 61-62, 64
        Carson, Colorado, 21
        Greely, Alaska, 68, 136
        McCoy, Wisconsin, 121, 124-125
        Wainwright, Alaska, 125, 136
40th Parallel, 1
Forward Operating Base Rhino, 135
Franks, General Tommy, USA, 135
Fremont, John C., 4-6, 8, 24

Gentleman, Lieutenant Colonel Alexander W., 51,
58-59, 60-61, 71
Goddard, Gunnery Sergeant Bernard G., 82
Godey, Alexis, 4
Goodman, First Lieutenant Edward C., 52
Goldsworthy, Captain James N.A., RM, 83-84, 88;
Major, 87, 112
Gow, First Lieutenant Douglas W. "Doug," 83
Gray, Major General Alfred M., Jr., 97-98, 105, 116,
123, 124
Gray, Robert L. "Bob," Jr., 83
Great Basin, 1, 2, 4
Grouse Meadow, 5, 55, 94, 141
Guantanamo, 14
Guy, Colonel John W., 101-102, 131

Haberman, Staff Sergeant Harold F., 27-28, 32-35

Haebel, Major General Robert E., 110
Hall, Colonel David B., 138
Hall, Major Michael S., 11
Hayman, Sergeant Major Charles L., 105
Heck, Major Matthew J. "Matt," 105
Heinl, Colonel Robert D., 16, 37, 44
Henderson, Gunnery Sergeant Lonnie, "Moose," 74-75, 83
Henness Pass, 9
Hermle, Colonel Leo D., 14
High altitude strike teams (HASTs), 136
Highway 4, 113
Highway 108, 24, 27, 37, 45, 52, 55, 63, 66, 91, 103
Highway 182, 107
Highway 395, 23-24, 26, 29, 30, 33-34, 36, 52, 63, 65, 103, 110, 120, 129, 132
Hill, Mary, 1
Hitler, Adolf, 12, 15
Hoffman, Major General Carl W., 95
Hoke, Sergeant William E., 83
Holcomb, Major General Thomas, 14
Hoover Wilderness Area, 83, 113
Hopkins, Colonel John I., 90, 111-113, 120
Horse Creek Canyon, 72
Houghton, Major General Kenneth L., 90-91
Hoye Canyon, 58
Hubbard, Colonel Donald B., 23-24, 26-29, 31-32, 34, 36-40, 141
Humboldt River, 4

Imjin River, 41
Indians, groups
       Maidu, 2
       Miwok, 2
       Paiute, 2, 4
       Washo, 2; see also Washoe, 6, 8

Jacques, Sergeant Major Maurice J., 42
Jenkins, First Lieutenant Harry W. Jr., 83-84, 102; Colonel, 111-112, 115-116, 119; Major General, 114-116, 120-121, 131,
Jenkins, Lieutenant Colonel Sidney F., 44, 48-49, 51
Jenkins, Mark, 135-136, 141
Johnson, First Lieutenant Richard, W. "Dick," 23-24, 31-32, 141
Johnson, President Lyndon B., 85
Jones, Major General Thomas S., 133, 141
Jones, Second Lieutenant William K., 15, 17

Kandahar Airfield, 135-136
Karch, Brigadier General Frederick J., 85

Karzai, Hamid, 137
Keeling, Brigadier Andy, RM, 112
Kelley, Captain Paul X., 62; general, 109, 114
Kennedy, President John F., Jr., 76, 79-80
Kennedy Meadows, 9
Kern, Staff Sergeant, 120
Kiel Canal, 98
Kilfoyle, Staff Sergeant John F., 86
Kimball, Secretary of the Navy Dan A., 36
Knapp, Lieutenant James V. "Jim," 74
Knudson, Captain George A., 77, 82, 95
Kodiak Island, 17-18
Kola Peninsula, 97-98
Korean Peninsula, 19, 23, 41, 43, 72, 76
Kozeniesky, Major Craig, 135-136
Krulak, Colonel Victor H., 42

Laden, Osama bin, 135
Lake Bonpland, 6
Lake Tahoe Basin, 1
Lamar, Sergeant, 128
Last Outpost, 71
Laxalt, Paul, 87
Leavitt Meadows, 7, 9, 24, 55, 79, 86
Lee, First Lieutenant Vincent R., 73
Lehman, Secretary of the Navy John F., 104
Leonard, Zenas, 4
Lewis, Ernest, 5
Life magazine, 35
Lightfoot, Gunnery Sergeant William R. "Bill," 74
Litzenberg, Colonel Homer L., 19
Liversedge, Brigadier General Harry B., 18
Lorzing, Major John E., 88
Louis, Saint, 4
Lynch, Brigadier General Jarvis D., Jr., 118

McAninch, Lieutenant Gregg, 125
MacArthur, General Douglas, USA, 19
McCulloch, Brigadier General William L., 93-94
McLennan, General Kenneth, 101-102
Mahon, Color Sergeant, RM, 105
Mannila, First Lieutenant Richard R., 82
Marine Barracks
       Adak, Alaska, 17, 44, 129
       Pendleton, California, 20, 36, 39-40
       Hawthorne, Nevada, 39, 82, 103
       San Francisco Naval Shipyard, California, 84
       Washington, D.C., 109
Marine Corps Air Station, El Toro, California, 28, 127
Marine Corps Bases and Depots
       Recruit Depot, San Diego, 78

Supply Center, Barstow, 49, 70
Twentynine Palms, California, 95
Marine Corps Commands and Units
Air-Ground Task Forces
Fleet Marine Force, Atlantic, 42, 99, 103
Fleet Marine Force, Pacific; Western Pacific; Troops, 22, 27, 28, 39, 42, 47, 87, 93
I Marine Amphibious Force, 90, 93, 111
II Marine Amphibious Force, 99
III Marine Amphibious Force, 16, 85
1st Marine Brigade 12, 16, 48, 95
1st Provisional Marine Brigade, 13-14
3d Marine Brigade, 18, 36, 27, 41, 139
4th Marine Amphibious Brigade, 98-99, 106, 112, 115-116, 117-118, 121
9th Marine Expeditionary Brigade, 85
15th Marine Expeditionary Unit, 135-136
26th Marine Expeditionary Unit, 135-136
36th Marine Amphibious Unit, 98

Air
1st Marine Aircraft Wing, 19, 48, 75, 85
2d Marine Aircraft Wing, 48
3d Marine Aircraft Wing, 45, 48, 58, 102
Marine Aircraft Group 40, 112
Marine Medium Helicopter Squadron 266 (HMM-266), 112
Marine Medium Helicopter Squadron 566 (HMM-466), 129
Marine Observation Squadron 6 (VMO-6), 66

Ground
1st Marine Division, 12, 16, 18-20, 22-23, 38, 41, 43-44, 48, 56, 65, 67, 73-75, 77-78, 85, 87, 89-90, 93-95, 99, 102, 111, 128, 132
2d Marine Division, 12, 43, 48, 56, 62, 87-88, 97, 105, 108, 112, 119-120, 123-125, 127, 138, 140
3d Marine Division, 41-43, 48, 75, 84-85, 89, 102, 118, 137
4th Marine Division, 40

1st Marine Regiment, 31, 40, 99
2d Battalion, 1st Marines, 87, 89-91
3d Battalion, 1st Marines, 91-92
2d Marine Regiment, 111-112, 114-116, 119-120, 123-125, 138
1st Battalion, 2d Marines, 87, 112
3d Battalion, 2d Marines, 88, 128
3d Marine Regiment, 40, 73, 138, 140
3d Battalion, 3d Marines, 73, 140
4th Marine Regiment, 87
1st Battalion, 4th Marines, 111

2d Battalion, 4th Marines, 49
5th Marine Regiment, 78, 89, 95
1st Battalion, 5th Marines, 51
2d Battalion, 5th Marines, 23, 45, 62, 67, 72-73
3d Battalion, 5th Marines, 95
6th Marine Regiment, 12-13, 14-17, 62, 127, 135
1st Battalion, 6th Marines, 16
3d Battalion, 6th Marines, 127
7th Marine Regiment, 45, 68, 90, 93-94, 111
1st Battalion, 7th Marines, 67
2d Battalion, 7th Marines, 45, 90, 111
9th Marine Regiment, 26, 111
3d Battalion, 9th Marines, 26
1st Battalion, 10th Marines, 116
2d Battalion, 23d Marines, 102
1st Battalion, 25th Marines, 85
3d Battalion, 26th Marines, 62

1st Amphibian Tractor Battalion, 78
1st Engineer Battalion, 132
1st Reconnaissance Battalion, 65, 91
1st Shore Party Battalion, 132
1st Air Naval Gunfire Liaison Company, 89
1st Force Reconnaissance Company, 90
2d Defense Battalion, 40
2d Parachute Battalion, 62
2d Reconnaissance Battalion, 88
3d 4.5 Rocket Battery, Force Troops, FMF Pacific, 45
3d Raider Battalion, 21
5th Defense Battalion, 12
7th Engineer Battalion, 40-41, 65, 132
Force Engineer Battalion, 96
Parachute Regiment, 62
Regimental Landing Team 7 (RLT-7), 18, 89
Special Operations Command, 141

1st Replacement Draft, 67
6th Replacement Draft, 21, 27
14th Replacement Draft, 23, 27-28, 39
15th Replacement Draft, 29, 36
17th Replacement Draft, 33
19th Replacement Draft, 36
20th Replacement Draft, 36
21st Replacement Drafts, 36
26th Replacement Draft, 42

Marine Corps Gazette, 11, 35, 77, 127, 130
Marine Corps Schools and Training Center
Amphibious Warfare School, 26, 62, 107, 120

Command and Staff School, 129
Development and Education Command;

Training and Education Command, 105, 118, 133
Infantry Training School, 44
Landing Force Development Center, 62
Staging Battalion, 88
Staging Regiment, 26, 29, 38-39
Staging and Replacement Command, 20, 23, 30
Training and Replacement Command, 20-21, 23, 26, 29, 32, 39

Marine Corps Mountain Warfare Training Center, 40, 80, 83, 89, 95, 100, 103, 111, 127-131, 133, 138
Maritime Prepositioning Ships (MPS), 103
Marjanov, Gunnery Sergeant John, 74, 132-133, 137
Marston, Brigadier General John, 12-14, 16
Martin, Colonel Glen E., 67-72, 77
Mattis, Brigadier General James N., 135
Mason, Colonel Richard B., 7-8
Milavic, Staff Sergeant Anthony F., 73-75
Military Airlift Command, 90
Military Assistance Advisory Group, 67, 77
Mill Creek Canyon, 5
Miller, Lieutenant General John H., 103
Miller, Staff Sergeant, 128
Milligan, Brigadier General Robert F., 116
Mize, Major General Charles D., 94; Lieutenant, 95
Mojave Desert, 1, 3
Mono County, 9, 25, 68, 79, 85, 120
Mono Lake, 9
Montoya, Gunnery Sergeant Raymond A., 75
Moor, Robin, 12
Moore, Captain Walter "Mu Mu," 21, 23
Moore, Marvin K., 83
Moraga, Ensign Gabriel, 3
Morris, Captain John B., 73
Moriarty, Captain William S., 82-83, 88
Mountains
Diablo, 6
Joseph, 3
Lassen, 1
Matterhorn Peak, 112-113
Whitney, 1, 121
Mountain Leader's/Leadership Course, 47-48, 51-54, 56-57, 63-65, 68-74, 78-79, 90, 110, 112-113, , 116, 120, 124, 130-131, 136, 138
Mountain Corps Mountain Warfare Training Center, 24, 40, 73, 76-77, 80, 83, 85, 87, 89, 91, 94-96, 100-103, 105, 110-111, 118-119, 122, 126-133, 135-141,
Mundy, Brigadier General Carl Jr., 116, 125, 128
Myatt, Major General J. Michael, 128
Navy Commands and Units

Commander-in-Chief, Atlantic, 97
Commander-in-Chief, Pacific Forces, 85
Commander-in-Chief, Pacific Fleet, 18
Naval Air Station at Fallon, Nevada, 52, 56, 90-91, 112, 140
Naval Air Station Lakehurst, New Jersey, 62
Naval Air Station Lemoor, California, 90
Navy Arctic Test Station, Point Barrow, 17
Naval Construction Battalion, Port Hueneme, California, 87, 109
Naval Dispensary and Dental Clinic, Camp Pendleton, 49
Naval Engineering Facilities Command, 120
Pacific Fleet, Pearl Harbor, 123
Seabees, 46
Supreme Allied Commander, Atlantic (SACLant), 112
12th Naval District, 25, 39, 50-51

Neal, Staff Sergeant Theodore E. "Boone," 74, 83
Nixon, President Richard M., 89
Norway Air-Landed Marine Amphibious Brigade, 117
Nye, James W., 9

Obama, Senator Barak H., 138; president, 140
Operations
Anorak Express, 98
Battle Griffin, 127
Cold Winter 1985, 112, 115, 117
Desert Shield and Desert Storm, 125, 127, 137
Enduring Freedom, 130, 135, 137-138, 140, 146
Starlite, 85
Workup, 98
Killer, 41, 67
Ripper, 41, 67
Osgood, Lieutenant Colonel William H., 102-103, 104-106, 108; Colonel, 103-104, 108-109, 111
O'Toole, Colonel Paul W. Jr., 129-130

Palazzo, Lieutenant Colonel Louis J., 139
Palmer, Master Sergeant Chad J., 76
Payne, John, 45
Pate, General Randolph, McC., 48, 58-59, 60-61, 73

Pickle, Francis, "Frank," 9
Pickel Meadow, 23-38, 40-48, 51-52, 59, 64-66, 68, 71-73, 77, 82, 85, 90-91, 103, 105, 107, 110-112, 114, 119-120, 124, 127-135, 137-138, 140-141
Polak, Colonel Raymond L., 129-130, 137

Polk, President James K., 7-8
Portolá, Don Gaspar de, 3
Prudhoe Bay, 93
Pruess, Charles, 4-6
Puller, Brigadier General Lewis B. "Chesty," 27, 30-31, 36, 40, 99
Pyramid Lake, 4

Quartararo, Sergeant Alan, 135
Quille, De Dan, 8

Raue, Technical Sergeant Carl H. Jr., 56-58, 68
Reagan, President Ronald W., 103, 107, 109
Reno, Nevada, 23, 25, 32, 42, 51-52, 66, 71, 76, 82-83, 87-88, 90-91, 103, 112-113
Reykjavik Harbor, 12
Richards, Petty Officer, 120
Richardson, Major Rodney C. "Rod," 123, 125-126, 136
Ridgely, Major General Reginald H., Jr., 59, 61, 65
Riney, Colonel Francis "Frank," 101
Ripley, Colonel John W., 123-124
Robeson, Major Edward J., IV, 102, 106, 110
Robinson, Major General Kenneth L., 108-109
Roise, Lieutenant Colonel Harold S., 23, 45
Roosevelt, President Franklin D., 12, 14, 78
Roosevelt, President Theodore, 25
Rumsfeld, Secretary of Defense Donald H., 137
Russ, Martin, 43
Ryffel, Lieutenant Colonel George G., 28, 37-39, 47

San Bernadino Range, 20
Sanchez, Lieutenant Colonel Eleazar O., 139
San Diego, California, 3, 12, 29
San Jacinto Mountains, 21, 22
Sardo, Brigadier General Americo A., 100-101
Saw Tooth Ridge 51, 55, 72, 74
Scheer, Staff Sergeant Carl E. "Pappy," 74
Schmuck, Lieutenant Colonel Donald M., 40-43, 48, 95
Schneider, Corporal John J., 27
Schumacher, Colonel Russell W. Jr., 129, 137
Schwankl, Colonel Joel G., 129,137-138
Schwenk, Brigadier General Adolph G., 90
Scott, Lieutenant Hugh L. III, 83
Serra, Junipero, 3
Shanghai, China, 49, 86, 132
Sheehan, Captain James P., 82
Sherman, Lieutenant William T., 7
Sheridan, Gunnery Sergeant John C., 73
Shepherd, General Lemuel C., Jr., 33, 40, 42
Ships
    Alki, 11-12

    Bataan (CVL 29), 78
    Bismarck, 12
    Consolation (AH 15), 73
    Gurkha, 83
    Prinz Eugen, 12
Shoup, General David M., 79
Sierra Nevada, 1, 3-4, 7, 9, 30, 32, 34, 41, 48
Sitler, Lieutenant Commander, USN (MC), 128
Skipper, Major Kenneth J. "Ken," 77-78
Smith, Jedediah S., 3
Smith, Knut, 53
Smith, General Holland, M., 12
Smith, Brigadier General Norman H. "Norm," 118, 136
Smith, Lieutenant Colonel Oliver P., 16-17; Major General, 19, 22, 39
Smith, Major General Ray L., 136
Snell, Major James "Jim," 123
Straehl, First Lieutenant Richard L., 86
Strahan, Colonel Robert W., 130-131, 133
Stanislaus River, 4, 7, 9
Shapley, Major General Alan, 67-68
Shutler, Major General Philip D., 98
Sommers, Sergeant, 125
Sonora Pass, 5, 7, 9, 24, 66, 103, 130
Stark, Admiral Harold R., USN, 12
Steele, Captain Orlo K., 84; major general 131, 133, 136
Stennick, Colonel John F., 113, 118-119, 121-122, 130, 137
Stoneburner, Sergeant Major Harry A., 76
Stone, Irving, 8
Strawberry Flat, 9
Subic Bay Naval Base, Philippine Islands, 71
Suid, Lawrence, 45
Summit Meadow, 41
Survival, Evasion, Resistance and Escape (SERE), 78
Survival, Evasion, Resistance and Escape (SERE) Course, 80-81, 87-88
Sweetwater Range, 91
Swenson, Lieutenant Colonel Lester V. "Swede," 85-86

Tactical Area #1, 29
Tactical Area #2, 59, 65
Taylor, Staff Sergeant George, 89
Tent Camp #2, 29-30
Territorial Enterprise, 8
The Basic School, 29, 78, 102, 116, 118
"The People's Pool," 53, 65
38th Parallel, Korea, 18, 23, 67
Thomas, Col James M. "Jim," 133, 135-137
Toiyabe National Forest 25, 36, 51, 79, 107

Tooby, Color Sergeant Steven, 136
Topaz Family Housing complex, 110
Totman, Clayton O., 43-45
Trahern Party, 7
Trainor, Lieutenant General Bernard E. "Mick," 35, 136
Treaty of Guadalupe Hidalgo, 1848, 7
Trinidad, Cpl T., 83
Truckee, California, 66
Truman, President Harry S., 41
Tucker, Colonel Phillip E., 123, 129
Turley, Captain Gerald H. "Gerry," 75
Twin Lakes, 51, 55, 72-73, 83
Twining, Brigadier General Merrill B., 20-21, 23, 25

Utter, Lieutenant Robert A., 53
U.S. Forest Service, 25

Van Huss, Lieutenant Colonel Earnest A. "Ernie," 113, 119
Varmette, Thomas M. "Tom," 125
Vehicles
        BV-206, 115, 117, 121, 125-126
        Light Assault Vehicle 25, 107
        Amphibious Cargo Carrier M76 "Otter," 51-52, 70
        Thiokol Trackmaster, 70, 117, 132
Valleys
        Antelope, 87, 110
        Bridgeport, 4-5
        Carson, 8
        Eagle, 8
        Hudson River, 73
        Owens River, 1
        Sacramento, 4, 6
        Smith, 91
        Squaw, 67

Washoe, 8
Yosemite, 2, 4
Vozka, Corporal Henry 75-76

Wagner, Hans, 53
Walker, Joseph R., 4
Walker, Ralph V. Jr., 53
Walker River, 2, 7, 9
Walt, Major General Lewis W. "Lou," 85
Wawrzyniak, Captain Stanley "Ski," 71-73
Weapons
        M198 155mm howitzer, 116
        Gun, chain, 25mm, 107
        Mortar, 81mm, 90, 107
        Howitzer, 105mm, 107
        Rifle, Recoilless, 106mm, 90, 94
        Rocket antitank, M-220, 107
Wedertz, Frank, 4
Weinberger, Secretary of Defense Caspar, 104, 107
Wells, Colonel Timothy C., 125, 138
Wester, Lieutenant Colonel Sean D., 139
Westerman, James M. "Jim," 63
West, Francis J. "Bing," 136
West, Sergeant William T. "Billie," 83
West Walker River, 5, 9, 24, 37, 45, 55, 58, 76, 79, 86, 120, 135
Wheeler, Lieutenant Colonel Kurtis P. "Kurt," 121-122
White Shod Course, 88
Wiedhahn, Captain Warren Jr., 66
Wilkin, Sergeant Martin, 125
Wilkinson, Colonel Frank R., Jr., 78-82, 85
Wilson, General Louis H., Jr., 95, 99
Wonsan Harbor, 19

Yudam Ni, 23

Ziglar, Gunnery Sergeant Coy D., 77

The Authors

MajGen Orlo K. Steele conceived, researched, and wrote this work based on some 35 years of U.S. Marine Corps service and experience. He is retired and lives with his family in Grass Valley, California, not far from the Mountain Warfare Training Center.

LtCol Michael I. Moffett represented the Field History contribution to this effort. He is retired and lives with his family in New Hampshire. They are pictured with Marines at the MWTC.